A Century of Chicano History

A Century
of Chicano History
Empire, Nations, and Migration

Gilbert G. Gonzalez
Professor
University of California, Irvine

Raul A. Fernandez
Professor
University of California, Irvine

ROUTLEDGE
NEW YORK AND LONDON

Published in 2003 by
Routledge
29 West 35th Street
New York, NY 10001
www.routledge-ny.com

Published in Great Britain by
Routledge
11 New Fetter Lane
London EC4P 4EE
www.routledge.co.uk

Routledge is an imprint of the Taylor & Francis Group.
Printed in the United States of America on acid-free paper.

The following chapters were previously published in *The Pacific Historical Review*:

"Chicano History: Transcending Cultural Models" (Vol. 63, No. 4, 1994)
© 1994 by the Pacific Coast Branch, American Historical Association
Reprinted from *Pacific Historical Review*
Vol. 63, No. 4, by permission of the University of California Press

"Empire and the Origins of Twentieth Century Migration from Mexico to the
United States" (Vol. 71, no. 1, 2002)
© 2002 by the Pacific Coast Branch, American Historical Association
Reprinted from *Pacific Historical Review*
Vol. 71, No. 1, by permission of the University of California Press

10 9 8 7 6 5 4 3 2 1

Library of Congress Cataloging-in-Publication Data

Gonzalez, Gilbert G., 1941–
   A century of Chicano history : empire, nations, and migration / Gilbert G. Gonzalez,
   Raul A. Fernandez.
      p. cm.
   Includes index.
   ISBN 0-415-94392-2 — ISBN 0-415-94393-0 (pbk.)
   1. Mexican Americans—History—19th century. 2. Mexican Americans—History—
20th century. 3. Immigrants—United States—History—19th century. 4. Immigrants—
United States—History—20th century. 5. United States—Relations—Mexico. 6.
Mexico—Relations—United States. 7. Mexico—Emigration and immigration—History.
8. United States—Emigration and immigration—History. I. Fernandez, Raul A., 1945–
II. Title.

   E184.M5G645 2003
   973'.046872—dc21

2002037050

. . . he [the migrant] *is forced to seek better conditions north of the border by the slow but relentless pressure of United States' agricultural, financial and oil corporate interests on the entire economic and social evolution of the Mexican nation.*

Ernesto Galarza, 1949

Contents

Acknowledgments

We have many to thank for their numerous unselfish contributions that assisted us to make this book better than we alone could ever have achieved. Colleagues, friends, and family deserve our heartfelt thanks. At the University of California, Irvine, we benefited from the support of fellow faculty, students, and staff, among them John Liu, Ester Hernandez, Jeanette Castellanos, Louis Desipio, Anna Gonzales, Ken Pomeranz, Patricia Hamm, Barbara Abell, Gillian Kumm, Edna Mejia, Stella Ginez, and the faculty and students in the Labor Studies Program and Chicano Latino Studies Program. From beyond the walls of UC Irvine, the critical commentary of Jon Panish, Gema Guevara, John Mason Hart, David Johnson, Richard Gibson, Myrna Donohoe, Victor Quintana, Henry Pope Anderson, and José Alamillo helped us to clarify and strengthen our arguments. Finally, we wish to thank two very special colleagues who helped in no small measure to improve our book. Our thoughts are with two departed colleagues, Jeffrey Garcilazo and Lionel Cantu. Lionel gladly loaned his books and offered his critical ideas without hesitation, and Jeff's dissertation was a most valuable source of information, which we depended upon on numerous occasions.

More than critical insights were at play: we were privileged to have the unwavering support of our respective partners, each expert in her particular field. Frances Leslie and Nancy Page Fernandez assisted with their active collaboration at several key junctures. Among other contributions, Nancy recommended readings, which assisted in developing key chapters in the book, and Frances prepared the illustrations. Both were often abruptly put on notice to hear our ideas, frequently in incipient stages of maturation, and to make sense of them. Their observations usually invariably led to further conceptual development.

Research requires financial assistance, and this work depended on the backing of a number of support programs. The University of California SCR 43 research funds administered via the UCI Chicano Latino Studies Program as well as support from the UCI Committee on Research and the UCI Labor Studies Program made possible the completion of critical phases of the research. We are particularly indebted to the staff at the UCI Main Library Interlibrary Loan Department, who always responded positively to the many requests for materials used in writing this book.

Last, we express our deep appreciation to the editorial staff at Routledge, in particular Karen Wolny and Sara Folks. They were a pleasure to work with and helped us steer the manuscript from draft to book. Not only the editorial staff deserves mention; the outside press reviewers also offered valuable commentary and suggestions for improvement, which after careful evaluation and selection we incorporated.

Introduction

One Hundred Years of Chicano History

This book explores the origins of the increasing Mexican-American population of the United States. We show how more than a century of economic domination of the United States over Mexico continues to produce economic and social dislocations, which are at the root of the mass northward migration of Mexicans to the United States, a constant wellspring of the Chicano population.

This work itself has been in the making for the past ten years. In the early 1990s, dissatisfied with the one-sided, culture-based approach of much of Chicano historiography, we set out to review and critique that body of writing. In addition, we sought to identify economic-historic structures as a guide to contextualize Chicano social and cultural history. After a prolonged period of manuscript revisions, we published an article, appearing in the *Pacific Historical Review* in 1994, that presented three main arguments. The first was that Spanish and Mexican society in the pre-1848 U.S. Southwest possessed a feudalistic character. Second, the dating of the beginning of Chicano history to the Treaty of Guadalupe Hidalgo in 1848 was without merit, as it avoided the significant break between one historical event—the demise of the old Spanish and Mexican rule in the area—and the rise of a new, separate in time, migration-based population more than fifty years later. Third, the urban emphasis on much of twentieth-century Chicano historiography responded to what was *au courant* in the U.S. academy, rather than being in synch with the predominantly rural character of the Chicano population during the first two-thirds of the twentieth century.

When that article was published we did not intend to write a book about the origins of Chicano history. We merely hinted at a more accurate periodization for Chicano history by stating that the Chicano population of the United States had developed under modern, "corporate" capitalism in the twentieth century. Although there is much that we would change in that article if we were to write it anew, it has been reprinted in at least three anthologies and has acquired, as it were, a life of its own. It is included here as chapter I because it set up for us the tasks we would complete several years and many pages later.

At first we thought the task of developing the argument of a different beginning for Chicano history would take merely another essay, so we embarked on research and writing without envisioning an entire book dedicated to the subject. In this second essay we delved in detail into the social dislocations brought upon Mexico by the economic domination of the United States beginning in the last quarter of the nineteenth century. The growth of and increasing power of large, monopolistic banks and industrial corporations in the United States at this time became the foundation of a new kind of American empire, and not just over Mexico. We also critiqued a wide variety of migration theories, all more or less based on the sociological notions of "push-pull." Those theories fail to account for the historical and structural unity between the effects of U.S. corporate investments in Mexico and the needs of U.S. agribusiness in the U.S. Southwest, both of which conditioned the internal and external Mexican migrations and the resulting appearance of a Chicano population in the Southwest.

In this perspective, the rise of the Chicano population cannot be viewed as something almost accidental, tied to a war with obscure origins in 1848, which brought neither migration nor an increase in Mexican-origin people. Rather, Chicanos become central to the construction of a twentieth-century U.S. hegemonic empire characterized by a neocolonial style of indirect economic domination over Mexico as well as other countries. The rise of the Chicano population is merely one side of a coin, the other side being the gradual destruction and disarticulation of Mexico as a sovereign nation. Our emphasis was on the macro networks of domination that caused the demographic dislocation of Mexico's population and set it adrift, as opposed to the contemporary sociological focus on micro factors and the agency of individual migrants.

Our research resulted in a second article, published in 2002 by the *Pacific Historical Review;* that article is included here as chapter II. But when we were about halfway through writing the essay, it became obvious that much more research and writing would be needed for our mission to be accomplished. The remainder of the essays that follow were developed to finish our task.

Chapter III studies a large sample of the "travel literature"—by Protestant missionaries, mining engineers, journalists, and so forth—that emerged as the United States built its economic empire in Mexico. This may seem like a topic quite distant from the origins of the Chicano population, yet this "travel literature" provides an important connection between empire-building and economic dislocation in Mexico and the reception that Mexican immigrants received as they began to settle in numbers in the United States. In this chapter we narrate how travel writers constructed a "Mexican problem," a story of cultural "deficits" in Mexico's national culture. Later, as Mexican settlements grew in the United States, an entire sociological subfield developed to address the need for the "acculturation" of the migrants. The "Americanization" projects that educators and social welfare workers imposed on Mexicans beginning in the 1920s took as their point of theoretical departure the "Mexican problem" as defined by the earlier travel literature of empire. Dozens of postgraduate theses—indeed, an entire subfield of sociology—used as their primary research materials the abundant writings from that travel literature. U.S. imperialism connected back to its domestic policies toward Mexicans in this country. Thus Chicano historical experience is inseparable from the transnational activities of the United States that shaped its domestic public policies toward Mexican migrants.

Inspired by recent literature on gender and migration, we relate, in chapter IV, how a profound gender consciousness permeated the policies of the United States as it managed migration from Mexico throughout the twentieth century. Migration flows have been gender-micromanaged at all levels: the Bracero Program (1942–64) was limited to males only; other programs required family migrations; the border industrial program on the U.S.–Mexico border has recruited millions of young women over the past three decades. Examining the gender consciousness of empire allows us to calibrate and nuance the scope and reach of migration studies that focus only on the gender subjectivities and personal agency of individual migrants.

If the origins of the Chicano population can be found right at the beginning and center of the U.S. transnational mode of domination, the Mexican-American migrants to the United States have also been central to the construction of the national economy of the United States for more than a hundred years. In chapter V we study the economic integration of the Mexican American into the fabric of U.S. monopoly capitalism. We take key examples from twentieth-century history to illustrate that far from being "marginal," Mexican Americans worked in the most significant agricultural and industrial sectors of the U.S. economy decade after decade. We provide examples from a variety of areas, such as railroad construction, key agricultural crops such as citrus and lettuce, and processing industries. The labor of Mexican Americans is present in every aspect of national life, not just in the large factories and other places of employment, but also in the homes of the American middle class, where Mexican, and increasingly Central American women, raise the children and clean the houses of middle America. The utilization of Mexican labor as an integral component of the U.S. economy goes beyond the political borders of the nation. More than one million Mexican workers, mostly women, toil in thousands of *maquiladoras* strewn all along the U.S.–Mexico border, legally unable to even fantasize about an "American dream" of "upward mobility" and "mainstream" living, as their labor is spent in "Greater U.S.A.," the expansion of the U.S. economy right into Mexico.

Just as we were finishing the first drafts of chapters III, IV, and V, the *Journal of American History* released a special issue purporting to take a new look at the parallel histories of the United States and Mexico. Ostensibly the goal of this special issue was to get away from the confines imposed on U.S. historians by the concept of the nation-state. Our reading revealed to us a very different strategy, namely that, much like the American travel writers of the late nineteenth and early twentieth centuries, the *JAH,* in this special issue, had become a nationalist voice for U.S. imperialism. As author Mary Louise Pratt has pointed out, much of the travel literature of U.S. empire sported a seemingly innocent "anticonquest" tone while accompanying the groundwork for U.S. economic expansion. Similarly, the *JAH* sports a "no empire" flavor: the United States and Mexico are treated as equals in history; U.S. domination is never mentioned, nor is the systematic destruction of the Mexican nation; tools of U.S. imperial domination such as NAFTA are hailed are harbingers of the withering away of the nation-state in general. Rather than recasting Chicano history, conventional wisdom was reiterated: Chicano history began in 1848, migration from Mexico is due to the workings of push-and-pull factors, and so on. In general, the most insipid platitudes of State Department and White House claptrap about "globalization" are repeated as revealed truth. In chapter VI we provide an antidote to the *JAH* "official history," and its naked apologia for U.S. empire.

We finished our research and writing just as former Coca-Cola Mexico president Vicente Fox actually became Mexico's president. The policies and programs launched by Fox, under close direction and scrutiny by the United States, showed yet another turn of the screw by the United States on Mexico's economy. The new Mexican administration promised to deepen NAFTA, continuing the speeded-up process of depopulating the Mexican countryside, launching additional millions of Mexican farmers onto the highways of migration, expanding the flow of Mexican migrants into the

"Chicano nation" constructed in the United States over the previous century, and providing corroboration thereby to our argument about the origins of Chicano history. The U.S. State Department, with the aid of U.S. imperial stalwart Jesse Helms, negotiated a new Bracero program with the Mexican government, the likes of which had not been seen since the early 1960s. After twenty years of abundant sociological studies focused on "agency," "networks," and other "micro," "no empire" studies, these events demonstrated the continuing role of "macro" factors as key to the understanding of Mexican migration to the United States. In addition, several months of intensive "discussions," between the United States and Mexico—read "directives by the United States to its junior partner"—belie any claim to the disappearance of the nation-state when it comes to U.S.–Mexico policymaking. These public displays do provide, on the other hand, ample evidence of the subservient role of Mexico and its elevated role as a tool of U.S. foreign policy, and of the deep connection between U.S. domination over Mexico and the past, present, and future course of Chicano history.

I
Chicano History
Transcending Cultural Models

Mainstream U.S. historians tend to ignore Chicano history, apparently considering it the domain of specialists.[1] But why should U.S. social historians want to put aside issues as important as the social origins of pragmatism, or the Civil War in Kansas, and turn their attention to Mexican-American history? In part the answer has to be that generally speaking, it might help, along with other contemporary directions in cultural studies, to break down barriers to historical understanding among the various groups that comprise the United States. More specifically, such study would open up new areas of comparative research by adding to the proposition that "capitalism did not come to every region [of the United States] at the same time nor on the same terms."[2] In this chapter, we are concerned with the second issue.

We believe that important insights might be drawn by comparing the nineteenth-century evolution of economic forms in rural New England, the slave South, and the territories acquired from Mexico after 1836. At this time such a comparison across the United States is still difficult, because much Chicano historiography has built on cultural and culture-conflict models focusing on race and nationality as the bases for social relations and, ultimately, for historical explanation. Clearly in the post-1848 years in the newly acquired southwestern frontier, Anglo settlers frequently treated the Hispanic population much like it dealt with the native Indian population: as people without rights who were merely obstacles to the acquisition and exploitation of natural resources and land.[3] And, to be sure, the violence of the conquerors was often met with the resistance of the

1

conquered.[4] But these cultural struggles and racial conflicts have become for many Chicano historians the principal bases for understanding Chicano history.

Culture-based explanations tend to minimize the role of economic factors, which are crucial in shaping social and cultural forms and very useful in drawing regional comparisons. Innovative scholarship by Rosalinda Gonzalez, David Montejano, and Douglas Monroy moves away from culture-based models and toward an emphasis on economic power and processes.[5] The goal here is to advance and elaborate some of these ideas on socioeconomic forms in a more systematic manner.[6]

We begin by critically analyzing approaches that describe the history of Chicano-Anglo relations as a story of cultural conflicts and racism. Using Marxist taxonomies when appropriate, we seek to emphasize the *systemic* roots of conflict between pre-1848 Spanish-Mexican society and post-1848 Anglo-imposed social economy.[7] The history of the Southwest or, for that matter, the United States should not merely consist of a juxtaposition of cultural views, such as the Chicano perspective, the Anglo perspective, the Asian perspective, or the women's perspective. It also should examine the conflictive shared history of a prevalent economic organization of society. This approach can lead to a paradigm of complex and intertwined Anglo and Chicano history rather than one of separate perspectives.[8]

Historians who subscribe to the culture-based paradigm ground their perspectives in particular characterizations of pre-Anglo southwestern Spanish and subsequent Mexican societies.[9] Some (e.g., Albert Camarillo, Pedro Castillo, Richard Griswold del Castillo, Arnoldo de Leon, and Robert Rosenbaum) describe those societies as pastoral, communal, peasant, traditional, frontier, or hacienda. A different group of historians who place more emphasis on economic factors (e.g., Juan Gomez-Quiñones, Montejano, and Antonio Rios-Bustamante) characterize this era as "early capitalist." All, however, agree that Anglo-American society is capitalist, and all use their own characterizations of the period as points of departure for their inquiry. We hope to explore further the nature of these societies from the perspective of social and economic relations.

If the period that begins in 1848 is viewed as one in which two distinct socioeconomic formations, one largely precapitalist and quasi-feudal, and the other predominantly capitalist in character, collide, the situation looks akin to the North-South conflict in the eastern United States. More than just a "rough and tumble," racially conscious Anglo society conquering and subduing quaint Mexican pastoralists, the conquest also can be viewed as one step in the economic (capitalist) transformation of the United States from East to West. In other words, as Montejano has pointed out, the Anglo conquest was also a capitalist conquest. Economic change took place on par with cultural transformation.

In the second half of this chapter we exemplify briefly how a perspective grounded in economic power and processes can also be applied to two other themes in Chicano history. First we address the significance of the nineteenth century for Chicano historiography. Some scholars, including Camarillo, Del Castillo, Carlos Cortes, Gomez-Quiñones, and most recently Mario Garcia, find the Anglo conquest of 1848 and the ensuing Spanish, Mexican, and Anglo conflict to be a historical watershed from which issues a continuous nineteenth- and twentieth-century Chicano history. We challenge this assumed continuity between the nineteenth and twentieth centuries. Second, we seek to provide an alternative perspective to the common emphasis on urban Chicano experience. Chicanos have been predominantly urban only since 1940 or so. Overlooking the rural history, scholars too often disregard the origins of socioeconomic structures that underlie the contemporary urban experience.

Our goal, then, is to develop a useful characterization of pre- and post-conquest societies. This approach, it is hoped, will help scholars to engage in a comparative analysis of U.S. regional histories; encourage the study of the social, economic, and gender relations among Spanish, Mexican, and Anglo peoples of the American Southwest; and perhaps even contribute to moving Chicano history "from margin to center" in U.S. history discourse.[10]

The Character of Southwestern Spanish and Mexican Society

The nineteenth-century transition from Spanish and Mexican rule to U.S. governance is critical to Chicano historiography. Scholars argue that we can understand the process of evolving relations between the Spanish-speaking and English-speaking peoples in the post-1848 era by studying their particular characteristics, but disagree about the characteristics themselves.

Two sorts of definitions of Spanish/Mexican society have been offered most often. Albert Camarillo provides a succinct example of the first: "Once the subdivision of rancho and public lands had begun, the dominance of the emerging economic system of American capitalism in the once-Mexican region was a foregone conclusion. The process of land loss and displacement of the Mexican *pastoral economy* was fairly complete throughout the Southwest by the 1880s [emphasis added]."[11]

In a second view, which emphasizes economic elements, Spanish/Mexican societies were "early capitalist." Gomez-Quiñones, for example, contends that the essence of Mexican society was an emerging capitalist order, a transition away from a formal, feudal social order.[12] A decade later David Montejano agreed with Gomez-Quiñones: Montejano suggests that feudalism "is . . . a misleading description" of the pre-1848 Southwest and that the Spanish-Mexican haciendas were "a form of early capitalism."[13]

Historians applying the first approach characterize Spanish/Mexican society less specifically than Anglo-American society. Vague terms such as "traditional" or "pastoral" define the former; a more analytic one—"capitalism"—the latter. The invading society is distinctly described as capitalist in economy, culture, institutions, and behavior. We would expect it either to conflict with opposing social forms or to merge with similar social forms. However, the existing categorizations describe Spanish/Mexican society without regard to specific economic structure. We cannot examine a conflict between a society whose economy remains vaguely described (pastoral or traditional) and one with a specifically described (capitalist) economy.

The terms "pastoral," "communal," and "traditional" do not explain Spanish/Mexican society any more than the terms "technological" and "individualistic" explain Anglo society.[14] Analytic terms should not be used regarding Anglo America without using the same degree of specificity when referring to Spanish/Mexican society. By default, this dichotomous mode of categorization leads toward a "culture conflict" model for interpreting the Anglo-Mexican encounter because a more sophisticated one based on conflicting economic systems is unavailable.[15]

Historians using the second approach—defining the pre-1848 Southwest as "early capitalist"—cite as evidence the existence of wage labor[16] and the "capitalist" character of the hacienda or rancho. The presence of a free wage laboring class is tenuous, however, and the characterization of the hacienda as a capitalist institution is debatable.

Several studies demonstrate widespread use of debt peonage, hardly the stuff of free labor. For example, Hinojosa's study of Laredo, Texas, reveals that "the indebted poor fled Laredo rather than submit to a peonage system which amounted to slavery. The frequency of calls for assistance in returning runaways suggests both the widespread use of peonage and the extensive escape from it."[17] Conversely, solid documentation for the prevalence of wage labor does not appear in the relevant literature. In fact, there is no entry for "wage labor" in the subject index of David J. Weber's *Mexican Frontier*, the most thorough work covering the 1821–1848 period.[18]

The descriptions of life in the Southwest prior to the Anglo conquest strongly suggest certainly precapitalist (if not outright feudal) relations, constructed on the foundation of Indian subjects. California Indians, working as servants or laborers, were greatly exploited by the landowners and lived at the bottom of the class hierarchy. New Mexico comprised *minifundia* farming communities in which poverty-stricken subsistence villagers were forced into sharecropping and servitude by the *latifundistas,* the dominant economic, political, and social actors. The latifundistas used extra-economic coercion to exploit labor.

The idea that a Mexican "working class" existed before 1848 may arise from the appearance of monetary compensation for labor services. However, the existence of money payment for labor services does not, in and of itself, create a capitalist, free wage labor social relation. Serfs and peasants at various times in precapitalist societies received monetary compensations. These labor forms generally were transitory and temporary, such as in periods of labor scarcity. The general practice was payment in kind or in labor services. Debt peonage, like money payment, can exist side by side with free peasantry, bound peasantry, and slavery.

Furthermore, we cannot identify a typical California rancho as an "early capitalist" enterprise. None of the servants, laborers, or artisans in the Mariano Vallejo, Bernardo Yorba, or Julian Chaves properties received a wage. Some were forced into labor through military raids. The Hacienda de los Yorbas (near present-day Santa Ana, California) was representative of the California rancho:

> The tradesmen and people employed about the [fifty-room] house were: Four wool-combers, two tanners, one butter and cheeseman who directed every day the milking of from fifty to sixty cows, one harness maker, two shoemakers, one jeweler, one plasterer, one carpenter, one mayordomo, two errand boys, one sheep herder, one cook, one baker, two washerwomen, one woman to iron, four sewing women, one dressmaker, two gardeners, a schoolmaster, and a man to make the wine. . . . More than a hundred lesser employees were maintained on the ranch. The Indian peons lived in a little village of their own. . . . Ten steers a month were slaughtered to supply the hacienda.[19]

Generally, ranches and villages in California, New Mexico, and Texas provided for most of the needs of the residents, both laborers and landowners. They functioned largely as self-subsistence units. Although some of the products of the hacienda—primarily livestock—were exported, landholders used the proceeds to satisfy their taste for luxury, not to accumulate capital.[20] In New Mexico, small landowners and communal village farmers performed their own labor, had no servants, and often sharecropped for the larger owners. Within the large, small, and communal landholding system, labor remained relatively unspecialized. In the large landholdings, owners extracted wealth through the labor of their peones; in the communal villages, families eked out a marginal existence by their own labor and generally relied on payment in kind for labor services outside the village.

Those who see "early capitalism" as dominant in the Mexican Southwest claim that the pre-1848 and post-1848 Spanish borderland societies differ not in quality but in quantity. In this perspective, linear change characterizes the historical process after 1848: a less-developed, early capitalist Spanish Southwest society merged with a higher stage of that same type of society—the U.S. capitalist. This merger is considered a "modernization process."

Modernization theory, as applied in Chicano history, depends largely on the view of the hacienda as a commercial institution and, therefore, capitalist.[21] The debate as to the nature of the hacienda in Mexico and Latin America has been long and laborious. The predominant view twenty-five years ago held the hacienda to be a feudal or quasi-feudal institution. In the past two and a half decades, this approach, which was largely based on Marxist approaches developed by François Chevalier and utilized by Woodrow Borah, came under strong attack from non-Marxists, particularly U.S. scholars trained in a functionalist tradition. They substituted eclecticism and empirical historicism for Marxist concepts and methods.[22] The question of the nature of the hacienda became part and parcel of the debate over the character of Latin American society in general. In general, these writers shifted the crucial test for the character of the institution from the manner of extraction of surplus labor within the confines of the hacienda (relations of production) to whether products of the institution entered the world labor market (relations of exchange).

While these very valuable debates helped clarify concepts and approaches, they did not change fundamentally, in our estimation, the view of the hacienda as an essentially noncapitalist enterprise. The influential Mexican historian Enrique Semo aptly described the economic essence of the hacienda by saying that it produced for the market during a period of world market booms and retracted to a self-sufficient enterprise during contractions.[23] This prodigious feat is something a capitalist enterprise cannot do.[24] Furthermore, regarding social relations between laborers and owners of the haciendas, twenty-five years of detailed investigations of this venerable Latin American institution have merely shown that forms of labor besides debt peonage could be found, including sharecropping, renting, service tenantry, and temporary wage labor. This is a far cry from a prevalence of capital/labor relations.[25]

Modernization theory, as well as "world systems" theory, assume that the essence of capitalism lies *not* in the social relations, property patterns, ideology, and political institutions of a society but rather in the existence of commercial relations. Wallerstein's "world systems" analysis has been justly criticized for making international commercial relations among countries the key to determining the capitalist character of a society and for failing to address local, regional, and national issues involving the pertinent class organization of local society.[26] Consequently, the claim that the Southwest was "early capitalist" stands on the evidence of connections with international markets. If one accepts the "international trade equals capitalism" argument, then the possibility for historical analysis of specific economic forms collapses. Long-distance trade and production for distant markets exist in nearly all human societies. Has history, to paraphrase Marx, been the history of capitalism—only *one* socioeconomic form? Modernization theory ipso facto obviates the question "Was the Southwest in the Spanish/Mexican period precapitalist, quasi-feudal, or capitalist?" In this view, the relations among Mission Indians, Pueblo Indians, Mexicans, Plains Indians, and Anglo Americans reduce to a relationship among various levels of capitalist society.

Despite differences in approach, the characterization of southwestern Mexican society by Chicano historians emphasizes cultural conflict as the basis for explaining Chicano history. The first approach does this by default because conquering and conquered societies are defined in a way that precludes discussion of systemic economic conflict. In the second and significantly more complex approach, economic conflict is belittled by stipulating economic differences only of degree between the two societies. In our view, the use of vague economic categories causes Chicano historians almost by forfeit to emphasize conflict based on cultural or racial models to treat national, cultural, or racial factors at the expense of underlying economic forms even as they sometimes incorporate mention of economic factors, even Marxist terminology. To be sure, each and every work of Chicano history cannot be wholly arranged into our scheme. A very important example is Ramon Gutiérrez's award-winning work on Spanish Pueblo and gender relations in colonial New Mexico that we cannot neatly place in the two groups above.[27] While Gutiérrez mentions the prevalence and, in fact, the increase of servile forms of labor in New Mexico toward the end of the eighteenth century, he focuses instead on gender systems and sexual practices as indicative of relations of domination and as keys to the construction, mediation, and defense of cultural identity. In his view, the Hispano-Anglo conflict can be seen primarily as a form of culture clash that can be explained without significant reference to systemic economic conflict.[28]

Our purpose is not to develop watertight classification schemes. Such an effort would be not only doomed from the start, given diversity within Chicano historiography, but also be of limited value in and of itself. Rather, we seek to use strands already present in some of the works mentioned and to build what we think would be a stronger analytic framework for the economic and social historian, a task to which we now turn.

On Relations of Production

Categories of political economy devised by Marx, with appropriate temporal and spatial specificity, help reveal that pre-1848 Spanish-Mexican society derived from Spain's social structure in the New World. That is, the social heritage of the southwestern Spanish/Mexican era derived from hierarchical and inherited class relations characteristic of the Spanish social order.[29] This is not to say, however, that the pre-1848 New World social formations replicated Spanish social relations exactly and had no history of their own. The New World manifested innumerable variations due to climate, topography, demography, and so forth, much as, in Spain itself, the large *dehesas* of Andalucia differed from the small peasant holdings of the Cantabrian range during the seventeenth and eighteenth centuries.

After the conquest of New Mexico, first the *encomiendas* and later the *repartimientos* formed the basis of colonial production. As an institution, the encomienda dates back to the colonization of Castile during the retreat of the Moors.[30] Its appearance in New Mexico reflects the traditional assignments granted to a Spanish conqueror—in this case to some of Oñate's top soldiers—including supervision of Indian subjects required to perform labor for the benefit of the *encomendero*.[31]

Additionally, large land grants were given to the more prominent Spaniards. Through the encomiendas, the Pueblo villages contributed an annual tribute in kind to the leading colonists, usually consisting of maize and cotton blankets. In New Mexico, the tribute accruing from the encomienda did not amount to much. The repartimiento—or apportionment of coerced labor required from the Indian population living near an encomienda—was utilized to the fullest extent by the settlers living on ranches, and so was more important to them than to the Spanish colonists.[32]

Were these class distinctions softened by interaction and a reciprocal spirit?[33] In precapitalist societies, the need to cooperate against the forces of nature, and the physical proximity due to geographical isolation (and lack of transportation), bred a form of paternalism in which the lord legitimately cared for his vassals and serfs. This aspect of precapitalist society was, of course, reinforced by religious tenets that rationalized the modus vivendi. From a romantic point of view, the nature of class relations in precapitalist societies can be favorably compared to the atomization and competitive mentality prevalent in a fully developed capitalist society.[34] Social historical analysis, however, should look not only at the daily exposition of benevolence or lack thereof, but also at the long-term path of a society's development and at the material chances of escape from a position of coerced servitude. In precapitalist situations, then, "benevolence" may be viewed as an instrument of continued domination rather than as an idyllic virtue from older, better times.

Although the legal history of property relations in the California settlement is similar in form to that of its older cousin to the east, its content varies considerably. Importantly, the "mission system" exercised land control during the years before and well into the Mexican period.

The missionaries of California confronted a situation different from those in New Mexico. In New Mexico, as in large parts of Mexico and South America, the Indian population was concentrated in native towns and villages, and the missionaries were able to take the faith to them. Under the mission system, the California Indians were clearly subjected to coerced, compulsory labor that bore a striking resemblance to slavery.[35]

The mission system ended in 1833 with secularization and the distribution of land and livestock holdings to private land-grant holders. The secularization of mission lands marked the second major pre-1848 period in the history of land tenure practices and social relations in California—the era of the ranchos.

The size and number of these ranchos and the social relations they engendered predominated for several decades. As discussed above, the rancho has been compared traditionally to the medieval English manor. We underscore again its self-sufficiency: Although a great deal of production related to livestock was exported, these exports satisfied the luxury needs of the rancheros and did not lead to the accumulation of capital.[36]

Arizona was settled as early as 1696, when Father Eusebio Kino founded a number of missions, including San Xavier del Bac, near present-day Tucson. By the end of his work, in about 1712, twenty-five years of quiet were shattered by the discovery of silver in Arizona. After this brief silver boom, Arizona's economy came to be dominated by livestock production. The regional settlement included missions and some haciendas. However, from the middle of the eighteenth century onward, the area was the target of constant campaigns by warring Indians, which made the maintenance of this frontier next to impossible. With Mexican independence and the disappearance of the defensive presidios, the area was abandoned and, from 1822 to 1862, suffered relative neglect.[37]

The case of Texas was at once different and similar. The settlements were small and dispersed mostly around San Antonio, La Bahia, and Nacogdoches. Recent work by Gerald Poyo and Gilberto Hinojosa, while not focused on the issue at hand, provides what seems like a checklist for the lack of capitalist characteristics: absence of laborers; lack of markets for products; backward agricultural technology; and local "elites" concentrating on raising cattle in an extensive manner, much like the Californios.[38] Montejano's detailed description of Texas border social relations supports a similar conclusion.[39] The population of Texas barely reached four thousand at the end of the eighteenth century. In the lower Rio Grande Valley (where the way of life was quite similar to that of early California), a "few Mexico landowners lived an idle and lordly existence based upon a system of peonage."[40] Already by 1830, Anglo Americans outnumbered Mexicans by ten to one. These included some independent farming settlers, the harbingers of a new social system, but also many who held slaves, planted cotton, and sold it. In Texas, then, two sets of relations—precapitalist and slavery—existed side by side.[41]

On Relations of Exchange

Commodity production—that is, organized production for sale in the marketplace, a primary objective of capitalist production—was nearly absent in the northern Mexican settlements. To be sure, there were trade contacts with the outside. Despite centuries of physical isolation, the Spanish/ Mexican Southwest maintained an interesting array of trade ties with surrounding economies.[42] This trade, however, cannot be considered capitalistic. Or better yet, as Douglas Monroy has put it, "the trade of the California coast in the early nineteenth century may well have been a part of the world market, but the territory was not capitalist—the market did not mediate between persons or things."[43]

In a conception of capitalism as a historically specific pattern of production, the laborers are separated from the means of production (in this case, land). Labor power becomes a commodity that is utilized to produce other commodities. Commodity production on the basis of a wage-labor class constitutes the distinguishing feature of capitalism. The scholars we critique use the term "capitalism," as Elizabeth Fox-Genovese puts it, "in a general, heuristic fashion to apply to concentration of wealth, participation in commerce, the presence of banks, and the quest for incomes."[44] Such definitions focus on ahistorical attributes of all or most economic activity and therefore tend to "conflate all historical experience."[45]

As in the case of some localities in classical antiquity and in medieval Western Europe, the intensification of commerce in the Southwest from 1831 to 1848 was not conducive to the development of local industry and manufacturing or to the growth of towns and handicraft industries.[46] One historian noted that in New Mexico, the landed oligarchy engaging in trade "became merchants as well as feudal lords."[47] Much of the revenue gained through trade was used to purchase luxury goods, manufactured items, and land. Consequently, the influx of revenue had little appreciable impact on the redistribution of land, division of labor, and technology in production. In fact, during the Mexican era, when trade expanded in New Mexico and California, class distinctions hardened, large land grants multiplied, and peonage increased.[48] Moreover, by 1846, foreigners dominated production by artisans, leading one contemporary to remark that, in spite of the high volume of trade in hide and tallow, "there are no capitalists in California."[49] It is difficult if not impossible to paint the rancheros as capitalists. Mariano Guadalupe Vallejo, the "proud oligarch of Sonoma,"[50] had his own private militia to guard his vast estate and forty-seven servants to tend to his wife and children.

How was the pre-1848 socioeconomic formation in the Southwest finally defeated? What was the social significance of the Mexican-American War? The answers to these questions are paradoxically both simple and complex: simple in that within a few years a different mode of the social organization of production predominated the southwestern economy; complex in that (with regional and chronological differences) a variety of social mechanisms and individual agents simultaneously influenced this change. In some areas, it is clear that economic forces—more specifically, differences in the methods governing the economic organization of production—were the principal determinants of social change. In other areas (or at other times), purely economic factors are obscured, and legal (and/or extraeconomic forms of coercion) predominate. This situation is not surprising if the process is, as we assert, one of social revolution. It is certainly more difficult to identify and to ascertain the impact of social forces in an epoch of upheaval and rapid flux than in an era of stability.[51]

Periodization: The Key in the Nineteenth Century?

The notion that Chicano history begins with the conquest of 1848 is a common thread running through a majority of works in Chicano history.[52] Moreover, Chicano historians nearly unanimously emphasize a continuity of Chicano history from that point to the present. It is cultural conflict between Anglos and Mexicans that occupies the explanatory center of the discourse.

Chicano historians typically apply concepts that inadequately identify significant differences between nineteenth- and twentieth-century Chicano history, just as they tend to leave vague the nature of the economic conflict between conqueror and conquered in the mid-nineteenth century. On the other hand, a shared "cultural" trait, such as being Spanish-surnamed or Spanish-speaking, provides prima facie evidence for continuity between the nineteenth and twentieth centuries.

The conquest of 1848 appears to be the key event that subordinated Mexicans and thus represents the beginning of Chicanos as a discrete population in the United States—the "Conquered Generation" in Garcia's terms.[53] Later immigrations entered a society that had institutionalized the separate and subordinated status of Mexicans. This view is most clearly advanced by Professor Camarillo. He states that "[t]he history of the Chicano people as an ethnic minority in the United States was forged primarily from a set of nineteenth-century experiences."[54] "The key to reconstructing the history of Chicano society in southern California," he continues, "is understanding the major developments of the half-century after the Mexican War."[55] He calls scholars' tendency to consider the nineteenth century fairly unimportant a "long-held but untenable" view. In sum, nineteenth-

and twentieth-century Chicano experience seems fundamentally more continuous than discontinuous.[56]

The "importance of the nineteenth century for understanding the twentieth-century Chicano experience" appeared "self-evident to historians," according to David J. Weber.[57] It does not appear self-evident to us. The argument can be made for northern New Mexico, where twentieth-century Mexican immigration played a less significant role. It perhaps may be extended ad hoc to other subregions, but not persuasively to the region as a whole.

One might question the importance of determining which period established the foundation for the modern Mexican-American experience. When Chicano history began and who should be included in this history are important issues because a major debate pivots on: Do Chicanos constitute another immigrant ethnic group (similar to the Chinese, Japanese, Koreans, Germans, Jews, and others), or are they a "nationally" self-conscious, "conquered," indigenous population who were dispossessed of their land, as were the American Indians? How are Chicanos similar to and different from other nondominant peoples? Are Chicanos unique?[58]

The idea that contemporary Chicano history continues from social relations established in the 1848 conquest and that the nineteenth century therefore is "key" to Chicano history has been generally adhered to although challenged by the recent published works of Monroy and Gutiérrez.[59] Historians applying the "conquered people" thesis traditionally link a series of nineteenth-century conditions to the experiences of the contemporary Chicano population. Among these conditions are: segregated barrios; racial prejudice, discrimination, stereotypes, and violence; subordinate status; distinct culture; and occupation. Camarillo and Griswold del Castillo, for example, see the barrios of today as originating in the conquest; de Leon examines Mexican culture in the Southwest as transcending the Mexican and Anglo-American periods; and Gomez-Quiñones examines Chicano working-class history from the seventeenth century to the present. Carlos Cortes summarizes the perspective: "Mexican Americans began as an annexed regional minority and continued so throughout the nineteenth century. They are still concentrated heavily in the Southwest. . . ."[60] Stipulating a "conquered" legacy throughout Chicano history distinguishes Chicanos from other minorities such as the Chinese and Japanese (especially in the nineteenth century), and parallels the involuntary origins of African Americans and American Indians.

Focusing on issues of economic development, however, would reveal important changes between the nineteenth century and the twentieth century. We can distinguish between the established Mexican society and the later Mexican immigrants, representing two separate epochs and populations in the history of Spanish-speakers in the Southwest.[61] This perspective supports Almaguer's recent assessment that "a major discontinuity exists between the nineteenth- and early twentieth-century Chicano experiences."[62]

Several facts support the perspective that major trends in twentieth-century Chicano history postdate the conquest. First, with the exception of New Mexico, the small number of Mexicans annexed by the conquest are inconsequential compared to the much larger number of late-nineteenth-century Mexican migrants to the region. Second, the parallels between the nineteenth-century Chicano experience and that of other nonwhite minorities are striking. Mexicans suffered segregation, violence (such as lynching), and exploitation, as did the "nonconquered" Chinese, Japanese, Filipinos, and Asian Indians.[63] Third, the massive economic transformations of the Southwest created a great demand for cheap, unskilled labor, which was met by a tremendous migration from Mexico beginning at about the turn of the twentieth century.

Certainly, the pattern of regional development in the United States greatly affected Chicano history. The growth of southern California in particular became intimately related with demographic shifts of the Chicano population. The extraordinary development of the western half of the southwest region—a result of mass migration—came with the growth of California agriculture and southern California industry, both of which would have been impossible without the various Colorado River water projects.[64] As Berkeley economist Paul S. Taylor so aptly put it in 1928, "Irrigation means Mexicans."[65]

Additionally, an analysis of twentieth-century water development and agribusiness would demonstrate a history common to domestic migrants from the eastern United States and to Mexican immigrants. The recent regional development of the Southwest has depended on massive east-to-west U.S. migration and south-to-north Mexican migration.

The often violent struggle between precapitalist Mexican and capitalist Anglo societies emerged after 1848 but faded by 1900 as a new, integrated economic order arose. The fifteen thousand Mexican citizens living outside of New Mexico either accommodated to the new society or were overwhelmed by Mexican migrants. The conquered group lacked sufficient numbers to have a significant impact in the Anglo era. Moreover, once they lost their land by the late nineteenth century, they suffered significant cultural disintegration. Except in New Mexico and southern Colorado, Mexican migrants provided a completely new period in the history of the Spanish-speaking people in the Southwest.[66]

The four thousand Mexicanos residing in Texas in 1836 were vastly outnumbered. The old center of pre-1836 Spanish-Mexican activity, San Antonio and surroundings, did not receive mass Mexican migration until the twentieth century.[67] The same occurred in Arizona and California.[68]

Whereas little migration occurred in the nineteenth century, massive migration characterizes the twentieth. These migrants entered a society organized upon corporate economic enterprises, within which the economic function and political activity of Mexican labor is circumscribed by the combined power of the state and corporate interests.[69] These factors shape the evolution of the Chicano community in the twentieth century.

Migration in the twentieth century altered the character of the southwestern Mexican community. By the 1920s, Mexican labor became the key to economic development, the Spanish-speaking population grew dramatically, and settlement patterns multiplied and expanded.

Earlier Anglo-Mexican social relations turned on the conflict between two distinct socioeconomic formations, but twentieth-century social relations centered on the internal class conflicts inherent to corporate capitalism. The economic issues affecting Anglo-Mexican social relations shifted from conflicting systems of production to class relations within the same system. Likewise, the political conflicts shifted from land issues in the nineteenth century to working-class concerns in the twentieth. These conflictive relations are expressed in the racial and ethnic dimensions of the contemporary Southwest. The Mexican community as we know it today developed in this new atmosphere of corporate capitalism, a twentieth-century phenomenon.

We hope that a focus on these economic changes leads historians to reexamine Chicano history's dominant periodization to date, which assumes a fundamental continuity between the nineteenth and twentieth centuries. That "group history" view, based on racial conflict and shared language, obscures broader and more explanatory themes based on economic transformations and their social consequences.

The Urban Emphasis

Until recently, Chicano historiography has emphasized the urban Chicano experience.[70] In a review of three principal works on urban Chicano history by Albert Camarillo, Mario Garcia, and Richard Griswold del Castillo, David J. Weber noted that "all three try to link their work to the mainstream of social and urban history while still focusing on the particularity of the Mexican-American experience."[71] These studies, known as "the new Chicano urban history," restored the past to the "region's largest minority." Moreover, in accomplishing these scholars' mission, the writers "established the importance of the city as the crucible of change in Chicano society and culture, and have provided a valuable corrective to the notion of Chicanos as an essentially rural people.[72]

The urban analysis extends back into the colonial period. Romo writes: "Chicanos have not always lived in urban areas, but since 1609, at least, when their Spanish-Mexican ancestors founded the pueblo of Santa Fe, they have contributed to and have been a part of the urbanization process in the Southwest.[73] Richard Griswold del Castillo concurs, adding that ". . . [d]uring Spanish colonial times probably a larger proportion of the region's population lived in pueblos, towns, and cities than did the population in other areas of the United States."[74] Chicano urban history, then, encompasses both the pre- and post-1848 periods, though primarily concerned with the post-1848 era.

Thus, historians tend to examine Chicano history since the Spanish settlements as a branch of urban history. Even small population centers, such as Tucson in 1850, are labeled "urban." Consequently, the significance of the terms "urban" and "rural" disappears as nearly every population group is considered "urban."[75]

Complex and Heterogeneous Settlement Patterns

Several important conditions in the Southwest argue for a new, more complex approach to Chicano history. Pre-1848 southwestern towns and pueblos can hardly be classed with contemporary industrial urban centers on the East Coast, primarily because precapitalist population centers differ significantly from cities and towns in a capitalistic social economy. As late as the 1930s, urban Chicanos made up only half of the Chicano population.[76] Martin Sanchez Jankowski writes, "Until the 1960s, Chicanos lived primarily in rural areas or were members of small or medium sized communities. During the 1960s and 1970s Chicanos became more urban."[77] Moreover, fully 70 percent of the southwestern population lived in rural areas at the turn of the twentieth century. We doubt that Chicanos were more urbanized at that time than the general population.

As a consequence of the emphasis on "urban" life, Chicano history focuses on industrial, blue-collar labor and neglects rural and semiurban Chicano communities and their histories. For example, Chicano communities of southern California, such as the many citrus picker villages, do not fit the urban history model and have received little attention.[78] Carey McWilliams, one of the few historians who recognize the important rural character of such communities, writes, "This citrus belt complex of peoples, institutions, and relationships has no parallel in rural life in America and nothing quite like it exists elsewhere in California. It is neither town nor country, neither rural nor urban. It is a world of its own."[79]

A focus on economic development such as we advocate would examine the underlying trends of the Southwest in the late nineteenth and especially the early twentieth centuries, when economic growth engendered a variety of community life, running the gamut from rural to urban. Emphasizing economic changes also would provide further impetus to a growing historiographic trend concerned with regional Chicano history in Texas, New Mexico, and California by identifying differences in economic development in these three regions.

At the turn of the century, rural or semirural Mexican population concentrations dotted the southwestern landscape. By the early 1900s, commodity production in large-scale agriculture, mining, and transportation assumed economic predominance. The newly evolving pattern of production location drew the Mexican population with it. Mexican and Anglo community development followed the economic patterns.

A variety of community forms appeared that were shaped by the industries that fostered them. For example, labor camps were constructed according to the needs of railroad, mining, agricultural, stock-raising, lumbering, and other industrial enterprises. Population centers sprouted beyond the older settlements of Los Angeles, San Diego, San Antonio, El Paso, and Santa Barbara.

Because the principal economic thrust occurred in the countryside, it comes as no surprise that the Mexican population would, like its Anglo counterpart, establish its residence, family life, and community in rural as well as urbanizing areas. Arizona mining towns, which employed considerable Mexican labor beginning in the late nineteenth century, differed in character from sharecropping communities of Texas, and from cities with a large commercial/industrial character such as Los Angeles. Communities often appeared only briefly, disappearing when a mine was exhausted, a track completed, or orchards subdivided. The Mexican community, affected by the demand for its labor power, settled according to the pattern of economic activity, with rural, semirural, and urban patterns being equally critical up to the 1940s.

Family and Gender Relations

Several urban historians have referred to camps—enclaves of Mexican laborers and their families. Unfortunately, no one has sought to study them in depth. The term "camps" was used extensively in the 1900–40 period as an identification for a Mexican community, especially in the rural and semirural areas. Camp life often conjured images of impermanence, migration, tent life, or marginality. Recent research by Gilbert G. Gonzalez demonstrates, however, that camps, such as those in southern California's citrus belt, remain as barrios today in spite of the suburban sprawl that has engulfed them. Camps often constituted clearly defined, permanent, stable, and well-structured Mexican villages. Camps existed not only in the southern California citrus belt but also in migrant agricultural areas (especially in sugar beet fields) and in mining, railroad, and construction regions as well. A brief review of camps and their relation to economic development and urban life demonstrates the importance of integrating the role of Chicano rural life into Chicano history.

Rural communities extended beyond camps as families migrated with or without a home base. Some permanent communities of the lower Rio Grande were substantially populated by migrating families, which certainly shaped the character of the cities and towns. Type of work also influenced camp life and community. Citrus growers, for example, were stable, permanent, year-round employers, whereas the contract system that structured family labor in agriculture was periodic, indeterminate, and unorganized (except in beet work). These factors would affect the organization of community and the families' strategies to structure and control their own lives.

Another common and related form of community life was the company town. Often a camp *was* a company town, but research has not yet recognized the extent to which many Mexican communities owed their existence to a single company or grower association. *Colonias* or barrios in the copper towns of Arizona; the Goodyear cotton town of Litchfield, Arizona; the beet fields of California and Colorado; the steel mills of Indiana; and the citrus-grower association camps of southern California were part of a larger pattern of company towns in the West, the Midwest, and the South.

There were variations within these categories, too. For example, the sugar beet company towns of Ventura, California, had a decidedly different atmosphere than the towns of the South Platte Valley, Colorado. Even within southern California, the citrus company towns varied from heavy, paternalistic intervention into daily life to a hands-off policy by growers.[80]

Issues relating to gender and family need to be assessed within this broad spectrum of community.[81] Employment and/or educational opportunities available to women and children varied in relation to the organization of labor in particular enterprises. These, in turn, affected family, culture, and ultimately community. In the regions where family labor was widespread, the independence of women as economic actors was sharply curtailed in comparison to their urban counterparts. Family labor also was largely absent in the citrus industry and therefore of little significance in maintaining production; however, women were widely employed in the packinghouses, paradoxically earning wages equal to those of their male counterparts, the pickers. This factor certainly distinguished female employment in citrus from that of migrant family labor, such as in cotton production. Women packers held a sense of self-worth based on their individual labor and talents that was all but impossible for women who worked as part of a family unit. The male head of the family was the sole wage earner, and wages were paid directly to him by his employer or the labor contractor, seldom to the individuals who composed the family. Thus women in family-picking labor rarely received individual compensation for their labor.

A measure of the wide distinction between the experience of women in cotton production and women in urban production appears when comparing the work of Ruth Allen to that of Vicki Ruiz. Allen's classic 1933 study of women in Texas cotton production noted that among Mexican women who did fieldwork for hire, only a small percentage "received the income from their labor. In the case of the . . . married women the husbands received all the income."[82] Among 110 women who worked in a family unit not one "reported that there was any arrangement to pay for her labor."[83] Allen further states,

> But even when the woman is a hired laborer, she has no individual economic existence. Her husband, father, or brother handles the financial affairs. She does not collect her own money; she does not know how much is paid for her services; she seldom knows how much cotton she picks a day or how many acres she chops. The wage paid is a family wage, and the family is distinctly patriarchal in its organization.[84]

Vicki Ruiz's 1987 study of California cannery and packing women of the 1930s and 1940s arrived at substantially different observations. In the Los Angeles area, Ruiz found that "many women had dreams of white collar careers," and although women workers sought work to augment family income, they labored as individual wage earners even if they generally received less than men for the same work.[85] At work women developed a "cannery culture," a consciousness of common interests that fueled the movement toward unionization where ethnic women affected "every facet of decision making."[86]

Citrus packers responded to their work in a similar fashion. One packer declared that the packinghouse offered "a greater opportunity for women" and provided "a sense of importance and purpose . . . I learned about my own rights."[87] Furthermore, she added, "it was better, a lot better than picking cotton . . . [picking cotton] was miserable . . . [in comparison] packing oranges was heaven . . . it was a step ahead . . . at least we had a stable life."[88]

In education received, there also has been substantial variation according to the economy. Educational opportunity in the urban setting was much more egalitarian than in the rural migrant settlements. Rural migrants were far less likely to attend school, or if attending at all, they tended to attend only a portion of the school year. Statistics for Texas taken in 1945 indicate that only half of Mexican children were enrolled in school. In part, this was due to a deliberate policy by boards of education across the state to bar Mexican children, especially migrant children, from enrolling in school. However, in citrus towns opportunities for schooling were greater due to the absence of family labor, but less so than in the urban context due to occasional migrations for agricultural work.

Dr. Ernesto Galarza recognized the political distinction between urban and rural Mexican communities—a distinction that divided some civil rights activists in the 1940s and as recently as the 1970s.[89] Cesar Chavez, for example, left the Community Service Organization in the mid-1950s because it focused attention on urban issues. Chavez sought to deal with the problems of the rural Mexican community, a decision with far-reaching and well-known effects on the history of farm worker unions and California agriculture. That urban and rural areas contain distinguishable issues is further underscored by the differing emphases on school reform during the 1960s and 1970s. Rural activists generally demanded integration, while urban activists turned toward separatism, community control of neighborhood schools, and bilingual education.[90]

Fortunately, the urban emphasis in Chicano historiography is waning. Some recent Chicano historiography takes a more complex approach. For example, Sarah Deutsch's analysis of the transition from rural to urban life, Vicki Ruiz's incorporation of gender issues in her examination of women's organizations in the agriculture-based food-processing industry, Richard Griswold del Castillo's biographical study of Cesar Chavez, Robert Alvarez's study of Baja California migrating families, and Arnoldo de Leon's several works demonstrate that some communities do not fall into the urban pattern described in the earlier literature.[91] Finally, Poyo and Hinojosa's recent *Journal of American History* article[92] demonstrates in its concrete study of early Texas settlements the complexity and enduring significance of those specific communities.

The above examples verify the need to expand the scope of historical study beyond the urban setting. By so doing, Chicano historiography will begin to study appropriately the varied processes through which communities are constructed, community life is organized, and social and gender relations have evolved.

In the preceding pages we have used concepts appropriate to the task of identifying the systemic nature of the economic conflict between the pre-1848 Spanish-Mexican settlements and the economic modes represented by the invading Anglos in the second half of the nineteenth century. The focus on economic transformations served as well to question the conventional periodization of Chicano history and to posit the nineteenth- and twentieth-century Spanish-speaking populations of the Southwest as largely two different populations. Looking further at the process of economic development in the twentieth century allowed us to distinguish the varied ways in which communities, community life, and social and gender relations developed. Behind our approach lies the conviction that culture and economic life should not be kept in separate historical compartments. Rather, studies of cultural and racial issues and conflicts can be usefully contextualized through the nuances of economic change.

Perhaps focusing the discussion of Chicano-Anglo conflictive social relations on questions of economic power and development can assist in showing Chicano history to be more than the distinct experience and contribution of one particular regional, ethnic group. It might lead to interesting comparisons of the process of capitalist development east-to-west as well as north-to-south in the United States. The kind of analysis made by southern historians about capitalist development in the South and its inherent conflicts might be generalized to the entire nation and to include gender relations. Thus it is first possible that one could take a first step in the long march of demonstrating Chicano history to be an integral component of U.S. social history as a whole—of import to all U.S. historians. Together with other, concurrent efforts to stimulate a multicultural history, it might serve to distinguish the common experiences across cultural group and gender histories. To paraphrase Cornell West, paying keen attention to economic structures can assist historians to contextualize cultural history.[93]

Notes

1. Chicano historiography has made impressive strides over the past twenty years. See, among others, the following studies: Pedro Castillo, "The Making of a Mexican Barrio: Los Angeles: 1890–1920" (Ph.D. diss., University of California, Santa Barbara, 1979); Albert Camarillo, *Chicanos in a Changing Society* (Cambridge, Mass., 1979); Juan Gomez-Quiñones, "The Origins and Development of the Mexican Working Class in the United States: Laborers and Artisans North of the Rio Bravo, 1600–1900," in *El trabajo y los trabajadores en la historia de Mexico*, ed. Elsa C. Frost (Tucson, 1979), 463–505; Richard Griswold del Castillo, *The Los Angeles Barrio, 1850–1890: A Social History* (Berkeley: University of California Press, 1979); Mario Garcia, *Desert Immigrants: The Mexicans of El Paso, 1880–1920* (New Haven, Conn.: Yale University Press, 1981) and *Mexican Americans: Leadership, Ideology, and Identity, 1930–1960* (New Haven, Conn.: Yale University Press, 1989); Robert J. Rosenbaum, *Mexicano Resistance in the Southwest* (Austin: University of Texas Press, 1981); Rodolfo Acuña, *Occupied America: A History of Chicanos*, 2nd ed. (New York: Harper and Row, 1981); Ricardo Romo, *East Los Angeles: A History of a Barrio* (Austin: University of Texas Press, 1983); Richard Griswold del Castillo, *La Familia: Chicano Families in the Urban Southwest: 1848 to the Present* (Notre Dame, Ind.: University of Notre Dame Press, 1984); David Montejano, *Anglos and Mexicans in the Making of Texas, 1836–1986* (Austin: University of Texas Press, 1987); Vicki Ruiz, *Cannery Women, Cannery Lives: Mexican Women, Unionization, and the California Food Processing Industry, 1930–1950* (Albuquerque: University of New Mexico Press, 1987). See also Carlos Cortes, "Mexicans," in *Harvard Encyclopedia of American Ethnic Groups,* edited by Stephan Thernstrom, Ann Orlov, and Oscar Handlin (Cambridge, Mass.: Belknap Press of Harvard University, 1980), 699; Arnoldo de Leon, *The Tejano Community, 1836–1900* (Albuquerque: University of New Mexico Press, 1982); Albert Camarillo, *Chi-*

canos in California: A History of Mexican Americans in California (San Francisco, 1984); John R. Chavez, The Lost Land: The Chicano Image of the Southwest (Albuquerque: University of New Mexico Press, 1984); Arnoldo de Leon and Kenneth L. Stewart, Tejanos and the Numbers Game: A Socio-Historical Interpretation from the Federal Censuses, 1850–1900 (Albuquerque: University of New Mexico Press, 1989); Thomas E. Sheridan, Los Tucsonenses: The Mexican Community in Tucson, 1854–1941 (Tucson: University of Arizona Press, 1986).

2. Nan Elizabeth Woodruff, "The Transition to Capitalism in America," review of Christopher Clark, The Roots of Rural Capitalism: Western Massachusetts, 1780–1860 (Ithaca: Cornell University Press, 1990), in Reviews in American History 20 (1992): 173.

3. Several historians, notably Albert Camarillo, Pedro Castillo, and Robert Rosenbaum, aptly utilize Hobsbawm's concept of "social banditry" to analyze the appearance of banditry among the poorer segments of the vanquished population in the region. See Pedro Castillo and Albert Camarillo, eds., Furia y Muerte: Los Bandidos Chicanos (Los Angeles: UCLA Chicano Studies Center, 1973); Rosenbaum, Mexicano Resistance.

4. For example, Las Gorras Blancas. There were also several periods of outright warfare in Lincoln and San Miguel Counties. See Acuña, Occupied America, passim. The Texas "vigilante" style of law enforcement, biased against the local Mexican population, led to many injustices and resentment for many decades.

5. Rosalinda González, "Distinctions in Western Women's Experience: Ethnicity, Class, and Social Change," in The Women's West, edited by Susan Armitage (Norman: University of Oklahoma Press, 1987), 237–52; Montejano, Anglos and Mexicans; Douglas Monroy, Thrown among Strangers: The Making of Mexican Culture in Frontier California (Berkeley: University of California Press, 1990). The question of the direction of Chicano history is the subject of several recent essays. See Alex Saragoza, "The Significance of Recent Chicano-Related Historical Writings: An Appraisal," Ethnic Affairs 1 (1987): 25; Gerald E. Poyo and Gilberto M. Hinojosa, "Spanish Texas and Borderlands Historiography in Transition: Implications for U.S. History," Journal of American History 75 (1988): 393–416; David J. Weber, "John Francis Bannon and the Historiography of the Spanish Borderlands," Myth and the History of the Hispanic Southwest Essays (Albuquerque: University of New Mexico Press, 1988), 55–88; Tomas Almaguer, "Ideological Distortions in Recent Chicano Historiography: The Internal Model and Chicano Historical Interpretation," Aztlan 18 (1987): 7–27.

6. Generally speaking, Chicano historiography developed somewhat separately from the ongoing writing by borderland scholars and focuses on the later period. For a detailed evaluation of the vicissitudes and "sociology" of these fields of study see David J. Weber, "John Francis Bannon and the Historiography of the Spanish Borderlands." See also José Cuello, "Beyond the 'Borderlands' in the North of Colonial Mexico: A Latin-Americanist Perspective to the Study of the Mexican North and the United States Southwest," in Proceedings of the Pacific Coast Council on Latin American Studies IX, edited by Krityna P. Demaree (San Diego, 1982), 1–24.

7. Novelty is difficult to achieve, of course. More than twenty years ago, Howard Lamar categorized parts of the Southwest as "feudalistic." See Howard Lamar, The Far Southwest, 1848–1912: A Territorial History (New Haven, Conn.: Yale University Press, 1966). Even earlier, Carey McWilliams, in his classic North from Mexico (New York: Greenwood Press, 1968), applied a similar characterization.

8. Rosalinda González provides several examples of integrating Chicana women's household labor and wage labor into the fabric of capitalism and agribusiness in the West. See her "The Chicana in Southwest Labor History, 1900–1975: A Preliminary Bibliographical Analysis," Critical Perspectives of Third World America 2 (1984): 26–61; "Distinctions in Western Women's Experience: Ethnicity, Class and Social Change," in Armitage, The Women's West, 237–51; "Chicanas and Mexican Immigrant Families, 1920–1940: Women's Subordination and Family Exploitation," in Decades of Discontent, ed. Joan Jensen and Lois Scharff (Westport, Conn.: Greenwood Press, 1983), 59–84.

9. For a recent treatise covering the history of the entire northern Mexico borderland under Spain's rule, see Oakah L. Jones Jr., Los Paisanos: Spanish Settlers on the Northern Frontier of New Spain (Norman: University of Oklahoma Press, 1979). The Mexican period (1821–46) is aptly described in David J. Weber, The Mexican Frontier, 1821–1846 (Albuquerque: University of New Mexico Press, 1982).

10. bell hooks, Feminist Theory from Margin to Center (Boston: South End Press, 1985).

11. Albert Camarillo, "Chicanos in the American City," in Chicano Studies: A Multidisciplinary Approach, edited by Eugene E. Garcia, Francisco A. Lomeli, and Isidro D. Ortiz (New York:

New Teachers College Press, 1984), 25. He writes: "The economic formations within the Mexican communities greater Mexican North in the seventeenth and eighteenth centuries can be characterized as early-capitalist, a period of a variety of co-existing economic forms and practices, the predominant tendency being the transition to capitalism."

12. See Gomez-Quiñones, "Origins and Development of the Mexican Working Class," 464.

13. Montejano specifically rejects the views of the pre-1848 Southwest as a feudal or even a pre-capitalist (and merely pastoral) society. See Montejano, *Anglos and Mexicans*, 312–13.

14. Robert J. Rosenbaum carefully attempts to define Mexican society by applying the term "peasant." However, peasants were only one segment of Mexican society in the pre-1848 Southwest. The term is misleading in that it narrowly defines the class nature of Mexican society while at the same time providing too general an interpretive design. See Rosenbaum, *Mexicano Resistance*.

15. Others might argue that "nationalist" impulses led Chicano writers to emphasize a "them vs. us" attitude. See, for example, Saragoza, "Significance of Recent Chicano-Related Historical Writings," 27.

16. Gomez-Quiñones notes that the landless sector "worked for wages in principle; these were sometimes real, more often fictional. Wage labor worked alongside indentured labor and even slave labor." He also states that the "majority of landless mestizos were laborers or *medieros* (sharecroppers). Persons were paid in subsistence, shares, goods, and small wages." See Gomez-Quiñones, "Origins and Development of the Mexican Working Class," 481, 501.

17. Gilberto M. Hinojosa, *A Borderlands Town in Transition: Laredo, 1755–1870* (College Station: Texas A & M University Press, 1983), 41. Weber notes that in New Mexico the practice of debt peonage was widespread, even more so in the Mexican than in the Spanish period. (See Weber, *Mexican Frontier*, 211–12). Cleland found the same in southern California, where the Indians were "the chief labor supply. . . . They lived and worked under a form of peonage similar in some respects to that so long in effect in Mexico. . . ." (See Robert Glass Cleland, *The Cattle on a Thousand Hills* [San Marino, Calif.: The Huntington Library, 1951], 81.) Gomez-Quiñones elaborates: "As ranchos developed [Indians] were hired out to the rancheros for a fee to the missions to do similar work on the ranchos as for the missions. None or little payment went to the laborers. . . . At most they received clothes, blankets, cheap trinkets and nearly always living quarters and food. Much of this they produced through their work." (See Gomez-Quiñones, "Origins and Development of the Mexican Working Class," 474.)

18. Antonio Rios-Bustamante makes the most cogent argument for capitalist development in the pre-Anglo Southwest, specifically Albuquerque, New Mexico; however, his own data contradict his position. Bustamante found 48.5 percent of the laborers were handicraftsmen and 23.8 percent were peasants; only 13.1 percent were day laborers. As he points out, even these day laborers often owned land and were "paid in produce." The description strongly resembles those of European villages at the height of the period generally known as feudalism. See Antonio J. Rios-Bustamante, "New Mexico in the Eighteenth Century: Life, Labor and Trade in the Villa de San Felipe de Albuquerque, 1706–1790," *Aztlan* 7, no. 3 (1976): 357–89.

19. Cleland, *The Cattle on a Thousand Hills*, 74. Señora Vallejo, wife of Don Mariano Guadalupe Vallejo, recalled that in their northern California hacienda, each of her sixteen children had a personal servant; she herself had two. In addition, twenty-seven other women ground corn, served in the kitchen, washed clothes, sewed, and spun: a total of forty-five servants in the master's house (ibid., 43). In New Mexico, the raiding party was employed to acquire servants from Navajos, Utes, or Apaches. Amado Chaves reminisced in 1927 that "many of the rich people who did not have the nerve to go into campaigns would buy Indian girls." (See Weber, *Mexican Frontier*, 212.)

20. There was some division of labor but, by and large, workers could move from one area of production to another (e.g., farming, sheepherding, carpentry, and construction). Under this simple division of labor, little specialization could occur. See Lynn I. Perrigo, *Texas and Our Spanish Southwest* (Dallas, 1960), 80–83.

21. To begin with, not all southwestern haciendas—or ranchos—meet this definition. Robert Glass Cleland compared the southern California ranchos with the English manor, noting that "each ranch was virtually a self-sustaining economic unit" (Cleland, *The Cattle on a Thousand Hills*, 42–43). Sheridan notes that the haciendas in and around Tucson were

"geared towards subsistence rather than commercial exploitation and expansion" (Sheridan, *Los Tucsonenses*, 14). Nancie L. Gonzalez's study of New Mexico attests to the self-subsistence character of production in villages (although surplus often was traded): "The small Northern Spanish villages were relatively isolated . . . from each other, and each one formed an almost self-sufficient unit, both in terms of economy and social structure" (Nancie L. Gonzalez, *The Spanish-Americans of New Mexico* [Albuquerque: University of New Mexico Press, 1967], 38–39). Robert J. Rosenbaum corroborates the findings of Sheridan, Cleland, and Gonzalez. He writes: "Most mexicanos engaged in subsistence agriculture solidly rooted in the traditions and social relationships of their village or land grant. . . . Producing a surplus for market was very low on their list of priorities" (Rosenbaum, *Mexicano Resistance*, 11).

22. See Eric Van Young, "Mexican Rural History since Chevalier: The Historiography of the Colonial Hacienda," *Latin American Research Review* 18 (1983): 12.

23. Enrique Semo, *Historia del capitalismo en Mexico: los origines, 1521–1763* (Mexico City: Ediciones Era, 1973).

24. During periods of crisis, capitalist enterprises may do one of several things (e.g., go bankrupt, close, disappear, get sold, or get absorbed). They do not, cameleonlike, become self-sufficient English manors.

25. Van Young, "Mexican Rural History," 24. This situation is quite typical of precapitalist societies. Wage labor, sharecropping, and other arrangements were known during Roman times.

26. The critiques are numerous, but see especially Eric Wolf, *Europe and the People without History* (Berkeley: University of California Press, 1981) and Peter Worsley, *Three Worlds of Culture and World Development* (Chicago: University of Chicago Press, 1984).

27. One of his principal aims, Gutiérrez explains, was not to be delimited by existing historiography but rather to initiate a "new dialogue." Ramon Gutiérrez, "Comments," Ramon Gutiérrez's *When Jesus Came, the Corn Mothers Went Away: Transnational Perspectives*, Pacific Coast branch, American History Association annual meeting, Corvallis, Oregon, August 14, 1992.

28. Gutiérrez, *When Jesus Came*, 325–27.

29. Perrigo, *Texas and Our Spanish Southwest*, 33–34, 44–45, 79–81.

30. Robert S. Chamberlain, *Castilian Background of the Repartimiento-Encomienda* (Washington: Carnegie Institution of Washington, 1939).

31. See James Lockhart, "Encomienda and Hacienda: The Evolution of the Great Estate in the Spanish Indies," *Hispanic American Historical Review* 49 (1969): 411–29, for a discussion of the juridical and practical relationships between *encomiendas* and land ownership.

32. The encomiendas and repartimientos required the native inhabitants to till the soil, to tend livestock, to work in mines, and to carry burdens in addition to the paying obligatory tribute. The general relative poverty of the New Mexico area has led to questioning the view that, here as well as elsewhere, Spanish Mexicans lived comfortably off the coerced labor of their Indian serfs (George I. Sanchez, *Forgotten People: A Study of New Mexicans* [Albuquerque: University of New Mexico Press, 1949], chap. 1). Whether they lived *comfortably* or not is an outside conditioning factor that does not alter the pattern of subjection that characterized the society. Here, as well as elsewhere in New Spain, the colonists lived off the labor of their Indian charges.

33. Camarillo, *Chicanos in a Changing Society*, 12, 13.

34. In this light, one can speak of the "benevolence" of precapitalist economic forms as specifically superior to that of capitalism. This is a dangerous road: from this ahistorical vantage point, slavery also was benevolent!

35. Varden Fuller, "The Supply of Agricultural Labor as a Factor in the Evolution of Farm Organization in California," in *Agricultural Labor in California*, Hearings before a Subcommittee of the Committee on Education and Labor, U.S. Senate, 76th Cong., pt. 54 (1940).

36. Under the mission system, the predominant forms of labor were religious forced labor and peonage in the presidios. As described by one ranchero, the Indian men tilled the soil, pastured cattle, sheared sheep, cut timber, built houses, paddled boats, made bricks and tiles, ground grain, slaughtered cattle, and dressed their hides for market, while Indian women worked as servants, brought up the children, and cooked every meal.

37. Odie R. Faulk, "The Presidio: Fortress or Farce?" *Journal of the West* 8 (1969): 21–28. For a contrasting view, see James Officer, *Hispanic Arizona, 1536–1856* (Tucson, 1987).

38. Poyo and Hinojosa, "Spanish Texas and Borderlands."
39. According to Montejano: At the time of independence in 1836 and annexation in 1848, one finds a landed Mexican elite, an ambitious Anglo mercantile clique, a class of independent but impoverished Mexican rancheros, and an indebted working class of Mexican peones. The new Anglo elite was generally Mexicanized and frequently intermarried or became compadres ("god-relatives") with landowning Mexican families. As one Texas scholar described the situation, the Anglo cattle barons established an "economic, social, and political feudalism" that was "natural" and not necessarily resented by those who submitted to it (O. Douglas Weeks, "The Texas-Mexican and the Politics of South Texas," *American Political Science Review*, 24 [1930], 610). Annexation had merely changed the complexion of the landowning elite (Montejano, *Anglos and Mexicans*, 8).
40. McWilliams, *North from Mexico*, 85.
41. Perhaps because, in all of these subregions, ranching prevailed, "pastoralism" has become a favored descriptive term among Chicano historians.
42. Before the Spanish *entrada* into New Mexico during the 1600s, trade had already taken place between earlier groups of regional settlers. In his first expedition, Coronado observed the existence of commerce between the Plains Indians and the Pueblos. The Plains Indians, skillful tanners of buffalo and deer hides, exchanged these goods regularly for Pueblo corn, cloth, and pottery.
43. Monroy, *Thrown among Strangers*, 101.
44. Elizabeth Fox-Genovese, *Within the Plantation Household* (Chapel Hill: University of North Carolina Press, 1988), 53.
45. Ibid.
46. The development of commercial capital has been erroneously associated with unremitting progress. Trade and commercial capital also can make their appearance among economically undeveloped, nomadic peoples, as evidenced by the Southwest before the Spanish invasion. In the case of the Southwest, manufacturing or industrial development did not occur as a direct result of increased commercial activity. (Weber makes this specific observation in *Mexican Frontier*, 144.)
47. Moorhead, op. cit., 194, cited in Weber, *Mexican Frontier*, 210.
48. Weber, *Mexican Frontier*, 209–12; Gutiérrez, *When Jesus Came*, 325–27.
49. Weber, *Mexican Frontier*, 146.
50. Ibid., 211.
51. One can identify two major contributors to historical change in the Southwest between 1821 and 1880: the development of commodity circulation, and the effects of usury capital. We have already discussed the development of commodity circulation as a weakening element. Usury capital as one example of a process that characterized the conflict between these two social economies is described in Raul A. Fernandez, *The United States-Mexico Border: A Politico-Economic Profile* (Notre Dame, Ind.: University of Notre Dame Press, 1977).
52. Weber correctly points out that the bulk of Chicano history focuses on Mexican Americans in the border region since the Mexican-American War. See Weber, "John Francis Bannon," 69. We note these important exceptions: Gutiérrez, *When Jesus Came*; Hinojosa, *A Borderlands Town in Transition*; and Monroy, *Thrown among Strangers*.
53. Garcia, *Desert Immigrants*. The fullest development of this notion is the "internal colony" model best represented in the works of sociologists Alfredo Mirande, *The Chicano Experience: An Alternative Perspective* (Notre Dame, Ind.: University of Notre Dame Press, 1985); Mario Barrera, *Race and Class in the Southwest: A Theory of Racial Inequality* (Notre Dame, Ind.: University of Notre Dame Press, 1979); and Chavez, *The Lost Land*. For an early critique, see Gilbert G. Gonzalez, "A Critique of the Internal Colony Model," *Latin American Perspectives* 5 (1974): 154–61.
54. Camarillo, *Chicanos in a Changing Society*, 2.
55. Ibid., 3.
56. Rodolfo Acuña, in the second edition of his *Occupied America*, the most widely adopted monograph for Chicano history courses, began to move Chicano history away from that position. We agree with Saragoza, however, in that "the 'them-vs.-us' character of *Occupied America* endured, and thus highlights continuity as the crucial element between the two epochs" (Saragoza, "The Significance of Recent Chicano-Related Historical Writings," 29).
57. David J. Weber, "The New Chicano Urban History," *The History Teacher* 16 (1983): 226.

58. Joan Moore and Harry Pachon argue that the Spanish- and Mexican-origin population of the Southwest has a unique history. See their *Hispanics in the United States* (Englewood Cliffs, N.J.: Prentice-Hall, 1985).

59. Monroy, *Thrown among Strangers*, and Gutiérrez, *When Jesus Came.*

60. Cortes, "Mexicans," in *Harvard Encyclopedia of American Ethnic Groups*, 699.

61. We note in passing that, in this age when terms of self-reference have acquired paramount importance, the term "Chicano" itself developed as a self-referent by working-class, immigrant Mexicans in the twentieth century (Camarillo, *Chicanos in a Changing Society*, x–xi). Also, old settlers and new arrivals considered each other to be culturally different.

62. Almaguer, "Ideological Distortions in Recent Chicano Historiography," 23.

63. We do not suggest that the experiences of these groups are identical. For example, the Asian experience was unique in that Asians were the only group to suffer total exclusion (1882 Chinese Exclusion Act, 1917 Barred Zone Act, and 1920 Immigration Act), as well as other legislative barriers from American society. We argue, in contrast, that Chicano history has tended to examine the distinctiveness of the Chicano experience at the expense of similarities it shares with other subordinated groups in the twentieth-century Southwest.

64. This growth cannot, of course, be limited to the utilization of the Colorado River. California's Central Valley and State Water Project and other western water projects are an integral part of the picture. See Marc Reisner, op. cit., passim; Johannes Hemlun, *Water Development and Water Planning in the Southwestern United States* (Denmark: Kulturgeorafisk Institut, 1969) and Charles W. Howe and K. William Easter, *Interbasin Transfers of Water* (Baltimore, Md.: Johns Hopkins Press, 1971). The western states of California, Nevada, Oregon, and Washington deviated from the national norm in terms of agricultural employment growth during the first sixty years of the twentieth century. For example, from 1938 to 1959, agricultural employment in the United States was cut roughly in half, but doubled in these four western states. Heavy capital investments, especially in irrigation, opened up large areas for cultivation. These developments in industry and agriculture stimulated a steady migration stream to California and elsewhere in the West from Mexico as well as from the eastern United States. The economic growth of the Central, San Joaquin, and Imperial Valleys in California worked like a magnet, attracting millions of agricultural workers from Mexico who would eventually settle in the United States or in the border cities of Mexico.

65. McWilliams, *North from Mexico*, 162.

66. The argument for discontinuity is not new. Moses Rischin, "Continuity and Discontinuities in Spanish-Speaking California" in *Ethnic Conflict in California*, edited by Charles Wollenberg (Los Angeles: Tinnon-Brown 1970), and Arthur F. Corwin, "Mexican American History: An Assessment," *Pacific Historical Review* 42 (August 1973): 270–73, made the argument nearly twenty years ago. Their views, however, were marred by an "assimilationist" approach. Chicano historians threw out the proverbial "baby with bathwater" in ignoring their views in their entirety.

67. De Leon and Stewart, *Tejanos and the Numbers Game*, 25.

68. Sheridan, *Los Tucsonenses*, 78. Hinojosa noted that in the later part of the nineteenth century, "Laredo's Mexican American society was taking on a new character. New waves of Mexicans and Mexican Americans from across the Rio Grande and from other parts of Texas also entered Laredo. These new immigrants did not have any personal ties or loyalties to the old ranchero class" (Hinojosa, *A Borderlands Town in Transition*, 120). Furthermore, argues Hinojosa, these immigrants reaffirmed their "Mexican-American identity." This identity had its roots in Mexico, not in the Southwest or with the old Mexican society. Consequently, research "on Mexican folklore in the late nineteenth century (shows) that Tejanos harbored a vibrant range of sentiments expressing profound loyalties to their national identity to Mexico" (De Leon and Stewart, *Tejanos and the Numbers Game*, 89). On the other hand, the native Mexican society, which had existed within semiautonomous provinces with only tenuous connections with the central government, had an identity with their *patria chica*. Indeed, Californios, Nuevo Mexicanos, Tucsonenses, and Tejanos each had a stronger identity with their respective provinces than with Mexico. David Weber noted that this amounted to a "virulent regionalism." He writes: ". . . Many of the leaders of frontier society took greater pride in their region than in their nation and saw themselves as a society distinct from central Mexico" (Weber, *Mexican Frontier*, 239–40). As a result, Cali-

fornios and Nuevo Mexicanos expressed hostility toward Mexicans and distinguished themselves from the Mexican-born. This was the case during the Mexican period as well as the Anglo-American periods. As distinguished from later migrants, the native Spanish-speaking groups were a separate community whose history was either short-lived (except New Mexico) or submerged by Mexican migrants.

69. Mark Reisler, *By the Sweat of Their Brow* (Westport, Conn.: Greenwood Press, 1976), chap. 1.
70. As evidenced by the works of historians Mario Garcia, Ricardo Romo, Richard Griswold del Castillo, and Alberto Camarillo, among others.
71. Weber, *Mexican Frontier*, 224.
72. Following from this, Weber concludes that "the new urban history has been part of a larger push to link the modern Southwestern United States more securely to its roots in the colonial period" (ibid., 226).
73. Ricardo Romo, "The Urbanization of Southwestern Chicanos in the Early Twentieth Century," *New Directions in Chicano Scholarship* (La Jolla, Calif., 1977), 183.
74. Richard Griswold del Castillo, "Quantitative History in the American Southwest: A Survey and Critique," *Western Historical Quarterly* (1984): 408.
75. We presume that the common definition of urban—that is, towns and cities with a population of twenty-five hundred or more—is preferred for historical and sociological analysis. Nevertheless, a definition of urban and rural is lacking in urban Chicano history studies, and the reader is left to distinguish between them. In the absence of a precise differentiation, rural and urban dwellers are merged into a single community, negating the real distinctions obtained when applying the commonly accepted definition of the term "urban."
76. One extensive analysis of the 1910, 1920, and 1930 censuses found that in 1930, "in the states west of the Mississippi, the average of the percent of Mexicans in urban communities, by states, is 36 percent . . ." and further, that the "distribution of Mexicans in western United States, in the principal region which they occupy, is largely rural." However, in the midwestern states (states east of the Mississippi), the Mexican community is largely urban, with 61 percent living in such areas. See Elizabeth Broadbent, *The Distribution of Mexican Population in the United States* (Ph.D. diss., University of Chicago, 1941), 61.
77. Martin Sanchez Jankowski, *City Bound Urban Life and Political Attitudes among Chicano Youth* (Albuquerque: University of New Mexico Press, 1986), 4.
78. Cesar Chavez and his rural union movement have been all but ignored by this urban history. Richard Griswold del Castillo and Richard Garcia try to close the gap in *Cesar Chavez: A Biography* (Norman: University of Oklahoma Press, 1995).
79. Carey McWilliams, *Southern California: An Island on the Land* (Santa Barbara, California: Peregrine Smith, 1973), 207.
80. One of the authors is currently investigating a form of community life that deviated significantly from the urban, blue-collar pattern: the citrus picker community of southern California. We focus attention on it because southern California barrios appear to many to be part of a large, urban complex. This may be true today, but it was not the case during the height of the citrus industry. In about 1940, 36,000 Mexican pickers and packers were employed by the 242 or so grower associations in California, principally in the southern part. We estimate that about 75,000 to 100,000 Mexicans dwelled in the camps, some of which existed since 1910.
81. Nancy Hewitt presents a powerful argument for examining women in the particular social and material circumstances of their communities in "Beyond the Search for Sisterhood: American Women's History in the 1980s," *Social History* 10 (1985): 299–321.
82. Ruth Alice Allen, *Labor of Women in the Production of Cotton* (1933; reprint, Chicago: University of Chicago Press, 1975), 231.
83. Ibid
84. Ibid., 234.
85. Ruiz, *Cannery Women, Cannery Lives.*
86. Ibid., 39.
87. Interview with Julia Aguirre, August 8, 1989, Placentia, Calif.
88. Interview with Julia Aguirre.
89. Ernesto Galarza, "Program for Action," *Common Ground* 10 (1949): 33.
90. Alan Exelbrod, "Chicano Education: In Swann's Way?" *Integrated Education* 9 (1971): 28.

91. Sarah Deutsch, *No Separate Refuge: Culture, Class, and Gender on an Anglo-Hispanic Frontier in the American Southwest, 1880–1940* (New York: Oxford University Press, 1987); Robert Alvarez, *Familia: Migration and Adaptation in Baja and Alta California, 1800–1975* (Berkeley: University of California Press, 1987).

92. Poyo and Hinojosa, "Spanish Texas and Borderlands."

93. Cornell West, "The Postmodern Crisis of the Black Intellectual," in *Cultural Studies*, edited by Lawrence Gronberg et al. (New York: Routledge, 1992), 6.

II
Empire and the Origins of Twentieth-Century Migration from Mexico to the United States

In this chapter we show how the twentieth-century appearance of a Chicano minority population originated from the subordination of the nation of Mexico to U.S. economic and political interests. We argue that, far from being marginal to the course of modern U.S. history, the Chicano minority, an immigrant people, stand both at the center of that history and of a process of imperial expansionism that originated in the last three decades of the nineteenth century and that continues today.

Several observations that challenge conventional interpretations of Mexican migration and of the Chicano experience derive from this approach. This century-long exodus of Mexicans to the United States has often been perceived as an "American" problem, affecting welfare, education, culture, crime, drugs, budgets, and so on, and solved through get-tough measures ranging from California's Proposition 187 to softer views such as those taken by immigrant rights agencies. In contrast, we take the position that migration is a Mexican national crisis. We argue that migration reflects Mexico's economic subordination in the face of U.S. hegemony and of the limitations placed on its national sovereignty by that domination. A century of mass border crossings signifies the breaking apart of the social fabric of the Mexican nation and its resettlement in enclaves across the United States as a national minority. Finally, the story of U.S. domination of Mexico dates to the last three decades of the nineteenth century.

The sociopolitical repercussions of this subordination were enormous. Domination of a new type by the United States increasingly undermined the social and political cohesion of Mexico, causing dislocation to its domestic agriculture and industry as well as migration to the United States–Mexico border and to the United States itself. In his 1911 classic exposé *Barbarous Mexico,* John Kenneth Turner addressed the dismantling of the Mexican nation. "The partnership of Diaz and American capital," he argued, "has wrecked Mexico as a national entity. The United States government, as long as it represents American capital . . . will have a deciding voice in Mexican affairs."[1] Washington preferred economic domination by U.S. corporations to the direct annexation of Mexico. As John Mason Hart has persuasively demonstrated, U.S. capital realized that policy objective and reigned supreme in the Mexican economy by the late nineteenth century.[2] Mexico became the first foreign country to fall under the incipient imperial umbrella of United States.

The practice of territorial conquest and expansion in pursuit of, or as a consequence of, commercial developments is very old; from the Romans to the Aztecs to nineteenth-century Britain, this characteristic is shared by nearly every imperial power in the history of the world. Over the past hundred-plus years, however, the United States, along with other global powers, developed an empire of a new type, a transnational mode of economic domination similar to yet different in important respects from previous imperial regimes.

While the United States has throughout its history engaged in numerous acts of territorial aggression and conquest—like other historical centers of power—its particular mode of empire building and maintenance emerged when the growth of large corporations and financial institutions included their direct involvement in alliance with local elites with the formally independent economies and politics of other countries. Simultaneously, these large conglomerates of finance and production had come to effectively dominate the government of the United States and freely used the power of the state to jockey for position with other world powers. The new twist in the practice of empire construction and management was aptly captured by the late U.S. secretary of state John Foster Dulles—who was directly involved in U.S. aggression against Guatemala and Iran in the 1950s—when he stated that "there [are] two ways of dominating a foreign nation: invading it militarily or controlling it financially."[3] In the case of Mexico, U.S. policy preferred financial control over military options.

Mexico and the U.S. Model of Empire Building

A transnational mode of imperial hegemony defined U.S. relations with the rest of the world throughout the twentieth century. Mexico provided the first testing ground. The United States first began to engage new mechanisms of empire in the late 1870s, when it became the senior partner in an alliance with the local Mexican elite personified in the figure of dictator Porfirio Díaz. Using a governmental threat of military intervention, large U.S. capital interests invested heavily in the construction of railroads in Mexico. The initial intrusions were quickly followed by massive investments in mining, especially copper, cattle farming, and cotton production. After Mexico, the United States would move swiftly to establish economic control and political influence over the rest of the continent, turning the landmass into its backyard. The United States launched the War of 1898 for a variety of motives: to make sure that no sovereign and independent nation appeared in Cuba upon the defeat of the Spanish empire; to establish a military presence guaranteeing the security of its investments while denying it to others; and to establish strategic outposts to secure and control commerce and investments in the Caribbean and in East Asia. U.S. political leaders defended the war with the rhetoric of providing support for the underdog—as in the case of recent interventions in Somalia, Bosnia, and Iraq—a rationale to allay public unease over war and to manipulate public opinion. The War of 1898 was followed quickly by the U.S.-supported secession of the province of Panama from Colombia, ensuring U.S. control of interoceanic trade. At the same time, large U.S. investments took place via the company town model in agriculture, railroad construction, and mining in Mexico and Cuba.[4]

The investment of U.S.-based corporations in Latin America, beginning at the turn of the twentieth century, in cooperation with archaic land-based elites and bolstered by the U.S. military and the threat of annexation, would transform the hemisphere into a series of neocolonial republics. Mexico became something of a laboratory for the imperial experiments; few events of significance in the history of twentieth-century Mexico were not decisively influenced by the power of United States economic, political, and, as a last recourse, military intrusion.[5] A few examples will suffice: the United States played a determining role in the outcome of the 1910 Mexican Revolution; after World War II the United States provided the money, propaganda, and logistics to control the labor and social movements in which the ideas of socialism were taking root not only in Mexico but throughout Latin America.[6] In the 1990s the United States established NAFTA to further secure its investments in Mexico and to restrict the use of that country for investments by its competitors. The freedom and security of U.S. capital remained a constant in U.S. policy toward Mexico in the twentieth century.

The establishment of U.S. imperial hegemony over Mexico and later Latin America at about the turn of the twentieth century has long been acknowledged in Latin America as central to local histories and identity.

the 1930s major Mexican and Latin American thinkers,
elos, Martí, Rodó, de Hostos, and others, placed U.S.
America as central to their essays on Latin America's fu-
l public awareness of the United States that pervades the
ics, and economics of Latin American countries is not
llel knowledge in the United States of its southern neighbors. In the academy, official U.S. historiography dates national emergence
into the global scene with World War I, privileging U.S. activity in Europe
over the decades of investment, interference, and invasions into Mexico
and other southern neighbors. As a subset of official U.S. history, the study
of the Chicano national minority has largely been constructed in an atmosphere in which "race matters," and culture, too, but empire does not. Insofar as the U.S. transnational mode of hegemony is acknowledged, it is not
seen as essential, or even related, to understanding the origins and development of the Chicano national minority.[7]

The Push-Pull Thesis:
The "Official" Line on Mexican Migration

The academic wisdom on Mexican migration to the United States established—since the first decade of the twentieth century—one basic theoretical construct: the push-pull thesis modeled upon conventional supply and
demand economics. The thesis reduced the causes to sets of conditions
within the sending country and the host country, conditions that *functioned independently* of each other. In one country a push (supply), or too
many people and too few resources, motivated people to consider a significant move; in the other country a pull (demand), usually a shortage of
labor, operated to attract the disaffected. In tandem they synergistically led
to transnational migration.

Following the political militancy and cultural nationalism of the late
1960s, numerous studies focused great attention on the origins of the Mexican population in the United States. The Chicano theme aroused the interest not only of the Chicano activists but also of academics attracted to
the issues raised by the regional political rebellion. Inevitably, immigration
struck a chord among nearly everyone involved and became a major topic
of discussion in the burgeoning field of Chicano studies. As the Chicano
studies, research agenda matured, immigration, particularly in the 1900–
1930 period, held a central place in many studies.[8] The original push-pull
thesis as enunciated by the U. S. Industrial Commission on Immigration in
1901, repeated by Victor S. Clark in 1908, and Manuel Gamio and Paul S.
Taylor in the early 1930s, became an article of faith among the new generation of academics destined to dominate the field to the end of the century.[9]

Many, if not most, academics simply made the 1910 Revolution the principal push factor operating in the 1900–1930 era.[10] Consequently, when in the late 1960s the UCLA Mexican-American Study Project engaged the question of immigration, the theoretical scenario had been set and the authors followed conventional wisdom: "The Mexican revolutionary period beginning in 1909–1910 spurred the first substantial and permanent migration to the United States. . . . By liberating masses of people from social as well as geographic immobility, [the Revolution] served to activate a latent migration potential of vast dimensions."[11]

To be sure, not every research study repeated previous studies verbatim. Research projects often emphasized particular conditions that modified the form in which push-pull would manifest. There *were* variations on the theme. A number of authors viewed the policies of Porfirio Díaz as similar if not parallel to the European elites' expropriation of peasants' lands and the simultaneous depeasanting of the countryside. Some see the extension of railroads throughout the nations as the key element that made migration possible. For others, the devastation of the 1910 Revolution and its aftermath precipitated the 1900–1930 migrations. A survey of the more significant studies of the past twenty years reveals the identification of a collage of factors that propel migration; seldom is the push viewed as the result of one factor alone. Currently, most students of Mexican migration and border studies agree that a complex of "push" factors operated at various times to create the conditions leading to Mexican migration over the course of the twentieth century.[12]

But regardless of the number of factors included in the push, the varying emphases, and the interrelations of factors within the push side of the equation, the crux for explaining Mexican migration during the 1900–1930 period focuses on a series conditions exclusive to Mexico. Some authors point to Porfirian economic policies as the major push agent; others identify the Porfirian era as one that kept peasants tied to the land and subject to the power of hacendados. Beyond that, whether it was Porfirio Díaz's land policies or the 1910 Revolution, or both, that created the push, the consequences of either one comprised the immediate supply conditions leading to migration: low wages, unemployment, poverty, or political oppression. The "pull" factors—high wages and labor demand in the United States—are taken as givens.

In about 1970 the push-pull thesis came under widespread critical scrutiny, resulting in some modification but primarily refinement, rather than substantial overhaul. Condemned as a neoclassical artifact, the push-pull thesis was ostensibly supplanted by a coterie of theoretical approaches to explain Mexican migration. The new paradigms—social capital theory, segmented market theory, new economics theory, and world systems theory—challenged push-pull. The first three contend that the old economic categories—wages, poverty, surplus population, and unemployment—inadequately explain the "push" of Mexican migration, particularly the long-term trends appearing since roughly 1970. World systems theory, on the other hand, contends that global capitalism reaching into the remotest corners of Mexico uprooted peasants from land and caused unemployment; both conditions drive migration. In spite of the constant disclaimer that push-pull can no longer explain migration, we shall argue below that the basic premises that comprised push-pull have not been completely uprooted by these modifications.

One is immediately struck by the longevity of that theoretical "model" first developed by government officials to interpret European immigration to the United States in the late nineteenth century. With some modifications, push-pull has been utilized throughout the twentieth century. Applied to the Mexican case soon after the rising border crossings during the early 1900s, the push-pull thesis survives to this day in altered form as the nearly exclusive theoretical design for understanding Mexican migration.

Most analysts of migration seem to view the "push" factors—Porfirian policies, the 1910 revolution, wages, surplus population, and so forth—as operating independently of the economic power of the United States. Implicit in the argument is the contention that an autonomous modernization process, not unlike that which occurred in Europe, led to Mexican migration to the United States. In short, older versions and modern variations of push-pull inherently presume that Mexican migration—from 1900 to the present—followed from independently stimulated economic progress in Mexico. Largely absent in discussions of migration are two questions: Is it appropriate to conflate all migrations into a single "one size fits all" paradigm? And if the forces of supply and demand work to eliminate economic disequilibria, why has there been an apparent permanent disequilibrium that no amount of migration from Mexico (or modernization therein) has been able to root out and that remains in effect after one hundred years?[13]

Economic Conquest: Porfirian Mexico, 1880–1910

A critical examination of the push side of the thesis requires that we analyze the economic policies carried out by the Mexican government in the 1880–1910 period and their social consequences. To investigate the origins of this migration flow from Mexico to the United States it is necessary to take another look at four processes at work in Mexico in the latter part of the nineteenth century: first, the building of Mexico's railroads by U.S. companies; second, the investment of U.S. capital in mining and smelting; third, the effects of the above modernization projects on Mexico's agriculture; and fourth, the displacement of large segments of Mexico's peasant population as a consequence of the foreign-inspired modernization.

We intend to show that foreign monopolistic economic interests—not the much-vaunted *científicos*—were the principal architects of the policies implemented by the administrations of Porfirio Díaz, and that these policies resulted in the subjection of Mexico to foreign economic domination. It was a domination of a new type: a transnational mode of economic colonialism. While Porfirian policies forcibly removed peasants from ancestral village lands, it would be wrong to assume that these were policies wholly designed in Mexico City. Like the construction of railroads, oil exploration and exploitation, mining, and agricultural investments by foreign capital, the removal of peasants from village lands emanated from the integration and exploitation of Mexican natural resources into foreign, primarily U.S., industrial production.

Not only its southern neighbor, but also all of Latin America fell under the gaze of U.S. foreign policy at the end of the nineteenth century. Mexico, it was believed, was the doorway to all of Latin America's riches, but only if the neighbor remained under U.S. economic tutelage. U.S. policy essentially followed the dictum of no less a patron of imperialism than Cecil Rhodes, who envisioned Mexico as the material fountain of empire. "Mexico," he once said, "is the treasure house from which will come the gold, silver, copper, and precious stones that will build the empires of tomorrow, and will make the future cities of the world veritable Jerusalems."[14] The United States changed the plural "empires" to the singular "empire."

The victory of the U.S. Union armies in 1865 failed to deter the cry for "all of Mexico" that lingered in the minds of adventurous entrepreneurs and their supporters in the U.S. Congress. In 1868 a spate of articles in the *New York Herald* and other metropolitan newspapers called on the United States to establish "a protectorate over Mexico." Voices of opposition to such a policy were heard; not all were enthralled by the easy victories of 1848 and the imagined expansion to the isthmus. Antiannexationists responded with an economic alternative free of any humanitarian impulses. William S. Rosecrans, speculator and promoter in Mexican railroads, while serving as minister to Mexico anticipated future U.S. policy toward Mexico in his response to the newspaper articles. Rosecrans urged that Americans abandon the notion of "all of Mexico." "Pushing American enterprise up to, and within Mexico wherever it can profitably go," he claimed, "will give us advantages which force and money alone would hardly procure. It would give us a peaceful conquest of the country."[15]

Rosecrans was not alone in contemplating a "peaceful conquest"; a number of his contemporaries engaged the discussion as to whether U.S.

economic interests required annexation. One prominent American investor, Edward Lee Plumb, wrote, "If we have their trade and development meanwhile we need not hasten the greater event [annexation]." The attitude of former president Ulysses S. Grant, an investor in Mexico's railroads, leaned toward the Rosecrans position. According to David M. Pletcher, "Grant's fragmentary writings about Mexico, however, suggest that in the last years of his life he developed toward that country an ideology of economic imperialism closely similar to that of other promoters."[16] Former U.S. commercial attaché Chester Lloyd Jones reiterated Rosecrans', Grant's, and Plumb's policy proposal decades later in a book, *Mexico and Its Reconstruction* (1921). "The economic advantage that would result to the United States from annexation," he contended, "as contrasted to that which may follow independence and friendship is doubtful. Mexican trade, both import and export, is already almost inevitably American and investments will be increasingly so. . . . A friendly, strong, and independent Mexico will bring greater economic advantages than annexation that certain classes of Mexicans fear and some citizens of the United States desire."[17] However, when Jones set down his policy recommendations, Mexico was well on the way to being "an economic satellite of the United States."[18]

Invading U.S. capital first conquered the Mexican railroad system (which for all practical purposes was an extension of the American system), then the mining and petroleum industries, and, concurrently, trade between the two countries. The social consequences of this conquest reverberated throughout Mexico in the form of mass removal of peoples from village lands, the ruin of former artisans and other craftsmen, the creation of a modern working class subject to the business cycle, and the appearance of a migratory surplus population. That migratory population first appears within Mexico in a rural-to-urban movement and a south-to-north movement; as the tide of U.S. investments grows, the migratory distances increase and cross over to the United States.

Mexico began to build its railroads during the administration of Benito Juárez (1867–72), who granted a concession to a British company to build a railroad between Mexico City and Veracruz. His successor, Sebastián Lerdo de Tejada, continued the Juárez policies but refused to allow railroad lines to be built toward the north for fear that they might become a military advantage to the United States. Following a period of political instability, military strongman Porfirio Díaz took over Mexico's government in 1876. Díaz inaugurated the period of economic liberalism—forerunner of the current NAFTA-style neoliberalism—by selling railroad concessions to large U.S. railroad companies in the northern states. Within three years after Díaz came to power, concessions to the United States provided for the construction of five railroads in Mexico—some twenty-five hundred miles—and carrying subsidies of more than $32 million. These lines went from south to north and provided a route to the interior of Mexico from which mineral ores and agricultural products was transported to the United States.[19]

These developments occurred simultaneously with the further development of railroads in the southwestern United States by the same corporate interests, who often competed against each other. Thus the Southern Pacific extended to Yuma, Arizona, by 1877, and in 1881 reached Deming, New Mexico, and El Paso, Texas, connecting at Deming with the Atchison, Topeka, and Santa Fe. By 1902, U.S. investments in Mexican railroads amounted to $281 million, with the northern states of Sonora, Coahuila, and Chihuahua the main recipients. By 1910 U.S. corporate capital had largely financed the building of fifteen thousand miles of track, providing a basic infrastructure that would ensure the transport of raw materials northward and technology south.

By the dawn of the new century the United States controlled the Mexican economy. According to U.S. consul-general Andrew D. Barlow, 1,117 U.S.-based companies and individuals had invested $500 million in Mexico. Railroads were the cornerstone of the modernization process—initiated, designed, and constructed via foreign capital. Fully 80 percent of all investments in railroads emanated from the United States.[20]

Railroads enabled a myriad of economic activities, principally those under foreign control, including mining, the export of agricultural products, and oil production. In 1902 Walter E. Weyl observed that railroads "permitted the opening up of mines" and stimulated "agriculture, and manufacturing by establishing foreign markets. . . ."[21] While foreign investments entered Mexico "at an astonishing rate," Mexican national markets for raw materials such as copper were practically nonexistent, or, in the case of coffee, sugar, and henequen, were severely limited. Consequently, U.S. enterprises, and those owned by Mexicans, marketed their commodities primarily in foreign outlets. Thus the railroads were indispensable for the increased export of extractive raw materials and agricultural products and the import of tools, machinery, and other products supporting the modernized sectors of the economy.

Previous to 1880, for example, copper was processed through the centuries-old patio method for deriving precious metals from ore. "Railroads," commented Marvin Bernstein, "aided mining from their very inception."[22] Aid, that is, to the detriment of established miners using archaic techniques. According to mining engineer H. A. C. Jenison, writing in the *Engineering and Mining Journal-Press* in 1921, railroads "made the more remote regions accessible, made the transportation of heavy machinery possible, and the shipment of low-grade ores to smelters profitable."

Consequently, about a sixth of rail mileage was "mineral railroad," but in general "most railroads counted upon mineral shipments."[23]

Under the stimulus of terms largely favorable to corporate investors rather than smaller individual stakeholders, U.S. capital assumed near-complete control in railroads, oil, agriculture, and mining, and had a large share of the financial structure in telegraphs, telephones, and urban transport. Mexico had passed into the hands of foreign economic interests. Related to Mexico's sovereignty, historian Robert G. Cleland wrote "[L]arge numbers of foreign companies, most of them which were American, entered Mexico. As the foreigner became interested in the industry, the Mexican gradually withdrew; little by little the important properties passed out of his control, until by 1912 of a total investment in the mining business estimated at $323,600,000 he could lay claim to less than $15,000,000." American investors held $223,000,000.[24] And of the total invested in that country, nearly 68 percent originated from foreign sources, its power multiplied by its control of key areas of the economy.

Every review of the evidence came to the same general conclusion: "Foreign investment [almost entirely of U.S. origin] was on the order of two-thirds of the total for the decade of 1900–1910; foreign ownership by 1910 has been estimated at half the national wealth."[25] U.S. interests were both dominant and strategically located in the economy: "American interests—the Hearsts, the Guggenheims, United States Steel, the American Corporation, Standard Oil, McCormick, Doheny—owned three-quarters of the minerals and more than half of the oil fields; they owned sugar plantations, coffee fincas, cotton, rubber, orchilla, and maguey plantations, and—along the American border—enormous cattle ranches."[26] For all practical purposes, the regional elites—the *comprador caciques*—and their representatives serving as the Mexican government provided the midlevel managing agency for foreign capital.[27]

Internal Migration: The First Step Toward Emigration

As in the past, Mexican wealth was concentrated in the semifeudal hacienda and remained so even as the railroads made the export of agricultural products to the United States and Europe a lucrative possibility. Enrichment without social change encouraged hacendados to transfer production from subsistence to cash crops for export. Coffee, fruits, henequen, hides, cattle, sugar, cotton, and other goods were traded beyond the local market to enter the international marketplace. For good measure, the large exporters received favorable transit rates that discriminated against domestic traders and forced the latter to produce for local consumption or not at all.[28] Hacienda export production, developed by and dependent on railroads, was equally significant for the effects on the peasantry. Evidence shows that the economic spur of the railroad promoted land expropriation laws, under the aegis of liberal land reform, and effected the legalized transfer of free peasant village holdings to nearby haciendas. Based on the locations of recorded violent peasant rebellions contesting land seizures between 1880 to 1910, *the majority of land expropriations during the Díaz era occurred along or nearby planned or operating railway routes.*[29] These activities, however, were entirely dependent on the effects of rail transport and production geared to foreign markets. Evidence points to similar patterns in other parts of Mexico. For example, studies have shown that in the northern state of Sonora, sales of empty public lands to speculators "faithfully mirror the history of the Sonora railroad."[30]

Interestingly, the railroads, which had little effect on industrial development, strengthened the precapitalist economic form, the hacienda. However, the hacienda, originally organized for self-sufficiency, engaged cash crop production on an extended scale to the detriment of staple crops, causing shortages of basic foodstuffs. Corn production fell by 50 percent and bean production declined by 75 percent between 1877 and 1910, forcing the nation to rely on costly imported staples. Yet, exports of raw materials such as henequen, coffee, sugar, hides, oil, and ores grew at an annual rate of 6.5 percent over the same period and dominated the rail traffic.[31] In 1910 Mexico was exporting 250,000 pounds of henequen a year, supplying midwestern farmers with twine for binding hay. While Mexico's foreign trade grew "tenfold between the mid-1870s and 1910," the average Mexican's diet fell below the levels of the pre-Díaz period as prices for staples rose much faster than wages.[32] The state-sponsored expropriations, the mass removal of hundreds of thousands of peasants from former village subsistence holdings, was the first phase toward the transnational migration that would occur a few years later. The first victims of Mexico's modernization—that is, economic conquest—were the peasants. As Friedrich Katz explained: "The expropriation of village lands as well as the demographic increase created large segments of unemployed laborers. . . ."[33] The army of dispossessed moved from village to town and city, and, as the northern mining districts opened up, the migrations moved from north to south.

By 1910 a total of 90 percent of the central plateau's villages owned no communal land; meanwhile, the haciendas "owned over half of the nation's territory."[34] No wonder that over the course of the Porfiriato the village-to-city migration would lead to a dramatic population growth in the provincial capitals, 89 percent, which outstripped the national increase of 61 percent.[35] The most dramatic increase occurred in the nation's capital.

Toward the end of the nineteenth century, migrating peasants began to settle in Mexico City in substantial numbers, forming communities of shacks and tenements in the impoverished zones there. The landed aristocracy, who preferred the amenities of the capital to life on their rural estates, lived apart, along wide, appealing avenues lined with town homes and palacelike residences. Large numbers of railroad "men" made their base of operations in the capital and comprised the city's American section. But it was the peasants who made the largest impact on the city. According to Michael Johns, "Railroads and expanding haciendas threw so many off their lands in the 1880s and 1890s that nearly half of the city's five hundred thousand residents . . . were peasants."[36] Daily, the new arrivals searched for quarters as best they could, cramming into overcrowded lodgings. An estimated twenty-five-thousand homeless moved into *mesones,* a form of nightly shelter for transients. Men, women, and children could be found sleeping on mats in single rooms, huddled against the cold. Others lived in more permanent quarters, tenements, or *vecindades,* which, while not as inhospitable as the *mesones,* were nonetheless overflowing. John Kenneth Turner estimated that at least a hundred thousand "residents" were without a stable shelter—that is, were homeless.[37]

From this pool, the city's aristocracy and foreign (mainly American) businesspeople selected their domestic servants: drivers, cooks, baby-sitters, housecleaners, laundresses—some sixty-five thousand who in 1910 made up 30 percent of the capital's workforce.[38] This growing labor pool not only supplied the city with workers but also would eventually supply other regions. Labor recruiters working for textile manufacturers, henequen plantations, railroads, mining, and oil operations also targeted displaced peasants. Many ended up in Yucatán henequen estates as virtual slaves working alongside many thousands of Yaqui Indians forcibly removed from their Sonoran homelands to make room for land speculators and railroad builders.[39] As railroads expanded their radius of operations and as ownership of mines shifted from small prospectors to Americans, the search for labor became a key element in the modernization process. Ironically, the very same modernization projects that removed peasants from the land also removed many more thousands from traditional occupations. Moises Gonzalez Navarro remarked that "the progressive disintegration of artesanal production wrought by modern industry was a novel occasion for men that, in effect, would allow him to sense the weight of personal circumstances."[40]

The northern trade routes from the central region, which normally occupied sixty thousand pack mules, underwent a profound change with the advent of railroads. Fred Powell, an authority on railroads, wrote, "Until the railroads, Mexico was the paradise of the packer."[41] Early Latin Americanists noted this change. Frank Tannenbaum wrote that in the past the "surplus crop was . . . loaded upon the backs of pack mules or in some instances on the backs of men and carried to the nearest trading center, often days of travel away. More recently it has been delivered to the nearest railroad station."[42] Walter E. Weyl confirmed the gradual displacement in his study. He wrote, "the muleteer is now relegated to a lesser sphere of activity and a lower position in the national economy. The driver of the mule car is slowly giving way to the trained motorman, and before long the vast army of *cargadores*, or porters, will go the way which in other cities has been trod by the *leñadores* and *aguadores*—'the hewers of wood and drawers of water.'"[43] Others besides mule packers were cast aside as wagon drivers, weavers, shoemakers, tanners, soapmakers, and others found that they could not compete against the new enterprises and imported goods and joined the army of dispossessed and unemployed, the burgeoning migrant labor pool. More recent work uncovered evidence for that pattern. Historian Rodney Anderson writes, ". . . the artisans added to the growing numbers of rural people forced off their lands by enclosure."[44]

Victor Clark noted in his 1908 study for the U.S. Bureau of Labor that underemployment and unemployment, interrelated with the internal demand for labor, caused a northward migration from the central plateau of Mexico along the railroad routes:

> The railroads that enter Mexico from the United States run for several hundred miles from the border through a desert and very sparsely settled country, but all of them ultimately tap more populous and fertile regions. Along the northern portion of their routes resident labor is so scarce that workers are brought from the south as section hands and for new construction. This has carried the central Mexican villager a thousand miles from his home and to within a few miles of the border, and American employers, with a gold wage, have had little difficulty in attracting him across that not very formidable dividing line.

Later in this study, Clark noted the demand for labor in the mines: "Like the railways, the mines have had to import labor from the south; and they have steadily lost labor to the United States." Clark interviewed one mining operator who brought eight thousand miners in one year from the south to work several mining properties in Chihuahua. Thus, on the whole, continued Clark, "there is a constant movement of labor northward inside of Mexico itself to supply the growing demands of the less developed states and this supply is ultimately absorbed by the still more exigent demand . . . of the border States and Territories of the United States."[45]

In his review of the Porfiriato, Mexican historian González Navarro wrote that the internal migrations were a "phenomenon seen for the first time" whose origin was found in the "human displacement from the countryside."[46] Approximately 300,000 persons left the south to settle in the north during the Porfiriato, a massive and permanent shift in the nation's population generated by foreign-controlled modernization.[47] One mining engineer lamented, "The call for labor is greater than can be supplied by the native population. . . ."[48] Another remarked, "The increase in number of mining operations in recent years has been so great as to make the securing of an adequate supply of labor a difficult problem."[49] Nonetheless, the employment statistics show a tremendous increase in the number of workers employed in the mines and smelters from roughly 1850 to 1900. At midcentury, scattered mines operated by small contingents of laborers toiled intermittently, often in a "hand-to-mouth affair," but by the century's end some 140,000 worked the mines and smelters, and most of these were internal migrants.[50] Another 30,000 to 40,000 were employed annually on the railroads in the 1880s and 1890s. It is no wonder that the population growth in the north superseded that of any other area of Mexico.[51]

Along the rail routes, cities such as Torreon and Gomez Palacio expanded enormously, as did ports such as Guaymas and Tampico, due to the transport of people and/or the export of goods. In 1883 Torreon was classified as a *ranchería*, a collection of ranches. By 1910 it had earned the title "city" with a population of more than 43,000. Nuevo Laredo grew from 1,283 in 1877 to 9,000 in 1910; and Nogales, which could not claim anything more than desert and some tents, blossomed into a thriving border port of 4,000 two years after the train passed through. Ciudad Lerdo offers an example of the power of the railroads to determine population placement—in this case, by their absence. In 1900 the city contained 24,000 inhabitants, but when the railroad bypassed it, the population declined to fewer than 12,000.[52]

The growth (or urbanization) of the city was the other side of the demographic shift from the central plateau to the north. In the case of the north, the population growth was most pronounced in the mining areas. Company towns such as Cananea, El Boleo, Nacozari, Navojoa, Copola, Concordia, Santa Eulalia, Santa Rosalía, Batopilas, and Esperanzas sprang from virtual wilderness into thriving mining camps within a few years. Albeit segregated, with Americans living apart from the Mexican labor force, the American employers believed that company housing was necessary to attract and control labor.[53] Cananea offers an example of one localized change occurring over a wide area of Mexico. A mining engineer reviewing the Greene Consolidated mining operations in 1906 wrote, "La Cananea presents a wonderful contrast to its earlier appearance . . . where eight years ago their were no persons other than a few warring prospectors . . . is now a camp of 25,000 persons with all the necessities and most of the comforts of civilization."[54] The Cananea operations required the labor of 5,500 regular men, with 8,000 to 9,000 listed as employees.

The Esperanza mining region in Coahuila experienced a similar profound change. In surveying the original site, the developer of the region found "cactus and mesquite desert with no trees, no houses (except a few 'jackals' [*jacales*, shacks]), and no water." In five years the area had grown to a population of 10,000, the mines employing 2,000. In roughly the same period, Batopilas grew from 300 to 4,000, employing 900 miners. Mulegè, a port near the copper boomtown of El Boleo, Baja California, demonstrates the secondary effects that mining had on the region. The small port grew from 1,500 in 1880 to 14,000 in 1910. Similarly, Nogales, Hermosillo, El Paso, and other cities that depended on mine-driven commerce paralleled the growth in the mining enterprises.

The reconfiguration of the centuries-old demographic pattern in Mexico comprises the first step in migrations to the United States. However, the economic forces that propelled the population shifts were not indigenous to Mexico; rather they emanated from foreign large-scale corporate enterprises operating under the protection of their home government's foreign policy.

Migration and Emigration

"In the southern section of the Western division immigration from Mexico has become an important factor," stated the 1911 *Report* of the Immigration Commission. Indeed, even before the launching of the full-scale battles of the 1910 Revolution (which were not to occur until 1913 to 1915), emigration had become a part of Mexican life. According to the available statistics, Mexican labor began to enter the United States in sizable numbers after 1905, partly as a result of the south-to-north internal migrations in Mexico. Later, migrations occurred in response to the economic depression in the United States that caused a slowdown of mining, motivating a northward migration. Data on Mexican migration show that the numbers declined between 1905 and 1907 from 2,600 to 1,400. However, the numbers rose steeply in 1908 to 10,638, reaching 16,251 in 1909 and 18,691 in 1910. But this tells only part of the story. In 1911 the Immigration Bureau noted that at least 50,000 Mexicans crossed the border annually without documentation. The cyclic pattern of migration of superfluous labor from Mexico began to take root.

The argument made for the "push" of the Revolution does not answer why the migrations, documented and undocumented, appear before the onset of

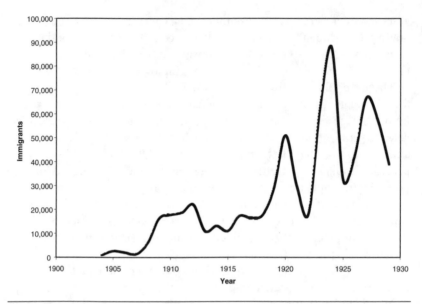

Figure 1. Mexican Migration to the United States, 1900–1929

Year	Immigrants	Year	Immigrants	Year	Immigrants	Year	Immigrants
1904	1,009	1911	18,784	1918	17,602	1925	32,378
1905	2,637	1912	22,001	1919	28,844	1926	42,638
1906	1,997	1913	10,954	1920	51,042	1927	66,766
1907	1,406	1914	13,089	1921	29,603	1928	57,765
1908	6,067	1915	10,993	1922	18,246	1929	38,980
1909	16,251	1916	17,198	1923	62,709		
1910	17,760	1917	16,438	1924	87,648		

the Revolution or why the migrations slow during the Revolution and spur in the 1920s, well after the fighting had terminated.[55] Again, the data show that the rise in migration occurred well before the intense period of civil war and that the numbers of emigrants declined with the onset of violence and major battles associated with the war. Thereafter, emigration returned to the pattern of the pre–civil war years but continued to grow more acute, corresponding with the pre-1910 movement. It is entirely probable, even without the 1910 civil war, that emigration would have moved in the same upward direction. This is precisely what has happened from the 1940s to the present day, without the violence of war. Thus the war probably exacerbated a preexisting condition rather than created it. (See figure 1.)

Moreover, the argument that the railroads as a transportation system inspired migration cannot withstand scrutiny. If railroads per se fostered the mass movement, then why did the migrations begin a quarter of a century *after* trains began running from Mexico City to the U.S. border? Second, if wages were the stimulant, then emigration should have occurred earlier rather than in the middle of the first decade, since wages were always lower in Mexico than in the United States. (This was particularly true during the Depression of the 1930s.) In addition, abundant evidence suggests that a major impetus to emigrate was the hacendado class, who perceived the dispossessed peasants as a potential political hazard and financed migration journeys. In El Paso, Victor Clark interviewed several young migrants and was surprised to find evidence of lending by "patrons" in support of emigration, "sometimes a political officer—in one case a judge—and sometimes a merchant, possibly also a landowner."[56] Years later, Paul S. Taylor also found evidence of lending to the unemployed. In Jalisco, Taylor noted, "Anyone with money engaged in the business of assisting persons to migrate" and that the "hacendados prefer to let the workers get away so they won't congregate in pueblos and ask for land."[57] Clearly, there are serious problems with the conventional mode of analysis. The usual "push" arguments together with the recent modifications simply cannot hold up to the evidence.

Recent "Refinements" to Push-Pull

In supporting their assertions, recent research by sociologists has pointed out that migration continued unabated over the post-1960 period when economic conditions in Mexico were relatively good. Studies analyzed noneconomic factors and questioned whether these factors impacted the decision to migrate. Framed in such a perspective, emphasis swung to the role of "agency" or the independent decision making of the migrants as they "negotiated" their migratory treks. Based on these premises, social capital theory configured transnational migrant networks linking communities divided by national borders. Migrants summoned motivations, constructed pathways, and provided the resources that propelled migrations over the long term. Theoretically, an institutionalized culture of migration embedded in the psyche of potential migrants establishes a social network across borders that feed migrations. Migration, in other words, exists autonomously above the economic and political life of Mexico. As migrants cross the border, they allegedly define the border on their own terms, thereby reconfiguring sociopolitical spaces. Ultimately, recent sociological models celebrated migration as "transnational resistance" to internationalized economic and political imperatives.

Accordingly, migration evolved into an institutionalized "self-feeding process" having a life of its own. Tautological in essence, migration is explained by migration; migrants migrate because, as "historical actors," they have voluntarily chosen to create a culture of migration. Nevertheless, the question of origins, or the factors that send the first migration, which leads to the second and subsequent migrations, is left by default to push-pull. The original sin, push-pull, prompts the first migrations, but once the sin is committed, the migration assumes a *self-generating* state. The only true national and/or transnational factor of significance of this theoretical construct is the migration itself. Rational choices made by migrants to acquire commodities, or to reestablish community, cultural lifestyle, and family ties, motivate migrations. International economic relations are relegated to the margins, and the economic domination we address here is ignored while the "independent" decision making of the migrants is centered.[58]

A second theoretical design arising from the critique of push-pull, the segmented labor market model, emphasizes an aspect of economics of the receiving country, precisely the structured dependence of the modernized, "postindustrial" forms of production, on the continued flow of cheap immigrant labor. The demand to satisfy an economic addiction, an insatiable thirst for cheap labor, drives migration. As in the previous theoretical construct, the adherents to this position contend that the old push conditions, wage differentials, a surplus population, and so on, are irrelevant. However, while the push side of the equation evaporates, the pull side—that is, the demand for labor in the receiving country—functions as before. Note that both theoretical models view the two economically interconnected countries as *economically independent of each other* and ignore transnational financial *domination* with respect to the process of migration. Like the original push-pull theory, its revisions separate the process of migration into two interacting but independent operations.[59]

A third model, new economics theory, contends that migration is explained "by measures of risk and the need for access to capital" rather than by the workings of the labor market.[60] According to Douglas Massey, "Considerable work suggests that the acquisition of housing, the purchase of land, the establishment of small businesses constitute the primary motivations for international labor migration."[61] Here the push argument seems to have been supplanted by factors other than wages; however, this theoretical model, as in the case with social capital theory, stands well within the old model. New economics theorists argue that the sending country fails to supply needed capital, land, and business opportunities. These contentions fit into the push-pull model as it was first articulated nearly a century ago: the host country has something that the sending country lacks, hence people migrate to satisfy a felt need, and a neoclassical equilibrium is established (or should be established).

Ultimately, the several critiques of push-pull theory fail to extricate migration theory from the former's clutches. Several basic assumptions replicate the old model. For one, migrants have a felt need, and Mexico cannot meet that need; thus a push. Second, the United States has the conditions and wherewithal to satisfy the migrants' yearnings; therefore a pull. Last, the national economies of Mexico and the United States are interactive (often described as "interdependent") but without domination exerted by either party; hence independently functioning push and/or pull.[62]

Finally, the world systems model causally links global capitalism with migrations. In this view, direct foreign investments generate economic development in sending countries that removes natives from farming lands or causes unemployment in traditional occupations, creating a body of migrants within the country. Saskia Sassen, perhaps the best-known theoretician of migration from a world systems paradigm, rightly points out how a foreign investment interested in export agriculture modernizes production, which simultaneously upsets traditional farming practices, removes small farmers from the Mexican countryside, and resettles them in cities. Some migrate to the northern states, where foreign-owned assembly plants advertise employment. Ultimately that same surplus labor migrates to the United States, where immigrant labor is in constant demand.[63]

Our basic differences with world systems theory as applied to Mexican migration to the United States stem from (1) the emphasis on direct investments, (2) the implicit argument that modernization via foreign financing equals the development experienced by Europe in the nineteenth century, and (3) the exclusive attention to the post-1960 period in theoretical presentation. First, direct investments are only one type of foreign capital that has affected the national economy of Mexico; other types of capital have serious consequences for the economy and society as well. For example, U.S. government lending programs; private philanthropic organizations such as the Rockefeller Foundation and others; and economic development programs (loans) run by the IMF and the World Bank, and the trade policies of the World Trade Organization, have a decided impact on the economy and society of Mexico. Second, world systems theory implicitly parallels notions of the great nineteenth-century European migrations that occurred via an indigenous capitalist modernization and consequent depeasanting of the land. We contend that foreign economic incursions led to a colonial status, resulting in neither an indigenous capitalist-driven nor dependent modernization, but rather one under foreign control that depeasants the land, removing them to other parts of Mexico and into the United States. Our third criticism responds to the notion that the post-1960s migrations are distinct from those of earlier decades. We argue that U.S. economic domination over Mexico remained more or less constant during the twentieth century. While world systems theory does point to the significance of foreign investments in the removal of people from the countryside and their migration to cities and northern assembly plants, the roots of migration accrue to global capital, or direct foreign investments, which "modernize" the Mexican economy. In essence, Mexico and the United States are sovereign nations as in the first versions of the push-pull thesis, each in their own way subject to the nuances of global capital and interdependent in the process. They ignore government-to-government lending programs, bank capital, massive foreign debts, and empire in that theoretical design; the world system is all one expansive undulating capitalist plain in which issues of inequality and domination become obscured.

Even though a general discussion of world systems theory is beyond the purview of this study, we would like to note the following points. We believe that the Achilles heel of world systems theory, and its predecessor, dependency theory, can be traced to their definitions of capitalism and of capitalists. According to these theories, the essence of capitalism lies not in the social relations, property patterns, ideology, and political institutions of society but rather in the existence of commercial relations. By this definition, most of Mexico was capitalist in the nineteenth century. By assumption Mexican elites become—in this view—capitalists—that is, people with potential for entrepreneurship and national independence, rather than obsequious comprador middlemen and hacendados who carry the bags for U.S. finance capital. By definition world systems theory grants the Mexican elites of the nineteenth century characteristics that assume a penchant for independence and self-reliance. The pitfalls of dependency theory were addressed in a series of debates in sociology, political science, and Marxist economics in the 1970s before the dependency model began to be used, all too uncritically, by Latin American historians. In particular, a modality of dependency theory—labeled "right dependency" (advocated by Brazilian sociologist Fernando Henrique Cardoso)—was critiqued for defending capitalist development behind a facade of "leftist" rhetoric.[64] It is a similar concept of capitalism and capitalists in world systems theory, which ipso facto elevates the degree of "agency" of Third World elites. It accords them, axiomatically, a higher degree of freedom and independence in their dealings with stronger nations, as in the case of Mexico's nineteenth-century advisers to dictator Díaz, the notorious *científicos*. In this manner, this theory obscures and obfuscates a history of imperial domination.[65] Lamentably, the major criticisms of world systems theory—in particular the criticisms of Eric Wolf and Peter Worsley—have not been appreciated by Latin American historians.

The core premise of push-pull—the imbalance of independent conditions in sending and host countries—still obtains in spite of critiques hurled against it. A real alternative to push-pull requires a reconceptualization of migration within the context of empire.

The Ebb and Flow of Migration, 1950–70

Analysis of the data on migration indicates that the flows are cyclical as well as long-term in nature. The push-pull thesis and its newer versions gloss over what accounts for this pattern of cycles, as it is unable to explain them. A "constant"—that is, a steady disparity in the level of income and wages, nor migrant networks and the like—cannot logically account for variations in the pace of migration. Rather, one must turn again to concrete historical developments to explain those changes.

Despite the upheaval of the 1910 civil war, U.S. investments in the 1920s either retained their position garnered during the Díaz years, or increased in significance.[66] With the coming of the global Depression that began in the early 1930s, economic activity by U.S. companies at home and abroad diminished. The evidence shows that migration from Mexico declines after 1930, following the 1910–30 generally upward pattern. The slowdown in migration lasts until the early 1950s, when it picks up again, with renewed vigor. To look for the causes of this rebound we once again turn to the pattern of U.S. economic activity in Mexico.

Beginning in the early 1940s, U.S. investments in Mexico began to rise once again but under new manifestations. The Depression of the 1930s brought to power in Mexico the incipient leadership of the future Partido Revolucionario Institucional under its paternalistic leading figure, Lázaro Cárdenas. Similar to the pattern established by Roosevelt's New Deal administration, the Cárdenas government used the economic power of the state as never before in Mexico to maintain and protect the free market/private property social contract.

Under the Partido Revolucionario Mexicano (forerunner of the PRI), foreign investment flowed once again: it tripled from 1940 to 1950, and doubled again by 1958.[67] But the profile of the investment was different. Guided by the governing party, the national government instituted in 1934 a major public finance and development institution, Nacional Financiera, which became the economic pillar of the economy. Nacional Financiera invested heavily in works of irrigation, highways, and electric power. Of the decades 1940 to 1970, a period of rapid economic growth in Mexico, it has been said that "[n]o financial institution in Mexico has contributed more to the economic growth of that country than Nacional Financiera."[68]

From the early 1940s on, U.S.-based banks and financial institutions began to invest in Mexico by way of loans to Nacional Financiera. Some of the lending institutions included the U.S. Export-Import Bank, the Bank of America, Chase Manhattan Bank, and eventually the International Bank for Reconstruction and Development (the World Bank). Between 1942 and 1959 more than $900 million (mostly of U.S. origin) had been invested in major works of infrastructure in Mexico by way of Nacional Financiera.[69] An analysis of Nacional Financiera funds reveals that, by l953, foreign loans accounted for the single largest—about one-third—source of equity funds available to the institution.[70] This allowed U.S. capital to maximize its leverage over decision making while minimizing risks: U.S. financial institutions were in the driver's seat of the economic policies of Nacional Financiera.

The investments financed by Nacional Financiera would have a tremendous impact on the structure of Mexico's economic and demographic patterns with consequences for migration to the United States. A significant proportion of the investment went into major irrigation projects, the most important of which were in the northern border states of Mexico. Development of the irrigation projects began in the early 1940s and included the Falcón Dam in the Rio Grande and the Rio Fuerte Irrigation Project in the state of Sonora. A tremendous increase in agricultural production took place in northern Mexico, simultaneous with the development of irrigation projects between 1940 and 1960. High rates of growth in cotton production in areas such as the Mexicali Valley made Mexico the largest cotton exporter in the world and brought the value of cotton production from 8 percent in 1940 to 24 percent in 1958.[71] Cotton production itself developed under the close control, through credit and marketing channels, of a major U.S. agribusiness giant, Anderson Clayton.

Control over Mexican cotton production was made effective because Mexican growers did not sell their product in the international market but through Anderson Clayton (and other U.S. enterprises), which monopolized the harvest and provided credit, seed, and fertilizers to the producers (much like Anderson Clayton did in California's San Joaquin Valley in the 1930s). This company also managed cotton production in the countries with which Mexico competed in the world market: Brazil and the United States. In the late 1960s this control enabled Anderson Clayton to engage in cotton "dumping," reminding the Mexican government who was boss.[72] The opening up of irrigated lands in Sinaloa and Sonora also allowed for the production of "winter vegetables" in those states beginning in late 1940, creating a few small pockets of U.S-agribusiness control. The opening up of the Pan-American Highway—another Nacional Financiera project—facilitated the marketing of Mexican vegetables in the United States. Thus the export of tomatoes from Mexico's northeast increased from fewer than 1 million pounds in 1942 to 14 million pounds in 1944.[73] But the denationalized character of this production was evident as other U.S. corporations joined Anderson Clayton in effectively taking over Mexico's agribusiness, from the production and sale of machinery and fertilizers to the processing and merchandising of agricultural goods. Among the better-known companies in control of Mexico's northern agriculture were John Deere, International Harvester, Celanese, Monsanto, Dupont, American Cyanamid, Corn Products, United Fruit, and Ralston Purina.[74] The method of political control that John Foster Dulles described was complete: Mexico was borrowing money from U.S. banks to develop irrigation projects and transportation, thereby making possible the growth of U.S.-controlled agriculture in the northern tier of Mexican states.

With the growth of agriculture came population shifts, continuing the pattern begun in the late nineteenth century. Outside of the tourist-driven economies of Acapulco and Quintana Roo, only three Mexican states, all border states, showed an astonishing rate of growth of 45 percent or more in the 1950–60 period: Baja California, 232 percent; Tamaulipas, 61 percent; and Sonora, 45 percent.[75] Between 1950 and 1960 the total population of the eight major *municipios* of the Mexican border—Tijuana, Mexicali, Nogales, Ciudad Juárez, Piedras Negras, Nuevo Laredo, Reynosa, and Matamoros—increased by 83 percent, from fewer than 900,000 to 1.5 million. By 1970 the population had reached a total of 2.3 million. Between 1960 and 1969 the population rise in the northern border states—Baja California, Sonora, Chihuahua, Coahuila, Nuevo Leon, and Tamaulipas—grew by 45 percent, in contrast with a figure of 31 percent for the nation as a whole. In 1970 fully 29 percent of the border population came from other parts of the country.[76] It is interesting to note that during the cotton boom years (1940–60), the border municipios where cotton was the main agricultural product—Mexicali, Cuidad Juárez, Reynosa, and Matamoros—registered the highest rates of population growth. On the other hand, during the years of the cotton crisis (1960–70), the same municipalities suffered a sharp drop in their populations.[77]

During the 1950–70 period further ties developed between countries formally equal and sovereign, but with one in a subordinate position while the other administered the transnational hegemony. The subordinated status of Mexico and specifically the changes in its political economy brought about by the economic and political activities of U.S. corporations and the U.S. government provided the opportunity to construct a giant agribusiness economy on both sides of the border that relied on the ready supply of cheap labor from the interior of Mexico. An evident consequence of this relationship was one of the most spectacular mass movements of people in the history of humanity. The northward migration of people from all corners of Mexico to its north, and for many, eventually to the United States, was motivated by the same general force, *the economic dislocation caused by U.S. capital—not an amorphous "global" capital—in Mexico*, the pace of the movement modulated in a cyclical manner by the relative intensity of U.S. economic intrusion. This movement turned the border area into a highly urbanized region. Simultaneously, migration constantly propelled the growth of the Chicano minority in the United States in a variety of forms: regulated and unregulated, legal and illegal, cyclical and long-term.

The Current Cycle, 1970–2000

As in the previous cycle, U.S. investments in Mexico shifted away from mining and railroads toward industrial manufacturing. U.S. corporations made their way through direct purchase into the most dynamic sectors of local industry, especially in the 1960s. This trend occurred most notably in consumer durables, chemicals, electronics, department stores, hotels and restaurants, and the food industry, in which United Fruit (later known as Dole), Heinz, Del Monte, and General Foods became very visible. Of the subsidiaries of U.S.-based corporations, 225 operated in the manufacturing sector.[78] U.S. investment in manufacturing concentrated around the Federal District, which accounted for 50 percent of the total manufacturing production of the country in 1975. As we will see, this would change in the ensuing years, but in the meantime Mexico's dependence on foreign loans continued to increase. Between 1950 and 1972 the foreign debt grew at an average annual rate of 23 percent, reaching $11 billion by the latter year.

A chronic balance-of-payments problem, a side effect of Mexico's reliance on the export of primary commodities and on foreign loans, made the situation worse. Beginning in the late 1960s, Mexico's hardly independent government had no choice but to accept lenders' terms. At the behest of international creditors, economic policies once again resulted in massive economic and demographic dislocation, contributing to a further increase of migration into its northern region, which became not only highly urbanized but also acquired a new role as a major "staging area" for further migration to the United States.

The Maquiladora Program

In 1967 Mexico took a giant step in the complete abdication of its economic sovereignty when it established the Border Industrial Program along its northern border. This program began the transformation of the entire area into a gigantic assembly operation. The sad story of the maquiladora program in all its sordid details has been told elsewhere.[79] Suffice it to say that, like a narcotic drug, which does not solve your problems while making you into an addict, Mexico has become dependent on

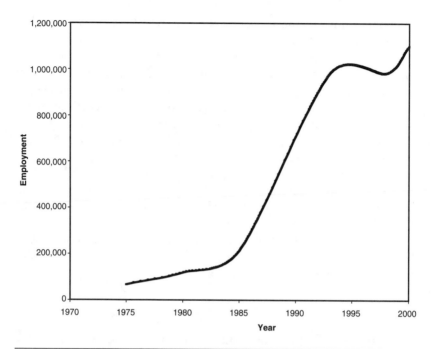

Figure 2. Maquiladora Employment, 1970–1999

Year	Employment	Year	Employment
1975	67,214	1993	546,433
1980	119,546	1998	983,272
1985	217,544	1999	1,100,000

its maquilas, which do not solve its unemployment problems nor allow the country to become self-sufficient, developed, and modern.

For the purposes of our argument, the maquiladora program served to make the border states of Mexico, and specifically its border cities, into entrepôts for the poverty-stricken, unemployed masses of the country. One cursory look at the employment figures and accompanying graph tell the tale. (See figure 2.)

The maquiladoras turned Mexico's northern border into an enclave with few links to the rest of the economy. Into the border area flowed duty-free manufacturing inputs to be assembled into final products, using cheap labor for entry into the United States or export to other countries. The northern tier of Mexico became a direct appendage of U.S. manufacturing, replicating the examples of railroads and mining in the Mexican economy during the early 1900s.

Simultaneous with the development of the maquiladora program, other significant changes began to affect Mexican agriculture. Between 1940 and the late 1960s, Mexico's countryside provided the basic food staples to its growing urban population. However, pressure from international lenders and agribusiness multinationals would change that. Mexico's central government began a policy of eliminating subsidies to small agricultural producers, who then began to abandon their farm plots to join the migration streams. Into the breach moved the United States, which turned the same agricultural lands into mechanized farms, producing export commodities to the United States. In the 1970s the rate of growth of basic staples such as corn, beans, and wheat began to fall behind the population growth. To cover the precipitous decline in food production, a problem not seen since the Porfiriato, the country was forced to import basic food supplies.[80] However, imports could not feed Mexico's people satisfactorily. Infectious diseases and other illnesses linked to malnutrition and economic underdevelopment became rampant by the late 1980s.[81]

NAFTA

The 1990s witnessed the signing of the North American Free Trade Agreement (NAFTA), the most recent and devastating example of how U.S. domination over Mexico continues to misdevelop and tear apart the socioeconomic integrity of that society. The U.S. government and major corporate interests promoted the NAFTA concept as a weapon in their trade competition with Europe, and especially Japan. Under the "free trade" slogan the proposed treaty would serve two purposes. First, it would guarantee a free hand to U.S. enterprises willing and able to invest in Mexico to take advantage of that country's cheaper wages. Mexico was to become an export platform of manufactured commodities for the United States and other markets around the world. Major U.S. corporations, in particular automobile manufacturers, stood to benefit greatly from this scheme. Second, the treaty would simultaneously deny in various forms and degrees to other economic powers the advantage of operations in and exporting from Mexico. Briefly put, the United States sought to create with Mexico (and Canada) an economic bloc to compete against Europe and Japan.

In their quest the United States could count on the leadership of Mexico's governing party, the PRI, and then-president Carlos Salinas. Under his leadership Mexico undertook a wide-ranging set of measures designed to make NAFTA a reality. First, to demonstrate resolute support for market-oriented policies and to attract foreign capital, the Mexican government began to break up numerous government enterprises and to lay off thousands of employees. Hundreds of state companies and institutions were sold or "privatized." The government enacted laws to "flexibilize" the labor market, including restrictions on wage increases, curtailment of vacation and sick-leave time, extension of the workweek, and increased management powers over firings and hiring of temporary workers (known in the United States as downsizing). The elimination of trade protection meant that by 1993, nearly 50 percent of Mexico's textile firms and 30 percent of manufacturers of leather products had gone bankrupt. By the time of the signing of the treaty, Mexico's population had become severely polarized in terms of wealth and income.[82]

The actual signing of NAFTA revealed that Mexico was only as strong a bargainer as the weakest of the 435 U.S. congressmen. U.S. president Bill Clinton could only succeed in obtaining a majority vote in Congress by guaranteeing each and every representative protection for his or her district against any competition that might result from NAFTA. A Texas congressman agreed to vote in favor of NAFTA only after Clinton promised that the Pentagon would add two more cargo planes to a production order previously awarded to his electoral district by the Department of Defense. A Florida representative voted for the treaty only after the State Department agreed to seek the extradition of an individual residing in Mexico who was accused of a crime in the United States. A lawmaker from Georgia opted for the treaty in exchange for promises by the Agriculture Department that limits would be imposed on increasing imports of peanut butter from Canada. In this manner even small U.S. producers of brooms were protected from Mexican competition. Throughout the entire humiliating process not a peep was heard from the Salinas government. In the end, "free trade" meant that Mexico would be completely open to U.S. goods, but U.S. producers were safely guarded against Mexico's products.

Rather than a free trade agreement, NAFTA could be better described as a "free investment" agreement. During the previous decade, tariffs levied by Mexico against the United States had steadily declined. NAFTA codified these changes, and, more important, it opened up investment opportunities in Mexico, protected against nationalizations, and eliminated all restrictions against U.S. ventures in Mexico. Of course, the "free investment" part would be limited under a section of the treaty titled Rules of Origin. These rules defined as domestic any inputs originating in Canada, the United States, and Mexico. Others (e.g., Japanese inputs) were henceforth classified as "foreign," and any products assembled with them were liable to export limits. In other words, after NAFTA it became more difficult for Japanese or European investors to ship products for assemblage into Mexico and export to the United States.

NAFTA was never envisioned as a developmental policy for Mexico. All announced plans, forecasts, and decisions of U.S. multinationals relied on the low wages prevalent in Mexico as the key variable involved. Further displacement of peasants, massive migration, and the destruction of what remains of domestic Mexican agriculture will follow on the heels of the complete opening to competition with the large U.S. agribusiness consortiums. Via NAFTA, Mexico agreed to subject all land to privatization—that is, sale and speculation. It returned, for example, Indian lands to the same juridical status that gave rise ninety years ago to Mexico's famed agrarian revolt.[83]

Almost to the day of the first anniversary of the signing of NAFTA, the newly installed administration of Ernesto Zedillo faced a catastrophic devaluation of the national currency. Mexico's image changed from an investor's paradise to a disheveled financial hulk, a virtual economic protectorate of the United States. The United States set up conditions for a bailout that were, according to newspaper reports, too sensitive to be published in Mexico. Eventually it became known that the U.S. plan required Mexico to hand over all revenues from its oil sales, and gave to U.S. banks a right to supervise and enforce further measures of austerity and privatization. Everything went up for sale—for example, bridges, airports, toll roads, ports, and telephones. In the meantime, thousands of farmers, businesspeople, and consumers went broke because they could not pay their debts and mortgages. Contemporary estimates indicated that in the first two months of 1995 nearly 600,000 jobs were lost. A whopping 30 percent of Mexico's labor force, 11 million people, was reported unemployed in mid-1995.[84]

The American embassy in Mexico, demonstrating the U.S. resolve to remain committed to its plans for Mexico, referred positively to rising unemployment and bankruptcies as the "Darwinian effects" of NAFTA. Embassy officials praised its "stabilizing" effects on the economy and called it the "bright spot" in the Mexican catastrophe. The United States, taking advantage of the plummeting wage levels in Mexico relative to the dollar, benefited enormously as 250 companies opened up shop in the border area in the first three months of 1995. Apparently Mexico should have been grateful that, in exchange for millions of unemployed and thousands ruined, a handful of Mexicans—a new generation of migrants—obtained jobs toiling for a miserable wage assembling products in border cities for reshipment to the United States. In the long run, the devastating effects of NAFTA on Mexico's remaining agricultural production and national urban manufacturers will throw into the migration highways an even larger number of people desperately looking to make a living, thereby enlarging at a faster pace the mass of Mexican migrants in the United States. NAFTA is a particularly telling example of the unity of push and pull, and the role of U.S. domination in dismembering Mexico and creating a Chicano national minority in the United States.

Conclusion: A Network of Domination

Under NAFTA, a steadily dropping manufacturing employment (outside of the maquila sector) points to the deindustrialization of Mexico. While in 1981 manufacturing employment stood at 2,557,000, it fell to 2,325,000 in 1993 and to 2,208,750 by 1997, a 13.6 percent drop from 1981. This also brought lower living standards, as many workers moved from permanent to lower-wage contingency work that lacked benefits and union protection. The destruction of Mexico's industrial base is particularly pronounced in the area of capital goods. From 1995 to 1997 alone, following the peso debacle, 36 percent of the 1,100 capital goods plants closed down. In all, 17,000 enterprises of all kinds went bankrupt shortly after the crisis exploded. Meanwhile, employment opportunities in the lowest-paying categories ballooned by 60 percent, dragging 5 million people to the official "extreme poverty" category. Manufacturing production has been reduced to the maquiladora sector, situated largely in the northern confines of the country, and to an increasingly concentrated manufacturing system dominated by a few U.S. industrial giants involved in production for export.[85]

The debacle in national industry repeated in agriculture with catastrophic consequences. According to a Mexican analyst, the opening of the agricultural markets by the NAFTA treaty led to the rapid ruin of what remained of Mexico's production of basic staples, and to the dumping of cheap U. S. corn, wheat, and beans into Mexico. One hundred years of U.S. empire building has produced what three hundred years of Spanish rule could not accomplish: the complete inability of the Mexican nation to produce enough to feed its own people. The migratory consequences are staggering: millions will be forced to leave Mexico's countryside in the next decade.[86]

The demographic impact of U.S. transformations in Mexico's economy has already caused a dramatic shift in the nation's population distribution. Since the 1960s, the northern municipios have featured one of the fastest-growing populations in the world. There appears no end in sight to this phenomenon: the population, which topped 4 million in 1995, is expected to double by 2010 and to more than triple by 2020. Ciudad Juárez, for example, has grown five times since 1970, reaching a population of 1 million. According to an Associated Press report, each day "an estimated 600 new people arrive from Mexico's poor provinces hoping for work" in Ciudad

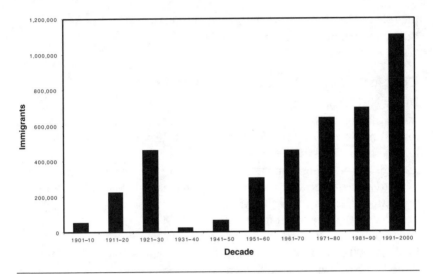

Figure 3. Twentieth-Century Immigration from Mexico to the United States.
Source: U.S. Immigration and Naturalization Service Statistical Yearbook 2000.

Juárez, or nearly 220,000 new arrivals a year. Internal migrants in desperate straits will later surface as international migrants confronting the dangers of the militarized border.[87]

Today this process intensifies the Mexicanization in the many barrios across the United States, forging a distinct demographic form with immigrants either outnumbering the second generation or reaching a level of parity not seen since the 1930s. Migrants are the fastest-growing sector of the Chicano population, approximately 40 percent born in Mexico, up from 17 percent four decades ago.[88] (See figure 3.) Had it not been for the Great Depression and World War II, the migratory movement of the 1900–1930 period would have proceeded without respite. That interruption made possible a distinctive Mexican-American generation and later the Chicano generation. However, once migration resumed its previous pace, a cultural pattern that first surfaced in the 1920s reappeared in the 1960s. We foresee that Mexicanization is overwhelming the older enclaves, remaking older barrios into immigrant centers and thus reforming the older ethnic politics, particularly the Chicano version forged out of the 1960s. Migration elbows out the 1940s-to-1960s variations of ethnic politics and replaces it with a politics deeply affected by an immigrant society.[89]

If there were any theoretical doubts about the false dichotomy between push-and-pull factors in the case of Mexico, the maquila program, NAFTA, and the agricultural collapse have erased them. For the most part, historians and social scientists have not chosen to critique push-pull in this manner. Rather, as we discussed above, social science perspectives have chosen, in head-in-sand fashion, to focus away from these "macro" factors toward the agency of migrants who, having constructed networks of migration, are regarded as the self-generators of migration. To be sure, Mexican immigrants have taken on active roles and made significant choices in the construction of their lives, families, and communities. But it defies common sense and the evidence to suggest that the explanation for Mexican migration to the United States lies within the immigrants' subjectivity. A simpler and more powerful explanation for Mexican migration to the United States, and the consequent development of the Chicano national minority, should focus on the one hundred years of economic domination by centers of transnational economic power in the United States. Bit by bit, this tighter and tighter network of domination has succeeded in disarticulating the Mexican economy, destroying its domestic industry as well as local agricultural production, creating demographic dislocation, and, in the process, turning an increasing portion of its population into a nomadic mass of migrant workers who eventually emerged as the Chicano national minority. The rise of the Chicano national minority was not an event marginal to U.S. history; quite the opposite, it was central to the construction of a U.S. neocolonial empire.

Epilogue

In chapter I we challenged the widespread view that contemporary Chicano history originates in the aftermath of the 1848 conquest.[90] By focusing on economic transformations we questioned the conventional periodization of Chicano history and argued that the nineteenth- and twentieth-century Spanish-speaking populations of the Southwest were largely two different populations. A focus on the War of 1848—the presumed starting point of Chicano history—obscures the relationship between the establishment of U.S. hegemony over Mexico, which comes many decades later, and the development of the Chicano national minority in the United States in the twentieth century.

One needs to distinguish the annexation of 1848 and the ensuing institutional integration of the territory into the United States from the economic conquest of the late nineteenth and early twentieth centuries. Rather than the commonly held belief that the Mexican-American War of 1848 led to the construction of the Chicano minority, this study proposes that the origins of the Chicano population evolved from economic empire led by corporate capitalist interests with the backing of the U.S. State Department. The political and economic repercussions of the war virtually ended by the last decade of the nineteenth century. Furthermore, at no time did the 1848 annexation cause continuous internal migration, the mass population concentration along the border, the bracero program, low-wage maquila plants, Mexico's agricultural crisis, and, more important for this study, the decades of migrations to the United States. Those historical chapters, derived from the economic subordination of Mexico, forged the modern Chicano national minority.

Notes

1. John Kenneth Turner, *Barbarous Mexico* (Chicago: Charles H. Kerr, 1911), 256–57.
2. John Mason Hart, *Revolutionary Mexico: The Coming Process of the Mexican Revolution* (Berkeley: University of California Press, 1997), chapters 5 through 7.
3. As quoted in *The Monitor* (Ottawa, Canada), September 1995.
4. See, for example, the following: Jonathan C. Brown, *Oil and Revolution in Mexico* (Berkeley: University of California Press, 1993); William E. French, *A Peaceful and Working People: Manners, Morals, and Class Formation in Northern Mexico* (Albuquerque: University of New Mexico Press, 1996); G. M. Joseph, *Revolution from without: Yucatán, Mexico, and the United States, 1880–1924* (Durham, N.C.: Duke University Press, 1988); Ramon Eduardo Ruiz, *The People of Sonora and Yankee Capitalists* (Tucson: University of Arizona Press, 1988); Mark Wasserman, *Capitalists, Caciques, and Revolution: The Native Elite and Foreign Enterprise in Chihuahua, Mexico, 1854–1911* (Chapel Hill: University of North Carolina Press, 1984).
5. A number of studies look at the characteristics of the cooperation between Mexico's elites and powerful U.S. monopolies that descended on Mexico at the end of the nineteenth century. In addition to those listed in note 4, see Robert Freeman Smith, *The United States and Revolutionary Nationalism in Mexico, 1916–1922* (Chicago: University of Chicago Press, 1972) and Hart, *Revolutionary Mexico*, chapters 5 and 6.
6. See, e.g., Clarence Clendenen, *The United States and Pancho Villa: A Study in Unconventional Diplomacy* (Ithaca, N.Y.: Cornell University Press, 1961); Friedrich Katz, *The Secret War in Mexico: Europe, the United States, and the Mexican Revolution* (Chicago: University of Chicago Press, 1981); Gregg Andrews, *Shoulder to Shoulder? The American Federation of Labor, the United States, and the Mexican Revolution* (Berkeley: University of California Press, 1991); and Hart, *Revolutionary Mexico*.
7. Gilbert G. Gonzalez, *Mexican Consulates and Labor Organizing: Imperial Politics in the American Southwest* (Austin: University of Texas Press, 1999).
8. On this see Mario Barrera, *Race and Class in the American Southwest: A Theory of Racial Inequality* (Notre Dame, Ind.: University of Notre Dame Press, 1979), 68–69.
9. U.S. Industrial Commission, *Reports of the Industrial Commission on Immigration*, vol. 15 (Washington, D.C.: U.S. Government Printing Office, 1901), lxxxix. The report's conclusions about the cause of migration were based on the testimony of a former commissioner of immigration of the Port of New York. As a witness before the U.S. Industrial Commission he stated, "Those people who come for settlement in this country have a desire and feel the ability in themselves to expand, to look out for larger and better fields for their activity than they can find at home," p. 183; Victor S. Clark, *Mexican Labor in the United States*, Department of Commerce and Labor, Bureau of Labor Bulletin, no. 78 (Washington, D.C., 1908), 505; Manuel Gamio, *Migration and Immigration to the United States: A Study of Adjustment* (Chicago: University of Chicago Press, 1930), 171; and Paul S. Taylor, *A Spanish-Mexican Peasant Community, Arandas in Jalisco, Mexico* (Berkeley: University of California Press, 1933), 40.
10. For a summary of sociological critiques of the "push-pull" theories see Alejandro Portes and Robert L. Bach, *Latin Journey: Cuban and Mexican Immigrants in the United States* (Berkeley: University of California Press, 1985); Stephan Castles and Mark J. Millen, *The Age of Migration* (New York: Guilford Press, 1993); Ewa Morawska, "The Sociology and

Historiography of Immigration" in *Immigration Reconsidered: History, Sociology, and Politics*, edited by Virginia Yans-McLaughlin (New York: Oxford University Press, 1990), 192.

11. Leo Greble, Joan W. Moore, and Ralph C. Guzman, *The Mexican-American People: The Nation's Second-Largest Minority* (New York: Free Press, 1970), 63.

12. The examples of push-pull are many; the following are but a few: Leo R. Chavez, "Defining and Demographically Characterizing the Southern Border of the U. S." in *Demographic Dynamics of the U. S.-Mexico Border*, edited by John R. Weeks and Roberto Ham-Chande (El Paso: Texas Western Press, 1992); Douglas Massey et al., *Return to Aztlan: The Social Process of International Migrations from Western Mexico* (Berkeley: University of California Press, 1987), 108; Mark Reisler, *By the Sweat of Their Brows: Mexican Immigrant Labor in the United States, 1900–1940* (Westport, Conn.: Greenwood Press, 1976), 14; Arthur F. Corwin and Lawrence A. Cardoso, "*Vamos al Norte:* Causes of Mass Migration to the United States," in *Immigrants and Immigrants: Perspectives on Mexican Labor Migration to the United States,* edited by Arthur F. Corwin (Westport, Conn.: Greenwood Press, 1978), 39; David Maciel and Maria Herrera Sobek, "Introduction," in *Culture across Borders: Mexican Immigration and Popular Culture,* edited by David Maciel and Maria Herrera Sobek (Tucson: University of Arizona Press, 1998), 4; Camille Guerin Gonzales, *Mexican Workers and American Dreams: Immigration, Repatriation, and California Farm Labor, 1900–1939* (New Brunswick: N.J.: Rutgers University Press, 1994), 27–30; George J. Sanchez, *Becoming Mexican American: Ethnicity, Culture, and Identity in Chicano Los Angeles, 1900–1945* (New York: Oxford University Press, 1993), 20, 39; Richard Griswold del Castillo and Arnoldo de Leon, *North to Aztlan: A History of Mexican Americans in the United States* (New York: Twayne Publishers, 1996), 60–61; Antonio Rios-Bustamante, ed., *Mexican Immigrant Workers in the United States* (Los Angeles: UCLA Chicano Studies Research Center Publications, 1981); Frank D. Bean, Rodolfo de la Garza, Bryan Roberts, and Sidney Weintraub, eds., *At the Crossroads: Mexico and U.S. Immigration Policy* (Lanham, Md.: Rowman & Littlefield, 1997).

13. There are a few exceptions. Mario Barrera's 1979 work *Race and Class in the Southwest: A Theory of Inequality* (Notre Dame, Ind.: University of Notre Dame Press) briefly pointed out that the push-pull notions were difficult to separate. Alejandro Portes also points to weaknesses in his chapter "From South of the Border: Hispanic Minorities in the United States" in Virginia Yans-Mclaughlin, ed., *Immigration Reconsidered*. Portes generally identifies the role of U.S. expansion and intervention in Mexico, which he lumps with "postcolonial" societies. Upon closer examination he appears to be referring to the territorial acquisition following the Mexican-American War of 1846. He specifically places the origin of the northward migration on the activities of labor recruiters, not on the social dislocations caused by U.S. investments. Interestingly, Saskia Sassen also emphasizes the "emergence of multinational labor market" consequent to the "internationalization of capital." She writes that the investments by U.S. railroad and agricultural corporations and the Border Industrial Program "are all processes which created a labor market." The U.S.–Mexico border artificially divides this "labor market"; hence migration responds to the international labor marketplace. Saskia Sassen, "U.S. Immigration Policy toward Mexico in a Global Economy," in *Between Two Worlds: Mexican Immigrants in the United States,* edited by David Gutierrez (Wilmington, Del.: Scholarly Resources Books, 1996).

14. Quoted in P. Harvey Middleton, *Industrial Mexico: Facts and Figures* (New York: Dodd, Mead, 1919), frontispiece; for a slightly different version see Alfred Tischendorf, *Great Britain in Mexico in the Era of Porfirio Diaz* (Chapel Hill: University of North Carolina Press, 1961), 75.

15. David M. Pletcher, *Rails, Mines, and Progress: Seven American Promoters in Mexico, 1867–1911* (Ithaca, N.Y.: Cornell University Press, 1958), 38.

16. Ibid., 38, 79–80.

17. Chester Lloyd Jones, *Mexico and Its Reconstruction* (New York: D. Appleton, 1921), 299, 310. Mexican elites anticipated the policy design. One-time Mexican representative in Washington Matias Romero proposed an economic conquest in an 1864 speech before a gathering of New York City's prominent citizens. Guests included the largest capitalists: names such as Aspinwall, Astor, Fish, and Clews filled the list. Romero advised: "The United States are the best situated to avail themselves of the immense wealth of Mexico. . . . We are willing to grant to the United States every commercial facility. . . . This will give to the United States all possible advantages that could be derived from annexation, without any of

its inconveniences." Matias Romero, *Mexico and the United States* (New York: G. P. Putnam's Sons, 1898), 385.

18. Pletcher, *Rails, Mines, and Progress*, 3.
19. Ruiz, *The People of Sonora*, 14–15; also, Wasserman, *Capitalists, Caciques, and Revolution*, 108–9.
20. In his authoritative 1921 review of Mexican railroads Fred Wilbur Powell stated, "Mexican railroad development was *the result of foreign capital and enterprise*, attracted by national franchises or 'concessions' and encouraged by subsidies [emphasis added]." Fred Wilbur Powell, *The Railroads of Mexico* (Boston: Stratford, 1921), 1.
21. Walter E. Weyl, *Labor Conditions in Mexico*, Bulletin 38, U.S. Department of Labor (January 1902), 52.
22. Marvin D. Bernstein, *The Mining Industry in Mexico, 1890–1950* (Albany: State University of New York Press, 1964), 35.
23. Ibid., 33. Booster advertising offering sure bets on Mexican investments cajoled American investors. Railroads, it was said, guaranteed lucrative profits and vast wealth awaiting the enlightened administration of the American investor. David M. Pletcher, "The Development of the Railroads in Sonora," *Inter-American Economic Affairs* 1 (1948): 1–2. One pamphlet published by the U.S. government announced that ". . . the opening up of new mining districts is largely due to Americans, both through the improved mining methods and through the development of railroads built by our capital." International Bureau of the American Republics, *Mexico: Geographical Sketch, Natural Resources, Laws, Economic Conditions, Actual Development, Prospects of Future Growth* (Washington, D.C.: U.S. Government Printing Office, 1904), 233.
24. Robert G. Cleland, "The Mining Industry of Mexico: A Historical Sketch," *Mining and Scientific Press* (July 2, 1921), 13; also, Wasserman, *Capitalists, Caciques, and Revolution*, 76.
25. John Sheahan, *Patterns of Development in Latin America* (Princeton, N.J.: Princeton University Press, 1987), 297.
26. Henry Bamford Parkes, *A History of Mexico* (Boston: Houghton Mifflin, 1970), 309, cited in Barrera, *Race and Class in the Southwest*, 69.
27. On this see G. M. Joseph, *Revolution from without*, 30, 51, 62; also, Wasserman, *Capitalists, Caciques, and Revolution*, 46.
28. John Coatsworth, *Growth against Development: The Economic Impact of Railroads in Porfirian Mexico* (DeKalb: Northern Illinois University Press, 1981), 123–24.
29. Ibid., 158 (our emphasis); John Mason Hart makes this same point in his classic *Revolutionary Mexico*. Hart writes: "In the midst of land seizures associated with the planning of the new railroad system, peasant uprisings ranged from Chihuahua in the north to Oaxaca in the south," 41.
30. Coatsworth, *Growth against Development*, 170. See also French, *A Peaceful and Working People*, 37–47; Ruiz, *The People of Sonora*, 16–17; and Wasserman, *Capitalists, Caciques, and Revolution*, 109.
31. Coatsworth, *Growth against Development*, 145.
32. Michael Johns, *The City of Mexico in the Age of Díaz* (Austin: University of Texas Press, 1997), 14.
33. Friedrich Katz, "The Liberal Republic and the Porfiriato, 1867–1910," in *Mexico since Independence*, edited by Leslie Bethel (New York: Cambridge University Press, 1991), 101; see also Hart, *Revolutionary Mexico*, 169.
34. Roger D. Hansen, *The Politics of Mexican Development* (Baltimore, Md.: Johns Hopkins University Press, 1971), 27; Nathan L. Whetten, *Rural Mexico* (Urbana: University of Illinois Press, 1948), 89.
35. Gonzalez Navarro, *El Porfiriato*, 20.
36. Johns, *The City of Mexico*, 64.
37. Turner, *Barbarous Mexico*, 116.
38. Johns, *The City of Mexico*, 30.
39. Evelyn Hu-Dehart, "Pacification of the Yaquis in the Late Porfiriato: Development and Implications," *Hispanic American Historical Review* 54, no. 1 (February 1974): 77.
40. Moises Gonzalez Navarro, *Historia Moderna de Mexico, El Porfiriato*, vol. 4 (Mexico City: Editorial Hermes, 1957); see also Hart, *Revolutionary Mexico*.
41. Fred Wilbur Powell, "The Railroads of Mexico," in Robert Glass Cleland, *The Mexican Yearbook, 1920–1921* (Los Angeles: Times-Mirror Press, 1924), 164.

42. Frank Tannenbaum, *The Mexican Agrarian Revolution* (Washington, D.C.: Brookings Institution, 1929), 126.
43. Walter E. Weyl, *Labor Conditions in Mexico*, Bulletin 38, U.S. Department of Labor (January 1902), 91.
44. See Rodney D. Anderson, *Outcasts in Their Own Land: Mexican Industrial Workers, 1906–1911* (De Kalb: Northern Illinois University Press, 1976), 48–50.
45. Clark, *Mexican Labor in the United States*, 470–71; see also French, *A Peaceful and Working People*, 42–43.
46. González Navarro, *El Porfiriato*, XVII, 25.
47. Friedrich Katz, "The Liberal Republic and the Porfiriato, 1867–1910," 89.
48. E. A. H. Tays, "Present Labor Conditions in Mexico," *Engineering and Mining Journal* 84 (October 5, 1907): 622.
49. Allen H. Rogers, "Character and Habits of Mexican Miners," *Engineering and Mining Journal* 85 (April 6, 1906): 700.
50. See Robert G. Cleland, "The Mining Industry of Mexico: A Historical Sketch," *Mining and Scientific Press* (July 2, 1921): 640.
51. J. Fred Rippy, *Latin America and the Industrial Age*, 2nd ed. (New York: G.P. Putnam's Sons 1947). Quote cited in Jonathan Brown, "Foreign and Native-Born Workers in Porfirian Mexico," *American Historical Review* 98 (June 1993): 798.
52. González Navarro, *El Porfiriato*, 23.
53. Rogers, "Character and Habits of Mexican Miners," 701. See also Brown, *Oil and Revolution in Mexico*, 80–81. Brown writes that the Veracruz state population increased by 280,000 between 1890 and 1910, the oil boom years cited by personages such as Edward Doheny, developer of the Veracruz area oil explorations.
54. Dwight E. Woodbridge, "La Cananea Mining Camp," *Engineering and Mining Journal* 82 (October 6, 1906): 623.
55. See French, *A Peaceful and Working People*; Brown, *Oil and Revolution in Mexico*; Wasserman, *Capitalists, Caciques, and Revolution*; Ruiz, *The People of Sonora*; Smith, *The United States and Revolutionary Nationalism in Mexico*.
56. Clark, *Mexican Labor in the United States*, 472.
57. Taylor, *A Spanish-Mexican Peasant Community*, 44.
58. See, e.g., Nestor Rodriguez, "The Battle for the Border: Notes on Autonomous Migration, Transnational Communities, and the State" in *Immigration: A Civil Rights Issue for the Americas*, edited by Suzanne Jonas and Suzie Dod Thomas (Wilmington, Del.: Scholarly Resources Books, 1999); for a variation on the theme see David M. Reimers, *Still the Golden Door: Third World Comes to America* (New York: Columbia University Press, 1985), 128–29; Vicki Ruiz, *From out of the Shadows: Mexican Women in Twentieth-Century America* (New York: Oxford University Press, 1998), 163; Pierette Hondagneu-Sotelo, *Gendered Transitions: Mexican Experience of Migration* (Berkeley: University of California Press, 1994); Douglas Massey, "The Social Organization of Mexican Migration to the United States," in *The Immigration Reader: America in Multidisciplinary Perspective*, edited by David Jacobsen (New York: Oxford University Press, 1998), 213–14; and David Jacobsen, "Introduction," in *The Immigration Reader*. Jacobsen writes: Mexican migration reflects the earlier development of social networks that sustain it."
59. See, e.g., Wayne Cornelius, "The Structural Embeddedness of Demand for Mexican Immigrant Labor: New Evidence from California," in *Crossings: Mexican Immigration in Interdisciplinary Perspective*, edited by Marcelo M. Suarez-Orozco (Cambridge, Mass.: Harvard University Press, 1998), 141–42; and Smith, "Commentary," in *Crossings*.
60. Massey, "What's Driving Mexico–U.S. Migration," 953.
61. Ibid., 954.
62. See the following: Reimers, *Still the Golden Door*; also, Frank D. Bean, W. Parker Frisbie, Edward Telles, and B. Lindsay Lowell, "The Economic Impact of Undocumented Workers in the Southwest of the United States," in *Demographic Dynamics of the U.S.-Mexico Border*, edited by John R. Weeks and Roberto Ham-Chande (El Paso: Texas Western Press, 1992).
63. Saskia Sassen, "Foreign Investment: A Neglected Variable," in Jacobsen, ed., *The Immigration Reader*; also, Saskia Sassen, *Globalization and Its Discontents: Essays on the New Mobility of People and Money* (New York: New Press), 1998, chap. 6.

64. Mr. Cardoso has long since shed the facade and openly advocates the neoliberal open-door investment policy prescribed by the United States as the preferred model for economic development.

65. The critiques of world systems theory are numerous, but see in particular Eric Wolf, *Europe and the People without History* (Berkeley: University of California Press, 1981) and Peter Worsley, *Three Worlds of Culture and Development* (Chicago: University of Chicago Press, 1984).

66. Smith, *The United States and Revolutionary Nationalism*, 34.

67. Howard F. Cline, *Mexico: Revolution to Evolution, 1940–1960* (New York: Oxford University Press, l963), 244.

68. Benjamin Higgins, *Economic Development: Problems, Principles, and Policies* (New York: W. W. Norton, 1968), 643.

69. Cline, *Mexico*, 245.

70. Higgins, *Economic Development*, 645.

71. W. Whitney Hicks, "Agricultural Development in Northern Mexico, 1940–1960," *Land Economics* (November 1967): 396.

72. Raul Fernandez, *The United States–Mexico Border* (Notre Dame, Ind.: University of Notre Dame Press, 1977), 108.

73. Ibid., 123.

74. See David Barkin, "Mexico's Albatross: The U.S. Economy," *Latin American Perspectives* 2, no. 2 (1975); see also Hart, *Revolutionary Mexico*, epilogue.

75. Cline, *Mexico*, 86.

76. Raul Fernandez, *The Mexican-American Border Region Issues and Trends* (Notre Dame, Ind.: University of Notre Dame Press, 1989), 61.

77. Ibid.

78. Fernandez, *The United States–Mexico Border*, 108.

79. See Fernandez, *The United States-Mexico Border*, and *The Mexican-American Border Region*.

80. David Barkin and Blanca Suarez, "El Fin de la Autosuficiencia Alimentaria," in *Mexico: Nuevo Imagen* (Mexico City: Centro de Ecodesarollo, Editorial Nueve Imagen, 1982); Ruth Rama, "Some Effects of the Internationalization of Agriculture on the Mexican Agricultural Crisis," in Stephan E. Sanderson, *The Americas in the New International Division of Labor* (New York: Holmes & Meier, 1985).

81. Hart, *Revolutionary Mexico*. Hart writes on p. 378, "Mexico in 1987 constitutes an economic and social disaster . . . 70 percent of the children suffer from malnutrition. . . . The World Health Organization estimates that 107,000 Mexican children died in 1983 from three diseases for which immunization is available."

82. Carlos Heredia and Mary E. Purcell, "The Polarization of Mexican Society," paper prepared for the NGO Working Group on the World Bank, Development Group for the Alternative Policies, December 1994.

83. Gonzalez, *Mexican Consuls and Labor Organizing*, 12, 14–15; see also James D. Cockcroft, *Mexico: Class Formation, Capital Accumulation, and the State* (New York: Monthly Review Press, 1983), 91.

84. Gonzalez, *Imperial Politics*, chap. 6.

85. *International Report*, issue 34, vol. 12, no. 1, (March 1994); issue 35, vol. 12, no. 2 (June 1994); issue 37, vol. 13, no. 1 (February 1995); and issue 38, vol. 13, no. 2 (July 1995). Raul Fernandez, "Perspectivas del Tratado de Libre Comercio de Norteamerica," *Deslinde*, 13 (March–April 1993). James Cypher, "Developing Disarticulation within the Mexican Economy," *Latin American Perspectives* 28, no. 3 (May 2001), 11–37.

86. Víctor S. Quintana, "La Catástrofe Maicera," *La Opinión* (April 17, 1999); Chris Kraul, "Growing Troubles in Mexico," *Los Angeles Times* (January 17, 2000). Kraul writes that due to corn imports from the United States, "one-fifth of the 250,000 families who were working the land in Guanajuato in 1990 have since left their farms . . . a population shift that has been repeated across Mexico." The Free Trade Agreement "mandated the end of the costly subsidy program." John Coatsworth, "Commentary," in Suarez-Orozco, ed., *Crossings*, 75–78; Philip Martin, "Do Mexican Agricultural Policies Stimulate Emigration?" in *At the Crossroads: Mexico and U.S. Immigration Policy*, edited by Frank D. Bean, Rodolfo O. de la Garza, Bryan R. Roberts, and Sidney Weintraub (Lanham, Md.: Rowman & Littlefield, 1997).

87. "A Call to Action Is Needed at U.S. Border," *Los Angeles Times* (May 9, 1999); Mark Stevenson, "Border Factories Target of Fury over Mass Killings of Women," *Orange County (Calif.) Register* (April 4, 1999); see also Roberto Ham-Chande and John R. Weeks, "A Demographic Perspective of the U.S.–Mexico Border," in *Demographic Dynamics of the U.S.–Mexico Border*, edited by John R. Weeks and Roberto Ham-Chande.

88. Frank D. Bean and Marta Tienda, *The Hispanic Population in the United States* (New York: Russell Sage Foundation, 1987), 110; Marcelo M. Suarez-Orozco, "Introduction: Crossings: Mexican Immigration in Interdisciplinary Perspectives," in Suarez-Orozco, ed., *Crossings*, 7; Gilda Laura Ochoa, "Mexican Americans' Attitudes and Interactions toward Mexican Immigrants: A Qualitative Analysis of Conflict and Cooperation," *Social Science Quarterly* (March 2000).

89. James P. Allen and Eugene Turner, using data available to 1990, have shown that in several enclaves of high concentrations of Mexicans and Mexican Americans in Los Angeles and Orange Counties (Consolidated Metropolitan Statistical Area), nearly 64 percent of those age 25 to 64 are immigrants out of a total population numbering 1.6 million. They also demonstrate that more than 37 percent of the same age group immigrated between 1980 and 1990. In other words, at least a third of the age group in these enclaves entered the United States in the post-1980 period. That such a high concentration of adults are immigrants will have a decided effect on the political orientation of the group. See James P. Allen and Eugene Turner, "Spatial Patterns of Immigrant Assimilation," *Professional Geographer*, 48, no. 2 (1996).

90. Gilbert G. Gonzalez and Raul Fernandez, "Chicano History: Transcending Cultural Models," *Pacific Historical Review*, 23, no. 4 (1994).

III
The Ideology
and Practice of Empire
The United States, Mexico, and Mexican Immigrants

In step with the emergence of U.S. economic domination of Mexico, a host of American writers crafted a sizable body of literature on Mexico for a receptive American audience. In their presentations, authors identified a critical mass of pathological cultural norms affecting Mexican society known generally by the term "the Mexican Problem." This central theme, coursing through the texts, allegedly explained the causes of Mexico's economic backwardness (in comparison to the United States) and prescribed intensive American intervention to overcome it. Written by a diverse collection of individuals—from travelers to businessmen and Protestant missionaries—the accounts ultimately found their way into the popular culture and government bureaucracies of the United States. That body of literature not only advocated the economic domination by the United States over Mexico but also served as a theoretical departure for various oppressive public policies applied to the Mexican immigrant community.

This chapter examines that imperial cultural expression that flowed freely from the pens of American authors and the public schooling policy that this system of ideas generated. The evidence demonstrates a close interconnection between that methodical mind-set and the educational history of the Mexican immigrant community. Thus a culture of empire, a transnational body of thought contributes significantly to the shaping of public education involving Mexican immigrants. In the final analysis, the origins of the Chicano minority (and thus Chicano history) and the educational experience of the Chicano community are inseparable from the economic colonization of Mexico. Although this chapter is limited to an imperial mind-set constructed by Americans and its impact on the Chicano educational experience during the first three decades of the twentieth century, the culture of empire impacted broadly on that community throughout the century.

"The Peaceful Conquest": The U.S. Empire and Mexico

As the American Gilded Age came to a close, the forcible acquisition of Cuba, Puerto Rico, and the Philippines, the "peaceful" annexation of Hawaii, and the plunder of Panama presaged a new era in U.S. foreign policy. Mexico rose to prominence in U.S. foreign policy not as an annexed territory, but as an economically conquered territory. Terms such as "conquest," "invasion," and even "colonization" defined the increasingly dominating presence of U.S. capital in Mexico. F. E. Prendergast, writing in an 1881 edition of *Harper's New Monthly Magazine*, expressed claims that many thought reasonable: "[I]t is evident that any progress in Mexico must come through colonization by some higher and more progressive race, or by the introduction of capital in large amounts to develop her natural resources by the aid of native races."[1] For many of Prendergast's contemporaries, both annexation and a "peaceful conquest" meant the same thing. Twenty-six years later, Nevin O. Winter described the role of "outside capital" as "another foreign invasion but with a pacific mission."[2] Winter's contemporary Charles R. Enock alluded to the "ubiquitous American," a "noticeable feature of Mexican business life . . . what may be termed the Anglo-Saxon—or rather the Anglo-American—invasion." On the eve of the 1910 Mexican civil war, the United States effectively governed the Mexican economy by controlling $1 billion in investments, nearly two-thirds of all investments. More, outright foreign ownership of companies operating in Mexico (led by the United States) was "estimated at half the national wealth."

Contrary to popular thought, the 1910 civil war (the Revolution) neither derailed nor significantly threatened the strategic position held by the United States; on the contrary, the latter emerged from the war not only unscathed but also even stronger. Historian Alan Knight notes that U.S. economic interests "emerged from the Revolution more concentrated and more powerful." The predominant form of Mexican revolutionary nationalism "was happy to coexist with large and rising doses of U.S. direct investment."[3] Consequently, the ties binding the Mexican economy to the United States deepened rather than deteriorated in the postrebellion period. Substantial increases in Mexico's percentage of imports from the

United States occurred between 1910–11 and 1924, from 55.2 percent to nearly 73 percent. Other data corroborate the increasing subordination of the Mexican economy to the by then northern world power. By 1930, U.S.-based interests controlled the most important sectors of the Mexican economy. "In most areas," according to Robert Freeman Smith, "the United States expanded its presence."[4]

Following the "invasion" of Americans and their investments, a wave of publications on contemporary and historical Mexico that highlighted culture, archeology, art, economics, and history appeared primarily in those countries conducting business—that is, investing—in Mexico. A new genre of published works appeared in the United States simultaneously with the rising presence of U.S. capital and personnel in Mexico. In 1881 the first works of travelers appeared in journals such as *Harper's New Monthly Magazine* and *Collier's*. Hubert Howe Bancroft's *History of Mexico* (1880) began a modern tradition of studies, popular and academic, devoted to Mexico (the forerunner of modern Latin American studies in academia). By 1900 a defined literature devoted to Mexico assumed a substantial niche among the reading interests of Americans. However, that imperial ideology, constructed on a debasement of Mexico and Mexicans and an exaltation of all things American, reflected a maturing national political and cultural identity shared by broad numbers of people of the United States.[5] That identity seldom if ever separated itself from the ongoing process of a cultural *and* economic colonization, termed Americanization in the literature, of Mexico.

Socioeconomic Context for Creating the "Other"

By the time American writers began to engage topics on Mexico, a substantial modernization process fostered by U.S. capital had taken root. New forms of production and social relations wrought by foreign capital changed the social face of Mexico and provided the material that fashioned writers' thinking. Beginning in 1880, the construction of railroads initiated the first large-scale contacts between Americans and Mexicans. Estimates of the number of laborers required to lay track and maintain them ran as high as 40,000 per month working under the supervision of U.S. foremen, engineers, and supervisors. With the completion of the rails connecting Mexico City with the northern border in the mid-1880s, mining flourished such that by the turn of the century 140,000 mine and smelter workers were regularly employed. Countless more found employment in foreign-owned oil fields, power plants, textile factories, cotton farms, coffee fincas, and road construction.

By 1900 a massive shift had taken place in the demography of Mexico as settlements formed within economic zones under the control of American corporations. Altogether, an estimated 300,000 Mexicans migrated from southern and central states to establish new residences in the north (and eventually immigrated into the United States as the same companies recruited them over the boundary).[6] As Mexicans migrated within Mexico, immigrating Americans entered in force; altogether an estimated 40,000 Americans settled in the largest cities and in the new settlements formed as a consequence of foreign-inspired economic activity. From Mexico City to the railroad town of Torreon, the smelting center of Monterrey, the border towns from San Diego to Brownsville, and the Tampico oil fields, Americans formed the largest contingent of foreigners on Mexican soil.

Across the northern tier of Mexican states new communities mushroomed in response to mining, oil exploration, and railroad expansion developed by U.S. capital. Within these cities, towns, and remote mining, railroad, and oil camps, a new type of social relation was introduced into Mexico distinguished by a social and economic segregation separating Mexican laborers (and Mexicans in general) from American personnel and their families. The latter founded exclusive "clubs" and professional associations throughout the republic. Mexico City had its highly visible American colony numbering about six thousand, with its obligatory private club and a women's club reserved for English-speaking residents. The colony enjoyed residences styled in the American motif and lounged in their clubs' recreational facilities. An author for *National Geographic* found the colony active and growing in 1902. "It sustains a well-equipped club, an excellent hospital, and has all the paraphernalia of a well-ordered society intent upon getting the most out of life, such as golf links, base-ball, women's clubs, afternoon teas, literary circles, etc."[7] Two societies circulated within Mexico City. Americans and Mexicans lived separate lives, and in doing so mirrored their separate and unequal functions in the foreign-dominated modernization process.

Analyzing class relations requires that we contextualize the proletarianization of the Mexican population. In mining, oil, and railroad camps and towns across northern Mexico the two nationalities inhabited strictly separate quarters. The foreign minority comprised a class to itself, the handsomely rewarded corporate employees and managers who worked for, and answered to, a board of directors in New York, Los Angeles, or Chicago. In short, a sharply segregated community emerged, defined by workers' huts (sometimes provided by the company) at one end. At the other was an American colony easily distinguished by roomy houses for married personnel and modern dormitories for single men, an ever-present and active "club" with tennis court, sometimes a golf course, and a school for American children run by an American teacher.

At the site of the El Ebano oil field, famous for its tremendous output, seven thousand workers were segregated from the American technical and administrative personnel. The Mexican Petroleum Company, for example, provided housing— "two-room cottages . . . all wooden, neatly painted"— for the permanent "peon" employees, most of whom were recruited from the central plateau region. However, beyond the limits of the company-built houses, the "floating" labor supply, those usually working for an independent contractor, lived as best they could in the style of the "ordinary thatched huts of the Tampico natives."[8] Company owner Edward Doheny's description of the married American employees' housing contrasted sharply with the simple one-bedroom houses of the common workers: "five-room cottages, well kept, well cared for and presenting very attractive appearance." Single American employees lived in "exceedingly attractive" dormitories and enjoyed "the most complete" clubhouse in Mexico. According to Doheny, the single men "have reading rooms, game rooms, billiard tables, tennis courts and complete bathing facilities. The clubhouse . . . is arranged for general receptions as well as for the ordinary living conditions of its inmates." Doheny asserted that his company made every effort "to keep their American employees contented."[9]

The same social divisions obtained at the mining camps. At Guggenheim's Velardeña, smelter workers paid $2.00 to $2.50 a month rent, depending on size. And nearby stood a company store that invariably ruined local merchants and gouged the workers through vouchers handed out at payday and redeemable only at the store. One unusual mine operator from Sinaloa recalled that the "greatest injustice worked upon the laborers . . . was the system of company stores. Especially this was true of the mining companies."[10] One report estimated that three-fourths of the miners' wages were spent for food and supplies at the well-known and very successful silver mine at Batopilas in Chihuahua.[11]

In the remote countryside, on mountain peaks, valleys, and *barrancas* (ravines), the mining camps with their American and Mexican quarters stood as vivid reminders of class bifurcation, an extension of impressive modern mining facilities and smelters and of U.S. hegemony. The Mexican town generally enjoyed minimal sanitation; often the mining, oil, or railroad company supplied a school, a handball court, perhaps a theater, and always a hospital. Hospitals were as much a part of the landscape as the housing allowed the miners. Accidents routinely jolted the camp. One engineer wrote that "Accidents are altogether too frequent. . . ." This certainly was the case at the Santa Gertrudis mine in Chihuahua: thirty-nine men were killed in underground accidents from 1915 to 1918. Some accidents caused massive casualties. At the San Andres mine in Durango, more than a hundred men were killed in an explosion in 1901. In nearly all cases the men were held responsible, the operators alleging that the men were too careless and irresponsible.[12]

The company manager served as the camp's administrator and held significant clout to enforce rules and regulations governing the "Mexican town." The head of Guggenheim's operations in Mexico confided that the smelting and mining conglomerate "found Mexican labor as a rule satisfactory. We have always taken a sort of paternal interest in them."[13] At the Tampico oil fields, one writer noted that the boomtown "is a monument to the genius and faith of the Americans who made it great." Here in the newly born social atmosphere, he continued, "the swaggering, free-money, noisy, busy atmosphere of the frontier, of the oil fields, of the white man on his bully-ragging, destructive, inconsequential 'education' of the dark brother round the world, permeates the place."[14]

Relations between Americans and Mexicans, in all of their manifestations, provided the real, material context that greatly influenced writers as they traveled through Mexico. Mexico, after all, was not just Mexico; Americans were now more important to the Mexican economy than were Mexicans. Writers never lost sight of that fact and orchestrated their stories to justify that powerful presence. However, the average American knew next to nothing about Mexico, which inspired a heavy didacticism among writers. For most writers, informing about Mexico's indigenous past seemed a perfect place to begin their story.

Mapping Mexico's Historical Record

Narratives, from professional and academic articles to travelogues and other books, commonly opened with a section, chapter, or chapters accounting for the historical origins of Mexico and its people. Historical texts integrated fiction and fact into a simple imperial narrative. Historical genealogy invariably began with the pre-Columbian era with such introductory chapter titles as "Ancient History of Mexico," "Aztec Land," "Ancient Mexico," "Prehistoric Mexico," or "The Dawn of Mexico: Aztecs and Toltecs." Particular attention accrued to the Aztecs and their imperial relations with other societies before the coming of the Spaniards. Discussions of religious practices (particularly the human sacrifices), costumes, traditions, music, economic life, and their archaeological remains must have riveted the attention of the average reader. Journeys to the ruins at Teotihuacan, Mitla, or Cholula provoked extensive passages attesting to amazement that such monuments could be contemplated, much less completed. Narratives then proceeded to the Spanish conquest and finally the national period. Here the cultural and genetic origins of Mexico as well as the economic presence of the United States alongside Mexican forms of production were positioned. Accounts of the Spanish conquest identified the institutions planted by the conquerors and reviewed an alleged record of cruelty and oppression against the Indian populations. Without fail, the key to explaining contemporary Mexico originated with the ruin of the indigenous societies at the hands of Spaniards and the subsequent birth of the syncretic, new Mexico. After three centuries of Spanish colonial oppression over masses of servile Indians, the Mexican nation emerged.

A view of contemporary Mexico inevitably precipitated. The story went something like this: Over the centuries, Mexico formed a cultural and biological hybrid, a cross between Indian and European that exemplified the worst of both worlds. In the words of one author, "it must be confessed that [mestizos] often exhibit the well-known tendency to follow the vices and weaknesses of both sides of their ancestry rather than the virtues."[15] To be sure, some dissonance appeared now and then in the assessment of Mexico's population. "In the opinion of most observers," added a more optimistic foreign service hand, "[the mestizo] is an improved stock as compared to the aborigines, quick to learn but inconstant in the applications of lessons taught."[16] Indians and mestizos, 80 to 90 percent of Mexico's population, neither of whom were of the "better types," formed Mexico's historical and contemporary dilemma.

Nothing seemed as important to understanding Mexico than its racial lines, which, depending on the source, came out to be something like 12 percent white (however tainted by Spanish "blood" inheritance), 33 percent mestizo, and the rest Indian. Only the top 12 percent were worthy of leadership, except in cases of "exceptional" ability of individual mestizos and Indians. That was the social side of Mexico. Writers focused keenly on the material or natural side, describing Mexico as a land of vast, untapped resources, minerals, soils, timber, climate, and cheap labor attractive to American investors who "blessed" Mexico with a billion dollars of their investment capital. A chapter or two on mines, cattle ranches, and plantations, and a long discussion on railroads underscored the significant place that foreign capital, particularly U.S. capital, held in the Mexican nation.

But there was much more to the analysis than that of breaking Mexico down into its essential parts, a society composed of whites, "mixed breeds," and "full-blooded" Indians living atop the richest natural resources in the world. Narratives examined the behavior patterns fixed within each component of the Mexican nation and eventually distilled the base qualities that made Mexico unique among nations of the world.

"The Latin Mind Is Essentially Oriental"[17]

In scrutinizing Mexico's historical record, and after traveling to its hinterlands and cities, authors quickly found the word "Oriental" ideal for cutting to the essence of the contemporary Mexican national character.

"Oriental" allegedly defined Mexicans and their culture and appeared in enough accounts to suggest that it had become a standard measure for comparing Mexicans to other cultures, particularly that of the United States. For certain, readers' attention responded to the expression. "Oriental" conveyed an image of an exotic, poor, strange, appealing, possibly loathsome, and for sure a subordinate people practicing an impenetrable culture. George B. Winton set the tone of his 1913 training guide for Protestant missionaries from the United States with a quote opposite the first page:

> Now with regard to the character of the people, they are as Oriental in type, in thought, and in habits as the Orientals themselves . . . we find that they are genuine Asiatics. They have some of the fatalism, the same tendency for speculation on the unpractical side of life and religion, the same opposition to the building of industries, the same traditionalism and respect for the usages of antiquity.[18]

"It is all Oriental," gushed one journalist for the *Boston Globe* (1888), "even to the barking dogs that howl through the streets."[19] George B. Winton found that "Mexicans have much in common with the people of western Asia and northern Africa. So manifest is the resemblance to the latter that, taken with certain traits of the stone and architecture of the pre-European period, it has suggested a racial connection with Egypt." Mary Barton expressed surprise at finding examples of an Orientalism that compared to the Far East. "The way the women do their hair," she exclaimed, "is Mongolian, and brought back memories of women I had seen on the great Tibetan frontiers, the women of Nepal, Sikhim, and Bhutan; many of the Mexican women have the same jolly laughing mien and the same short, squat type of figure."[20] Not one author defined with any precision the meaning of "Oriental" when applied to Mexico. "Oriental" could be a mere similarity, while for some "Oriental" meant an identity with direct links to the "Orientals" themselves. And so they left the reader with vague references to Asia, the Middle East, and Africa. Ambiguity seemed to suffice.

The absence of a consensus as to the exact qualities that gave to the Mexican an "Oriental" presence seemed not to deter authors. Seemingly, the "Oriental" discourse engendered in Europe and applied by Americans as they related tales of economic conquest appeared a distraction rather than a central and defining point for explaining Mexico. "Oriental" was more literary and abstract than substantive and descriptive. When it became obvious that a variety of general qualities went beyond "Oriental" and required a terminology that delved deeper (and more "accurately") into the cultural uniqueness of Mexico, "Oriental" receded into the background but certainly did not disappear. Authors did not need to search long for a more appropriate descriptive term; they found it in the Spanish word *peon*, meaning common laborer. The language of empire, one unique to the American experience, took on a life of its own.

Mexico: Land of "Sleepy Peons and Sad-Eyed Burros"[21]

The peon supplied a favorite subject matter for many a writer's ruminations. Peon came from the Spanish *peón*, literally meaning someone who walks rather than rides a horse (a *caballero*), a definition that writers gladly supplied for readers. Peon (in the English pronunciation) more easily connected to the realities of Mexico and replaced the old standby "greaser" which had surfaced with the pre- and post-1848 contacts between Americans and Spanish Mexicans of the old Southwest. Even the newly found "Oriental" was eclipsed, but not eliminated, in the growing discourse on Mexico. As the literature grew, "peon" eventually encompassed everything that exemplified Mexican and not remotely American, the preferred measure for comparing the Mexican to the American. Writers ultimately placed peon, Mexican, and mestizo on an equal par.

Percy F. Martin, author of several works on Mexico, assured the readers of *Mexico of the Twentieth Century* (1907)that the "great deterrent to the complete regeneration of Mexico has been the character of the native peons."[22] A frustrated observer writing for the *Independent* (1926) asked, "Who are these peons? What is their physical and mental condition? Are they any better, or worse, than Orientals or many races . . . ?"[23] Mining engineer Allan H. Rogers, unlike those who found "Oriental" a fitting description, expanded the range of analogies by comparing the peon with the plantation blacks of the U.S. South. He defined the peon in the following terms:

> of mild and humble nature, much like the southern plantation field hand before the war . . . like the Southern darkey, he lived in quarters at the home ranch or at outlying ranches under the supervision of a majordomo and from working constantly under the sun his skin, naturally dark, was blackened to the hue of the African.[24]

Comparing the peon to the "Southern darkey" reappears in various forms in the literature, and the alleged qualities residing within the former slave and Mexican peon were strikingly similar. More often authors devoted considerable attention to the quality of labor similar to those descriptions of black labor in the United States, as did the editor of *Engineering and Mining Journal* in the June 9, 1906, issue: "The Mexican peon," he wrote, "is characteristically a docile laborer . . . with only simple wants, which are easily satisfied. . . ."[25] Some saw in Mexican labor a knack for taking the "easy way" to the degree that the habit established a barrier to any satisfactory relationship between American employers and Mexican labor. A journalist for the *Nation* concluded that the Mexican harbors "a complete disregard for the basic need of work [and] regards it as an evil."[26] Engineer J. Nelson Nevius minced no words: "The Mexican laboring classes have a highly developed lazy strain in their blood."[27] That description was but one step removed from making the conscious comparison of the American blacks to peon labor. Thus an author of a *National Geographic* article borrowed from the American experience, alleging that the "Mexican peon knows that he is born to serve, as did the old southern darky."[28]

The vast army of unskilled laborers (although many were experienced miners) working on the modern forms of industrial production and transportation were invariably known to American bosses as peons, men and women who formed a new class of wage workers in Mexican society. A long litany of pathologies allegedly afflicted the cheap labor uprooted from their lands, then recruited, shipped, and employed willingly by U.S. companies. The roll call of pathological conditions was inconsistently explained, although no one bothered to notice. Peon laborers and their families, whether Indians or "half-breeds," were purported to be prone to excessive drinking and promiscuity and were lethargic, unambitious, docile, unintelligent, fatalistic, superstitious, cowardly, cruel, uneducated, but trainable under the right influence. As clarification for the nation's social conditions, authors often referred to one or all of three factors: the racial inheritance of defective genes, centuries of Spanish colonial oppression, and/or the effects of inhabiting tropical climates or oxygen-rare altitudes.

Writing for the U.S. Department of Commerce and Labor, Walter Weyl observed, "The most salient characteristic of the native labor is apathy . . . on the whole it is sufficiently general to be considered a national characteristic of great importance in everything pertaining to labor."[29] Twenty years later Wallace Thompson, author of five books on Mexico and Latin America and editor of the journal *Ingenieria Internacional,* arrived at the same conclusion in his economically motivated psychological treatise *The Mexican Mind: A Study of National Psychology* (1922). Among a formidable lineup of defects, Thompson found that apathy held the key to explaining Mexico's genetically determined economic doldrums: "Forever the lack of ambition for aught save idleness; forever the promise of *mañana* and the great things of tomorrow—these drag upon the wheels of what might be. . . . Apathy remains, outstanding as a characteristic of Mexico.[30] E. D. Trowbridge, general manager of the American-owned Mexican Light and Power Company and employer of many a peon, said in 1919: "The peons have little initiative [but] work well under supervision."[31]

Not infrequently, mean and vicious metaphors debased the subject peoples. "Mexicans are restless. The peon likes to ride," wrote Frederick Simpich in the *National Geographic* of July 1920. "Whenever they have saved money from a few days' work they swarm to . . . towns . . . running to and fro apparently as aimless as the inhabitants of a disturbed ant hill."[32] Hubert Howe Bancroft had said as much thirty-two years earlier: "[the] the least possible labor provides for these wants, and careless for the morrow, they squander the surplus on drinking. . . ."[33] By 1930 such thinking had become conventional wisdom. "Peon" easily segued into images of children, and in the scramble to define the Mexican, "peon" and "childlike" served well enough.

The Mexican-as-child theme appears frequently in narratives suggesting that from the perspective of the observer, Mexican customs and norms were inherently determined sets of actions and ideas. Perhaps no other commentator stated it as clearly and vehemently as did the racially obsessed Wallace Thompson in his *The Mexican Mind*. After Thompson cited compulsive sex drives as the Mexican norm, he engaged the matter of maturity. "The Mexican," he confidently professed, "seems to have a child's or a savage's unwavering grasp of the details of desire and of the things he hopes for—a heritage from the Indian which centuries of white rule and oceans of white blood have never eradicated."[34] He then extended the racially determined maturation thesis using the example of Mexican humor: "There is indeed true humor and a great deal of it in the Mexicans, although it is accented by but little levity, and is more often childlike and wantonly cruel."[35] Thompson was hardly original (but when it came to the discourse on Mexicans few, if any, were); four decades earlier Hubert Howe Bancroft asserted a similar line of thought: "The Mexican—the mestizo now being dominant and representative—has remained in a state of adolescence, as indicated by his capricious, thoughtless, and even puerile traits."[36]

Children by nature required supervision or parental control, and commentators explicitly linked the two. Listen for a moment to the paternal prodding of Marie Robinson Wright, who applied a twist to the father figure role: "The United States is the elder brother among American republics" and "the civilizing influence of the American people can be made of great benefit to them [Mexicans]."[37] The absence of those civilities deemed prerequisites for modernization (industrial modernization equated with civilization) enjoined observers to generalize around a grand theme, the "Mexican Problem." In an address at a conference on Mexico at Clark University in 1920, Professor George Blakeslee affirmed what others had felt for some time: "The outstanding fact is that there is a genuine Mexican Problem."[38] A year later sometime diplomat Chester Lloyd Jones pointed out that "a generation ago few Americans recognized that Mexico was a problem."[39] But by the twenties, the Mexican Problem had become an issue around which Americans closed ranks.

Blakeslee defined the problem by this question: "How may it [Mexico] develop into a law-abiding, capable nation?" Commentators answered in unison. The resolution to a society governed by boundless pathological behaviors originating from a childlike mental inheritance required paternal intervention, possibly permanently, by a higher authority. The "Mexican Problem," was for the United States to resolve, a burden placed by destiny on its shoulders. Cultural defects rooted in faulty genetic material, in part, created the "Mexican Problem," to be attended to by public and private individuals and organizations from the United States. But beneath all of the racialized and paternalist rhetoric, observers were asking: What are the internal prerequisites for optimal economic and political relations between Mexico and the United States? Or as Chester Lloyd Jones put it (in a chapter aptly titled "Why Mexico Is a Problem"), "The great natural wealth of Mexico makes it a region in which the adjustment of its political and economic relations with the rest of the world is of great importance."[40]

"The Americanization of Mexico"[41]

Americans gladly promoted themselves as the saviors of Mexico. A legion of authors maintained that relief for a society burdened by an inferior civilization required a rigorously observed open-door investment policy. Economic hegemony constituted the bedrock of the redemption process, or so thought U.S. citizens managing operations in Mexico. Mexico, it was commonly alleged, languished under the weight of masses of peons, Indians, and mestizos (terms often used interchangeably), who reproduced not only themselves to excess, but an abject culture as well, which in turn bred archaic and moribund economic institutions and violence-laden political practices. Reformation—that is, Americanization—meant adjusting Mexico to continued infusions of U.S. capital for the exploitation of Mexico's resources and labor power.

Publications confidently recommended the continuance of an ongoing process of economic and cultural Americanization of Mexico. "Modernization and Americanization are almost synonymous terms in Mexico," declared Edward Conley in an article aptly titled "The Americanization of Mexico." Conley listed the salubrious "effects of the American invasion":

> We have been the leaven in the loaf as it were . . . we have taught the Mexicans banking and the use of banks. We have built hydraulic power plants and taught the Mexicans how to utilize the enormous amount of energy which was going to waste in their waterfalls. . . .

> We have, by our example and our commercial products taught the
> peon to wear shoes and a hat, and have increased his wages all over
> the republic.[42]

Not only banking, clothing, and wages, but the family structure as well
"will be on the American basis." Conley optimistically concluded that
"each year the American way of living is taking a deeper hold on the Mexican people."[43]

However, although Mexico was on the path toward a U.S.-inspired template for modernity, not all observers felt that the tide had turned, or that
equality was achievable. Most thought that Mexico was still enthralled to
ancient customs that had outlived their usefulness and that posed obstacles to modernization. University of California scholars working for the
Doheny Research Foundation, for example, concluded in 1918 that "In
Mexico . . . the problem for the great mass is to provide the means for
awakening sluggish minds and bodies that are suffering for the most from
manana [sic]. They have first to learn to labor well and dutifully; which
means an interest must be awakened to the satisfactions to be realized
from settled industry and its fruits."[44] Thompson used slightly different
phrasing: "The desire to 'get things done' which spurs the Anglo Saxon is
missing. . . ." In a similar vein of thought, sociologist Edward A. Ross introduced his account with a terse warning: "[W]hat a paradise this Mexico
might be if it possessed the moral character and the social institutions of
the descendants of the Puritans. Nature has done her part. It is man that
does not fill out the picture."[45] Invariably authors prescribed continued
cultural instruction proffered by the United States for the sickly nation.

James Carson unequivocally insisted on reliance upon American influ-
ences to solve the "Mexican Problem," a pattern of defects rooted in the Indian, "the dregs of a once powerful and progressive race." "The great need
of the people today," he counseled, "is for vocational training, and the genius of the American for organization will supply this if he is given an opportunity to help the Mexican develop the vast riches of the country. This
is the only kind of intervention that is imaginable."[46] Not all found the task
easy or possible of success; pessimism seeped in. Nevin Winter lamented
that "Things cannot be changed to Anglo-Saxon standards in a year or two
years, or even a generation. To Americanize Mexico will be a difficult if not
impossible undertaking."[47] An equally discouraged William Joseph Showalter argued, "It will be a long, long climb until its population, four-fifths
Indians and half-breeds, will reach that point in their national destiny
where they can possess a government like our own."[48] Nevertheless, thought
others, the course must be kept. One ex-engineer with years of experience
in Chihuahua mines reminisced that Americanization was not an easy task
but that it was possible and that it must be carried out. He claimed that

though it "takes four years to make an American out of him [the Mexican]," the task cannot be jettisoned: "Make an American out of him or leave him to his happy indolence."[49]

That desired systematic intervention became the North American version of the "white man's burden." Americans declared loudly and proudly that economic predominance carried with it the responsibility for guiding that nation from a degenerative state to a higher level of civilization and into the twentieth century. Duty—or better, self-interest—commanded that Americans assume the task. The solution to Mexico's backwardness, the "Mexican Problem," could be nothing short of an economic and cultural reconstruction of Mexico, a version of Americanization on an international scale. Then, exclaimed Wallace Thompson, "Mexico will be a white man's land, more truly than she has ever been."[50] As a Mexican's land, Mexico would inevitably languish in a tangle of pitiful behavioral patterns.

All of these efforts, it should be pointed out, stood well within the economic policy concurred with by the governing elites of Mexico and administered by their senior partners and self-appointed mentors, U.S. corporations. Formal and informal U.S. policy toward Mexico sought nothing less than a cultural and political adaptation of Mexico to the exigencies of the dominant economic interests then operating in Mexico. Americanization consequently never envisioned a politically independent person or nation via Americanization reforms. Much like the educational programs designed by European powers for their colonial possessions, Americanization never envisioned the promotion of equality between colonizer and colonized.[51] Instead it meant to secure the relation through the reiteration of the need for a long-term "civilizing mission." Seldom, if ever, were Mexicans complimented for intelligence, inventiveness, or any other quality that might ensure an independent economic and political development. No one dared claim that Mexicans were the racial or cultural equals of Americans, or that they could go it alone without U.S. capital in the economic driver's seat. Mining engineer Franklin Wheaton Smith spoke for a great many "Mexico hands" when he surmised that "Mexico is not yet strong enough to undertake unaided its own development."[52]

Observers concluded that Mexicans were salvageable if given the right training, and to the degree that their inveterate or cultural natures allowed. Americans insisted that they were capable of, and the lone party responsible for, leading them to redemption. That redemption, however, never contemplated the severance of the economic ties binding Mexico to the United States. Rather, cultural Americanization strengthened the hegemonic economic position of the United States. Thompson concisely summed up the heart of the matter in *The People of Mexico* (1922), a work touted by Chester Lloyd Jones and Edward A. Ross for its "excellence." Thompson frankly admitted that American anxieties emanated from a single source:

> Her [Mexico's] resources, her gold and silver and oil, her henequen and rubber and coffee and lumber, her great labor supplies that wait so surely upon education and uplift, are forces which the white world cannot ignore. . . . Mexico cannot live in isolation, for her lands lie in the very heart of the world and her resources are sorely needed. . . .[53]

The scenario is loaded with traditional perspectives of morally (and socially) acceptable gender relations: the "strong male," Uncle Sam, and the "weak female," Mexico, could not live apart, nor could they live as equals. Mexico must, by nature, subsume "herself," to the regional alpha male. But the analogy that Thompson applied rather unconsciously figured decidedly within international relations saturated with political and economic power. Chester Lloyd Jones, for example, placed the "Mexican Problem" in a broader global context, one in which "the shortcomings of the weak are problems for the strong." Contextualized within the existing imperial relations between, or as Jones put it euphemistically, weak states and strong states, Jones explained the "Mexican Problem" within a framework of those European nations sharing a vital interest in the Middle East, the Far East, and Eastern Europe. In the sphere of European interests as in that sphere eyed by the United States, "the problem of the protection of foreign interests promises to be most important." As for the United States, which had established protectorates in Cuba, Panama, Puerto Rico, Santo Domingo, Haiti, and the Philippines, the relations with Mexico, "the most important of the Latin Republics," comprised "the outstanding factor in American international policy in the next decade."[54] America's problem centered on managing to maintain its vital control over economic resources of Mexico, an economic protectorate, while diplomatically dealing with the latter subjectively as if an independent, sovereign nation. That objective, the creation of an internal order in Mexico compatible with foreign capital, consumed vast amounts of the U.S. Department of State's energy. The United States opted for a high-wire act, maintaining hegemony shrouded by policy of "reciprocity."

From Porfirio Díaz (1880–1910) through the Great Depression, the open-door investment policy continued its historical course; the message remained the same while the messenger changed. Through the administrative changes and policy nuances in Washington, economic facts and figures demonstrated that as regards U.S.–Mexico relations, no substantial break occurred either in policy objectives or in economic relations between 1880 and 1930. Mexico remained an object for cultural and economic Americanization. Ideological practices and economic empire expanded in tandem. Without the economic conquest that body of imperial thought would have little purpose, no objective relation. Generalizing about Mexico and the Mexican people, labeling them lazy, indolent, apathetic, and in need of uplift made sense only in relation to the material economic conquest by the United States. Ideology of empire did not inspire a desire for empire; an oversupply of capital and decreasing rates of profit propelled economic conquest. Ideology justified the accomplished conquest and persuaded the American public that they were obligated to the task of conquest.

Imperial Ideology and Chicano Educational History

The ideology of empire, like the corporations that inspired it, transcended the border as migrants traveled north and into the labor camps and colonias across the Southwest and Midwest. The same corporations that had employed and housed Mexican labor would now do the same north of the border. Carey McWilliams noted that the two sides of the border held many geographic similarities such that migrants would feel as if they had never left their homeland.[55] However, more than the similarity of the border region greeted the migrating peoples. Mexican migrants worked for the same corporations that used their labor power in Mexico; the ideology that justified the exploitation of Mexico's labor and resources greeted them as well in the new environment. Mexican work meant the same in the United States as in Mexico—the poorest-paid and lowest category of labor. Migrants often lived in labor camps sponsored by the same mining, railroad, and agricultural corporations operating in Mexico. Rigid segregation north of the border reproduced the social relations dividing American from Mexican in the labor camps, towns, and cities within Mexico. Mexican migrants did not necessarily find an entirely novel environment in the United States. Many had experienced various dimensions of it in their country.

Unfortunately, the literature on Chicano history overlooks the imperial context. The example of the educational experience of the Chicano community is a case in point. Despite many advances in the literature on the educational history of Mexican immigrants and their descendants, a full treatment on the topic has not yet appeared. Not only has there been a lack of interest in the subject, but also the prevailing approach ensures problematic results. For the most part, extant studies tend to focus solely on national theoretical and practical issues and, consequently, remain strictly within a U.S.-bound perspective. The resulting historiography (not only in education studies but in general treatments as well) is incomplete and, furthermore, overlooks the deeper origins of the educational experience of the twentieth century's most important immigrant community. In the bargain, the full accounting of U.S. educational history falls short. An examination of one particular aspect of Chicano history, public education, and within education, the effort to effect an Americanization of that community, will be shown to have direct links with the expanding U.S. empire. Furthermore, that national educational experience cannot be adequately explained without placing the economic domination over Mexico at the center of that history.

Mexican immigrants and their families began entering the United States in large numbers soon after 1907–8. After settlement into colonias across the Southwest and Midwest, immigrant children outside of rural agricultural regions were obligated to attend public school. As educators searched for guidelines for educating these children, they came across many of the works discussed above. By the mid-1920s this literature had provided a theoretical foundation for the educational programs designed for the Mexican community. An identical list of cultural and genetic pathologies, the same "Mexican Problem" and need for Americanization, filtered through to boards of education, teacher training schools, administrators, and schoolteachers. Ironically, the ideology of empire flowed back into the United States and provided the "expert" opinion that shaped the educational policy applied to Mexican children and adults. At the service of public schools, that transnational ideology constructed a transnational "Mexican Problem." As in the case of the Americanization of Mexico, the Americanization of the immigrant community was expected to preserve the social relations of subordination and domination.

The Transnational "Mexican Problem"

In the late 1940s Carey McWilliams continued his tireless campaign to correct public and private injustices committed against minorities, in particular the Mexican-American community. His classic *North from Mexico: The Spanish-Speaking Peoples of the United States* (1949) offered the first historical account of the Mexican-American people and served as a model for historians of the Chicano experience who followed his path. Combining a scholar's penchant for research with a political perspective that can be described as democratic radicalism, McWilliams documented the oppressive conditions shouldered by Mexican Americans. Correcting a history of racialized oppression motivated McWilliams to engage in various activities on behalf of minorities. His research demonstrated that the political struggles undertaken by the Mexican community (which he actively supported and participated in) contributed to democratizing the culture and public policy of the United States.

McWilliams argued that a major factor in establishing the syndrome of oppressive public policies exemplified in segregated schools, disproportional rates of arrest for juvenile delinquency, and the general prejudice that infected the dominant society was the continual recourse to the "Mexican Problem." So pervasive was this comprehensive conceptualization of the Mexican-American community that McWilliams selected it for the title of the eleventh chapter of *North from Mexico*. He observed that "In the vast library of books and documents about ethnic and minority problems in the United States, one of the largest sections is devoted to 'The Mexican Problem.'" McWilliams noted that a surge of publications on the "Mexican Problem" appeared in sync with the settlement of Mexican immigrants throughout the Southwest. Armed with volumes of "data," social workers, educators, the courts, and the police concluded "that Mexicans lacked leadership, discipline, and organization; that they segregated themselves; that they lacked in thrift and enterprise. . . ." McWilliams made a pointed mention of a "mountainous collection of master's theses" and dissertations that reported on alleged (and oft-repeated) inferior intellectual, cultural, or biological qualities of Mexican adults and children.[56] Unfortunately for those who learned their first lessons in Chicano history from McWilliams, none thought to investigate the origins of the "Mexican Problem." He explained that as early as 1908 one finds mention of a "Mexican Problem," not in a specific way, rather in an indirect fashion. Victor Clark, for example, writing for the Department of Labor in 1908, commented on the cultural separation between the United States and Mexicans:

> The Mexican laborer is unambitious, listless, physically weak, irregular and indolent. On the other hand he is docile, patient, usually orderly in camp. . . . If he were active and ambitious, he would be less tractable and would cost more.[57]

The references to the "Mexican Problem" were everywhere. Militaristic-sounding language encased in articles and books with catchy titles peppered the literature, and these frequently suggested a quickly spreading social/racial problem. Frederick Simpich, for example, opened "The Little Brown Brother Treks North" with a picturesque sketch of migrating Mexicans honeycombed with traditional stereotypes. Simpich's depictions of migrants crossing the border mirrored popular conceptions of the period: "Strumming their guitars and wearing five gallon hats . . . invading our country in a vast army." He later described the "army" as "hordes crossing the Rio Grande" escaping the "impoverished peon class."[58] Writing an article titled "Pressing Race Problems of Texas," Texas A&M professor William E. Garnett declared that the "problems associated with the Mexican invasion of the State are . . . the most pressing race questions now confronting Texas."[59] Anthropologist Florence Rockwood Kluckhohn followed a similar theoretical path at the 1951 annual meeting of the American Association of Schools of Social Work. The Mexican, she warned (or so it seemed),

> In every respect . . . is different. His time orientation is neither the future nor the past but the present. Individualistic relationships have almost no meaning for him. . . . He accepts what comes in whatever situation with small thought that he has any power or will to overcome or master obstacles. The good person to him is not the successful one, the one who achieves, but rather the one who obediently and graciously plays out the role defined for him.[60]

Even "sympathetic" authors found the culture of the Mexican community lacking in those basic substances that guaranteed successful assimilation into American life.

McWilliams rightly pointed out that the "Mexican Problem" only covered up the core issues, the racial domination that established the relations between the Mexican community and the dominant society. However, while McWilliams correctly identified critical academic and public policy slogans that only served to "muddy the water," he overlooked the transnational origins of the "Mexican Problem." Here we must look to the authors who formulated the ideology of empire. The evidence shows conclusively that materials written about the "Mexican Problem" within the United States were deeply influenced by those authors who designed the "Mexican Problem" in reference to Mexico.

As the Mexican immigrant community formed in the early 1900s, policymakers and academics lacking information, expertise, and direction that would inform public policy in relation to Mexican immigrants tapped into the materials written about Mexico. In fact, in the "mountainous collection of master's theses" referred to by McWilliams, there is a heavy reliance on the materials written about Mexico examined earlier in this chapter. No fewer than twenty-five theses and dissertations written on the Mexican immigrant community between 1912 and 1957 either cited authors such as Wallace Thompson, George B. Winton, Edward A. Ross, Joseph K. Goodrich, and Percy F. Martin, among others, or they simply made a case of a "Mexican Problem," a cultural catastrophe awaiting Americanization.

Some, such as Jessica Hayden (who taught Americanization in southern California for a generation), frequently recited nearly verbatim Thompson's *The Mexican Mind: A Study of National Psychology*. Among the quotations sprinkled through her 1934 master's thesis on the education of the

Mexican community, she included the following from Thompson (she actually plagiarized Thompson here):

> There is an outstanding characteristic of the Mexican apathy [*sic*], which remains an infirmity of the will; forever the promise of man-ana—the great things of the morrow. It is this apathy of the will which drags upon the wheels of such progress as might exist. The yoke of this custom also lies upon the Mexicans everywhere with a weight which is impossible to explain to the American or European.[61]

Thompson said the same somewhat differently (a passage cited earlier):

> But for all this altruism and this concentration upon self as well, there is apathy. Forever the lack of ambition for aught save idleness; forever the promise of "*manana*" [*sic*] and the great things of the morrow,—these drag upon the wheels of such progress as might be . . . an infir-mity of the will, an inability to stir out of that helpless drifting. . . . Apathy remains, outstanding as a characteristic of Mexico.[62]

The well-known sociologist Emory Bogardus of the University of Southern California, who specialized in the study of Mexican immigrants, gained a national reputation through that specialization. Trained by the eminent sociologist Robert E. Park at the University of Chicago, Bogardus ventured west with sparkling credentials. One of his first publications, *Essentials of Americanization* (1919), contained chapters on each immigrant group in the United States. In the rather short chapter on Mexicans, Bogardus demonstrated little originality of thought. His opening sentence highlighted an unquestioned conceptualization widely discussed across the southwestern United States: " 'The Mexican problem' has developed rapidly since 1900."[63] The same litany of pathological conditions con-tained in the extant literature on Mexico found expression. However, Bogardus realized that his short, three-page examination of the "Mexican problem" left much unsaid. He desired that his work direct educators to-ward works that would shed greater light on the qualities that made for a Mexican. For each immigrant group examined he listed a short bibliogra-phy, and in the Mexican section Bogardus listed only eight works. However sparse the reading list, all were about Mexico and all written by experts on Mexico and Mexican culture, which only underscored the importance of studies of Mexico for "understanding" the Mexican immigrant. Among the cited works were Charles R. Enock's *Mexico*, Joseph K. Goodrich's *The Coming Mexico*, Frederick Starr's *In Indian Mexico*, and George Winton's *Mexico To-Day*.

Bogardus followed *Americanization* with *The Mexican Immigrant: An Annotated Bibliography* (1929). Here we find the full expression of the by then general reliance on the literature on Mexico. According to Bogardus, the "literature on the Mexican immigrant falls somewhat naturally into three classes."[64] The first were those relative to cultural background, the second were materials relating to Mexican communities in the United States, and the third were those relating to "interracial adjustments." In the first category, focusing on culture, Bogardus listed thirty-seven books and fifty articles, all written about Mexico and Mexicans in Mexico. Particularly telling was Bogardus' short descriptions of each work, which provide an insight into the reception given those works by a growing body of specialists on the Mexican immigrants and their community. A few examples demonstrate the manner through which these materials became standard texts for understanding the Mexicans. Of Frederick Starr's *In Indian Mexico*, Bogardus commented, "An eminent anthropologist gives a first-hand, reliable picture of one part of Indian Mexico after another, until the reader begins to feel at home among all the peoples who are described. An outstanding work, depicting culture traits clearly."[65] It mattered not that, among other things, Starr described the Otomi indigenous peoples as having "ugly dark faces." Of Edward A. Ross's *The Social Revolution in Mexico*, Bogardus offered a similar assessment: "Through the keen eyes and rich cultural backgrounds of an eminent and trained sociologist *(sic)* the Mexican people are portrayed." Wallace Thompson's virulent anti-Mexican stream of consciousness, *The Mexican Mind: A Study of National Psychology*, was described simply as "An analysis of the Mexican mode of thinking, their racial characteristics, habits of thought, and of action."[66] Not surprisingly, only three books relative to the Mexican immigrant community were available at the time. The overwhelming majority of pertinent sources available to interested parties were written by individuals who had little if any concern for the "Mexican Problem" affecting the American Southwest. Nonetheless, these works soon entered into the academic and public policy mainstream and helped to flesh out, then promulgate, the "Mexican Problem" critiqued by McWilliams.

Five years after the 1929 bibliography appeared, Bogardus published *The Mexican Immigrant in the United States* and included a chapter on the literature. He announced that selections were "made of those which are deemed the most important," and that an "understanding of the Mexican immigrant rests directly on knowing his culture traits." Listed were the same works found in his earlier bibliography, plus many more written since the earlier publication relative to Mexico.[67] By the mid-1930s the "Mexican Problem" had become a standard for addressing the ills wrought by the "invading army" settling into Mexican colonias across the Southwest and Midwest.

Peonism: The Orientalism of the U.S. Empire

We now begin to understand that the authors of the many theses, dissertations, articles, and books on the Mexican community mentioned by McWilliams sought direction about and information on their subjects from the literature on Mexico. This also explains why the Mexican immigrant was continually referred to as a "peon," a hybrid of Indian and European "stock," a group burdened with the same syndrome of cultural disorders described in the literature on Mexico. In the main, writers on Mexican immigrants traversed the same ideological path taken by writers on Mexico.

Not surprisingly, essays and articles introduced their subject with a reference to the peon and hybrid origins of Mexican immigrants. A graduate of the Sociology Department at the University of Southern California, John Keinle retraced the "blood lines" in his 1912 thesis "Housing Conditions among Mexican Population of Los Angeles." Citing Charles R. Enock's *Mexico* as authority, Keinle reported that the hybid character of Mexico produced an undigested mixture of the European, the mestizo, and the peon.[68] Grace Reeves cited a host of works on Mexico in her 1929 thesis "Adult Mexican Education in the United States," and it comes as no surprise that she would write, ". . . the Mexican is a composite of two ethnic groups: Spaniards and Indians. Modern Mexico may be divided into three parts, racially speaking . . . [those] purely European; the part that is Indian; and the mixed portion."[69] A graduate of the University of California Department of Economics advised in his 1914 thesis "A Survey of the Mexicans in Los Angeles" that "The Mexicans considered in this study are the peons . . . and are the source of nearly all the serious problems."[70] In step with an emerging trend, the author relied extensively on works on Mexico, including that of Charles R. Enock *(Mexico)* and Percy F. Martin *(Mexico of the Twentieth Century)*.

Frank Callcott's 1929 article "The Mexican Peon in Texas" opened with "There are two classes of peons in Texas, those who intend to make the state their home and those who come only for the cotton picking. . . ."[71] In her 1932 master's thesis "Methods of Teaching Mexicans," Betty Gould reported that Mexican parents in the schools she researched "were not of the better class of Mexicans. They represent, rather, the very lowest type, the day laborer, or peon."[72] In an article titled "Mexican Immigrants and American Citizenship" (1928), social worker Helen Walker noted that the "larger per cent of the Mexican population of Southern California represents the peon class." Naturally, as Walker and her contemporaries had read, peons were a people apart. She recounted an old theme: "The Mexican peon dislikes work. Work is work; joy is joy. The two are not the same. There is joy in play . . . but not in work."[73] A school superintendent of a southern California school district argued that the peon background explained much about the intelligence of Mexican children. "The educational status of Mexican peon parentage is very low," asserted the future Americanization teacher, "and the average pupil of Mexican peon parentage has less ability to do the work commonly offered in our schools than has the normal American pupil."[74] Moreover, maladapted parents reproduced Mexico's cultural pathologies within the family setting. Such were the reasons that Emory Bogardus offered when he recommended to his readers, "It is necessary to first of all to consider the Mexican immigrant in light of the family culture traits of the peon classes of Mexico."[75]

These and many more articles and studies not examined here varied imperceptibly, their script provided by their sources. Peons were a hybrid people infected with a cultural virus that rendered them a major source of America's social problems. The list seemed infinite: Mexicans were docile, violent, promiscuous, shiftless, thriftless, unambitious, unhygienic, fatalistic, imitative, clannish, superstitious, and shunned labor; they undervalued education, lacked leadership abilities, and were intellectually inferior. On the other hand, and to their credit, they were generous, happy and carefree, rhythmic, poetic, good with their hands, artistic, courteous, and responded well to authority. The bad, however, outweighed the good.[76]

One future school administrator defined the Mexican immigrant question on an economically unequal international plane. "Standards of conduct," she wrote, "and personal ideals in Mexico are very different from those in the United States. It is only natural to assume that a country that has progressed more rapidly than Mexico, has also a higher goal in personal ideals and standards of conduct."[77] Anthropologist Florence Kluckhohn posed a similar assumption thirty years later. Mexicans, she stated, follow a culture foreign to the United States, "a culture radically different from our own," and "some of the differences are obvious because they are so extreme."[78]

Noteworthy references to an alleged childlike nature appeared as well. Vera Sturges, an official with the southwestern branch of the YWCA, gave an address, "Adjustment of Mexicans to U.S. Life," at a national meeting of social workers. "Intellectually," she concluded, "[Mexicans] are children."[79] Another student of the "Mexican Problem" concluded that Mexican immigrants were a "child-like, timid, carefree people."[80] Bogardus concurred in his oft-cited *The Mexican Immigrant in the United States* and claimed that the immigrant "is somewhat like a small child brought up in a paternalistic home."[81] One school superintendent underscored the critical factor of parentage in his manual on methods for the education of Mexican adults and children. He noted that "Mexican peon laborers are a group of second-graders." Experts held that Mexicans as a group were children, beset with all the problems that children bring to parents, and therefore required paternal-like supervision.[82] Readers also were informed that "the children of the Mexican peon laborers do not have a home environment that is conducive to good health, to good morals, or to educational advancement."[83] A second school superintendent managing a district with a large Mexican population resonated with this lament:

> Almost all their parents are in the peon class and their standard of living is far below that of the average American family; their customs are much different from American customs; and probably most important of all, their intelligence as a whole is inferior to the average American's intelligence.[84]

No amount of training could repair the intellectual deficit, but not all was lost.

Americanization

A stern dose of Americanization via the public school system seemed the only remedy available for eliminating, or at least controlling, a potential social scourge. Los Angeles schools superintendent Susan B. Dorsey advised a 1923 gathering of district principals, "We have these Mexicans to live with, and if we Americanize them we can live with them."[85] The preferred method to achieve cultural cleansing was the segregation of Mexican children and adults into a coerced socialization process suited to their "temperament." The requirement for "success" in the United States, as Florence Kluckhohn and a host of others explicitly proposed, was the force-feeding of those standards capable of overcoming the "orientations of Mexicans in this country."[86] Wherever a sizable Mexican colonia appeared, school districts devised Americanization programs housed within state-mandated segregated schools.

By 1920 the segregated Mexican school had become a fixture in colonias and played a central role in the life of both Mexican and Anglo communities. On the surface, segregated schools appeared as neighborhood schools, but in reality they functioned as special schools designed to train Mexican children and adults in patterns of behavior and thinking compatible with those standards guiding the "successful" society. Schools for Mexican children taught a separate curriculum, emphasized English and American standards of conduct, vocational education over academic work, group discipline over individuality, and logically had lower expectations. Indeed, segregated schools were administered as a separate school system within a larger district. Here, distinct sets of educational criteria functioned.

Mexican schools were generally underbudgeted and overcrowded, administered and taught by inferior personnel, and embraced a different set of goals. In rural school districts the Mexican school operated on a separate schedule to allow children to join their parents in the fields or orchards. In some school districts, especially those in Texas, migrant children were simply too important to the agricultural economy and were denied entry into schools. But in those districts where Mexican schools were the norm, the successful child was one who ceased to act like a "typical" Mexican, spoke English, thought in English, and acted like an "American." Those who successfully shed the Mexicans' "peculiar" habits were rewarded with better grades and a show of teacher respect. And in the dominant society, such an Americanized individual earned the distinction "different Mexican" to set him or her apart from the unreformed Mexican, the carrier of the "Mexican Problem."[87]

Reforming the immigrant's community culture reached beyond the usual targets of children and adults to focus on women. The state of California adapted its program to the division of sexual labor by emphasizing the role of women as potential Americanizers. The state made extraordinary attempts to apply a program designed to make Americanization agents of Mexican women. Presumably, once Americanized—that is, once a mother/housewife kept a home, fed and raised her family, and tended a garden on the "American plan"—she would then automatically Americanize her family. And many Americanized Mexican women would lead the entire community toward cultural redemption.[88]

Despite the rhetoric about the linkages between Americanization and success on the one hand, and Mexican culture as the cause of the Mexicans' "failure" on the other, the Mexican school seldom if ever posited social change as a goal. Paralleling the arguments for the Americanization of Mexico, the Americanization of the immigrant community was expected to preserve the social relations of subordination and domination, relations that derived from the economic order. Moreover, in the minds of theorists and practitioners, Mexicans could never resolve their historically conditioned shortcomings without supervision. As in the case of a Mexico depicted by writers as dependent on U.S. capital and know-how, Mexican immigrants became objects for the theory and practice designed by the architects of state policy.

That so many individuals charged with administering and designing public policy affecting the Mexican immigrant community were dependent on articles and books written about Mexico underscores the significance of empire for understanding the Chicano experience. The "Mexican

Problem" resonated on both sides of the border to become a transnational "Mexican Problem." The interface of the "Mexican Problem" with the immigrant "Mexican Problem" was not lost on at least one writer. In *That Mexican! As He Really Is North and South of the Rio Grande* (1928), author Robert McLean reviewed the general characteristics of Mexican immigration with no unusual conclusions. Little ambivalence marked the commentary on the "Mexican Problem"; a seeming unity of opinion as well as a sizable literature indicated that the pressing matter was well fleshed out by the time McLean's book appeared. Like so many of his contemporaries with an interest in Mexican immigrants, McLean appropriated a thick body of information on Mexico and applied it to the immediate questions of Mexican immigrants. Understandably, then, McLean chose C. W. Barron's *The Mexican Problem* as the first entry in his book's brief bibliography. The script was well rehearsed, and the conclusions were inevitable. Barron wrote in conventional tones about the Mexican character, contending that "the larger part of the good people of Mexico are children who want to be in debt and at the same time carefree."[89] But McLean, unlike the majority of his peers who failed to make the connection between the two "Mexican Problems," went beyond merely parroting the immigrant's cultural ills to insightfully detecting the transnational scope of the "Mexican Problem." He closed a chapter with a paragraph titled "The Problem of That Mexican" (a variation on the theme), stating,

> With his inherited ignorance, his superstition, his habits of poor housing, his weakness to some diseases, and his resistance to others, with his abiding love of beauty, he has come to pour his blood into the veins of our national life. "That Mexican" no longer lives in Mexico; he lives also in the United States. The "Mexican Problem" therefore . . . reaches from Gopher Prairie to Guatemala.[90]

Despite McLean's prescience, most observers continued to think of the "Mexican Problem" in strictly national terms. The evidence, however, strongly suggests that the politics of empire and national political life intersected at critical points.

Conclusions

A systematic pattern of ideas rationalizing and advocating imperial domination eventually found its way into the sphere of socialization institutions of the United States. Unfortunately, this aspect of U.S. history has not been explored. We argue that Chicano history unfolds inseparably from development and maintenance of the U.S. empire. Unfortunately, this vital component of U.S. social history and Chicano history is silenced. Consequently, explanations for the differential outcomes between Chicanos and the dominant society are incomplete and therefore wide of the mark. The interconnections of the Chicano historical experience with the economic and political hegemony exerted by the United States over Mexico and of the ideology that that domination inspired need to be placed on the research agenda.

Notes

1. F. E. Prendergast, "Railroads in Mexico," *Harper's New Monthly Magazine* 63 (1881): 276. Prendergast repeated a popularly held notion of the preferred conduct of U.S. foreign policy. Contemporary and influential economist Charles Arthur Conant, for example, wrote, "The irresistible tendency to expansion, which leads the growing tree to burst every barrier . . . seems again in operation, seeking new outlets for American capital and new opportunities for American enterprise.

   "The new movement is not a matter of sentiment. It is the result of a natural law of economic and race development. The great civilized peoples have to-day at their command the means of developing the decadent nations of the world" Charles Arthur Conant, *The United States in the Orient* (1900; reprint, Port Washington, N.Y.: Kennikat Press, 1971).
2. Nevin O. Winter, *Mexico and Her People Today* (Boston: L. C. Page, 1907), 53.
3. Alan Knight, *U.S. Mexican Relations, 1910–1940* (San Diego: Center for U.S. Mexico Studies, University of California, San Diego, 1987), 26.
4. Robert Freeman Smith, *The U. S. and Revolutionary Nationalism in Mexico, 1916–1922*, (Chicago: University of Chicago Press, 1972), 34.
5. David Spurr notes a similar discourse in European colonization projects. His work illustrates how imperialism is basically similar regardless of widely differing contexts. See David Spurr, *The Rhetoric of Empire: Colonial Discourse in Journalism, Travel Writing, and Imperial Administration* (Durham, N.C.: Duke University Press, 1993), chap. 5.
6. Moises González Novarro, *Historia Moderna de Mexico, El Porfiriato*, vol. 4. Mexico City: Editorial Hermes, 1957, xviii, 25; see also Friedrich Katz, "The Liberal Republic and the Porfiriato, 1867–1910," in *Mexico since Independence*, edited by Leslie Bethel (New York: Cambridge University Press, 1991), 89.
7. John W. Foster, "The New Mexico," *National Geographic* 13, no. 1 (1902): 24; also, Ralph McA. Ingersoll, *In and under Mexico* (New York: Century, 1924), 138–39. Ingersoll recalls that the American women at Monte del Cobre mines, most of them wives of office personnel, "all wanted more than anything else to be back in that rarefied air that they had left, and were obviously putting up with things at Monte [del Cobre] and making the best of a bad deal."
8. Second interview with E. D. Doheny, May 20, 1918; interview 503. Doheny Research Foundation, Occidental College Special Collections.
9. Second interview with E. D. Doheny, May 20, 1918; interview 503.
10. Doheny Research Foundation. "Labor in Mexico." Box K, interview with Lewis Scott of the Batopilas Company, May 20, 1918; interview 486. Occidental College Special Collections.
11. Arthur R. Townsend, "The Ocampo District, Mexico," *Engineering and Mining Journal* 77, no. 13 (March 31, 1904): 515.
12. See Companía de Santa Gertrudis, SA. Campaign against Accidents. Report for December 1917. Doheny Research Foundation Collection, Occidental College Special Collections; "Mexico," *Engineering and Mining Journal* 71, no. 2 (January 12, 1901): 65; "Coal Mining in Mexico," April 13, 1901. Doheny Research Foundation Collection. Occidental College Special Collections; interview with Mr. Requena, May 18, 1918; interview 489. Doheny Research Foundation Collection, Occidental College Special Collections.
13. "Labor in Mexico," interview with Mr. Morse: interview 485. Box K, Doheny Research Foundation.
14. Wallace Thompson, *Trading with Mexico* (New York: Dodd, Mead, 1921), 207.
15. Chester Lloyd Jones, *Mexico and Its Reconstruction* (New York: D. Appleton, 1921), 18.
16. Robert McClean and Grace Petrie Williams, *Old Spain in New America* (New York: Association Press, 1916), 134.

17. George B. Winton, *Mexico Today: Social, Religious, and Political Conditions* (New York: Missionary Education Movement, 1913), 2.
18. Ibid.
19. Mary Elizabeth Blake, "Picturesque Mexico," in Mary Elizabeth Blake and Margaret F. Sullivan, *Mexico* (New York: Lee & Shepherd, 1888), 39. Coauthor Sullivan added: "As the mystic symbols on the monuments of Egypt have only begun to yield their secrets to the archeologist, we need not despair of yet knowing something of the antiquity of a country whose age is beyond present estimates, and whose earliest civilization, as indicated by her superstitions, architecture, costumes, and myths, was Oriental," pp. 199–200. A spurious Charles Reginald Enock wrote, ". . . it has been said that, from his headdress to his sandaled feet, the native Mexican is Hispano-Egyptian." Charles Reginald Enock, *Mexico* (New York: Scribner, 1909), 35.
20. Mary Barton, *Impressions of Mexico with Brush and Pen* (London: Methuen, 1911), 20.
21. William Joseph Showalter, "Along Our Side of the Mexican Border," *National Geographic* 37, no. 1 (July 1920): 71.
22. Percy F. Martin, *Mexico of the Twentieth Century* (London: Edward Arnold, 1907), x.
23. Frederick Simpich, "The Little Brown Brother Treks North." *Independent* 116, no. 39 (1926): 238.
24. Alan H. Rogers, "Character and Habits of Mexican Miners," *Engineering and Mining Journal*, 85, no. 14 (April 14, 1908): 700.
25. "The Riots at Cananea," *Engineering and Mining Journal* 81, no. 23 (June 9, 1906): 1099.
26. Eva Frank, "The Mexican 'Just Won't Work,'" *Nation*, 125, no. 3241 (July 17, 1927): 156.
27. Letter to the editor by J. Nelson Nevius, *Engineering and Mining Journal* 78, no. 6 (August 11, 1904) 213.
28. Frank H. Probert, "The Treasure Chest of Ancient Mexico," *National Geographic* 30, no. 1 (July 1916): 43.
29. Walter Weyl, "Labor Conditions in Mexico," Bulletin 38, U.S. Department of Commerce and Labor (January 1902), 12.
30. Wallace Thompson, *The Mexican Mind: A Study of National Psychology* (Boston: Little, Brown, 1922), 41.
31. E. D. Trowbridge, *Mexico: To-Day and To-Morrow* (New York: Macmillan, 1919), 273.
32. Frederick Simpich, "Along Our Side of the Mexican Border," *National Geographic* 37, no. 1 (July 1920): 63. Simpich was not the first to use the humans-as-ants metaphor. In 1899 Cy Harman published *The Story of the Railroad* (New York: D. Appleton), in which he described railroad construction laborers on the Mexican Central as "Red ants, fleece clad, from the mountains, naked ants from the Terre Caliente, and Black ants from Sonora," 218.
33. Hubert Howe Bancroft, *History of Mexico,* vol. 14 (San Francisco: History Company, 1888), 611.
34. Thompson, *The Mexican Mind*, 134.
35. Ibid., 171.
36. Hubert Howe Bancroft, *History of Mexico*, vol. 6 (San Francisco: History Company, 1888), 607.
37. Marie Robinson Wright, *Picturesque Mexico*, 444.
38. George E. Blakeslee, "Introduction," in *Mexico and the Caribbean,* edited by George E. Blakeslee (New York: Strechert, 1920), viii.
39. Jones, *Mexico and Its Reconstruction*, 1.
40. Ibid.
41. Edward M. Conley, "The Americanization of Mexico," *American Monthly Review of Reviews,* 32 (1907): 724–725.
42. Ibid.
43. Ibid.
44. "Mexico: An Impartial Survey," Doheny Research Foundation Papers (mimeo) (1918), History Archives, Los Angeles Public Library, 95.
45. Edward Alsworth Ross, *The Social Revolution in Mexico* (New York: The Century Company, 1923), 7.
46. James Carson, "Upon the Indian Depends Mexico's Future," in *Mexico and the Caribbean: Clark University Addresses,* edited by George E. Blakeslee (New York: G. E. Strechert, 1920), 38.
47. See Winter, *Mexico and Her People Today*. Winter wrote: "American intelligence and capital have done much toward bringing about the present prosperous conditions and will do

much more in the future, Mexico will find their neighbors north of the Rio Grande ready to lend a helping hand," 395.

48. William Joseph Showalter, "Mexico and Mexicans," *National Geographic* 25, no. 5 (1914): 493.
49. Ingersoll, *In and under Mexico*, 117–8.
50. Thompson, *The Mexican Mind*, 19.
51. See Frederick Cooper and Anna Laura Stoler, eds., *Tensions of Empire: Colonial Cultures in a Bourgeois World* (Berkeley: University of California Press, 1997), 7.
52. Franklin Wheaton Smith, "Present Condition of Mining in Mexico," *Engineering and Mining Journal* 86, no. 14 (October 3, 1908): 655.
53. Thompson, *The People of Mexico*, 407.
54. Jones, *Mexico and Its Reconstruction*, 4.
55. Carey McWilliams, *North from Mexico: The Spanish-Speaking Peoples of the United States* (Philadelphia: J. B. Lippincott, 1949), 9–10.
56. Ibid., 206–97. One example, from a doctoral dissertation written in 1942, exemplifies a general trend in the graduate student literature. In his University of Texas doctoral dissertation on the education of Mexicans in Texas, Perry M. Broom described some of the generalized behavior patterns of Mexicans: "Tendencies toward imitation, conservatism, submission to authority, and emotional instability all color the 'Mexican' personality." Perry Morris Broom, "An Interpretative Analysis of the Economic and Educational Status of Latin Americans in Texas" (Ph.D. diss. University of Texas, Austin, 1942), 167.
57. McWilliams, *North from Mexico*, 9–10.
58. Frederick Simpich, "The Little Brown Brother Treks North," 237–38.
59. William E. Garnett, "Immediate and Pressing Race Problems of Texas," *Southwestern Political and Social Science Association* 6, *Proceedings* (1925): 32.
60. Florence Rockwood Kluckhohn, "Cultural Factors in Social Work Practice and Education," *Social Science Review*, 25, no. 1 (March 1951): 40.
61. Jessie Hayden, "The La Habra Experiment in Mexican Social Education" (master's thesis, Claremont College, Claremont, Calif., 1934), 27.
62. Thompson, *The Mexican Mind*, 41.
63. Emory Bogardus, *Essentials of Americanization* (Los Angeles: University of Southern California Press, 1919), 179.
64. Emory Bogardus, *The Mexican Immigrant: An Annotated Bibliography* (Los Angeles: Council on International Relations, 1929), 1.
65. Ibid., 5.
66. Ibid., 6.
67. Emory Bogardus, *The Mexican Immigrant in the United States* (Los Angeles: University of Southern California Press, 1934), 99.
68. John Keinle, "Housing Conditions among Mexicans in Los Angeles" (master's thesis, University of Southern California, 1912), 3.
69. Grace Reeves, "Adult Mexican Education in the United States" (master's thesis, University of Southern California, 1929), 51.
70. William Wilson McEuen, "A Survey of the Mexicans in Los Angeles" (master's thesis, University of Southern California, 1914), 3.
71. Frank Callcott, "The Mexican Peon in Texas," *Survey* 44 (June 26, 1920): 437.
72. Betty Gould, "Methods of Teaching Mexicans" (master's thesis, University of Southern California, 1932), 3.
73. Helen Walker, "Mexican Immigrants and American Citizenship," *Sociology and Social Research* 13, no. 1 (September–October 1929), 466. Walker published a series of articles that she derived from her master's thesis written at the University of Southern California in the late 1920s. "Mexican Immigrants" was taken from her thesis.
74. Merton E. Hill, *The Development of an Americanization Program* (Ontario, Calif.: Chaffey Union High School District Board of Trustees, 1928), 56. Hills's study originally appeared as a doctoral dissertation at the University of California, Berkeley, and was reprinted by his employer.
75. Bogardus, *The Mexican Immigrant*, 24.
76. The master's theses and doctoral dissertations that took up various themes concerning the "Mexican Problem" or that cited authors of works on Mexico numbered no fewer than twenty-six. Along with those noted in the body of the text, the following graduate studies

also made one or more such claims or citations: James Kilbourne Harris, "A Sociological Study of a Mexican School in San Antonio, Texas" (master's thesis, University of Texas, Austin, 1927); Mary Lanigan, "Second Generation Mexicans in Belvedere, California" (master's thesis, University of Southern California, 1932); Anne Christine Lofstedt, "A Study of the Mexican Population in Pasadena, California" (master's thesis, University of Southern California, 1922); John N. Kaderli, "A Study of Mexican Education in Atascosa County with Special Reference to Pleasanton Elementary School" (master's thesis, University of Texas, Austin, 1938); Emma E. Valle, "The Adjustment of Migrant Pupils in a Junior High School" (master's thesis, University of Texas, 1953); Grace Elizabeth Reeves, "Adult Mexican Education in the United States" (master's thesis, Claremont College, 1929); Albert Turner Kaderli, "The Educational Problem in the Americanization of the Spanish-Speaking Pupils of Sugar Land, Texas" (master's thesis, University of Texas, Austin, 1940); Charles Dinnijes Withers, "Problems of Mexican Boys" (master's thesis, University of Southern California, 1942); Marvin Ferdinand Doerr, "Problem of the Elimination of Mexican Pupils from School" (master's thesis, University of Texas, Austin, 1938); Charles Clifford Carpenter, "A Study of Segregation versus Non-Segregation of Mexican Children" (master's thesis, University of Southern California, 1935); Lawrence Otto Barfell, "A Study of the Health Program among Mexican Children with Special Reference to the Prevalence of Tuberculosis and Its Causes" (master's thesis, University of Southern California, 1937); Herman A. Buckner, "A Study of Pupil Elimination and Failure among Mexicans" (master's thesis, University of Southern California, 1935); Gladys Riskin Wueste, "A Survey of Factors Relating to the Education of the Children of Migratory Parents of Eagle Pass, Texas" (master's thesis, University of Texas, Austin, 1950).

77.   Gould, "Methods of Teaching Mexicans," 116.

78.   Kluckhohn, "Cultural Factors," 40.

79.   Vera Sturges, "The Progress and Adjustment of Mexicans to U.S. Life," *National Conference on Social Welfare Proceedings* (1920): 483.

80.   Clara Gertrude Smith, "The Development of the Mexican People in the Community of Watts, California" (master's thesis, University of Southern California, 1933), 9.

81.   Bogardus, *The Mexican Immigrant in the United States*, 52.

82.   Ibid., 43.

83.   Hill, *The Development of an Americanization Program*, 65.

84.   John Branigan, "Education of Overage Mexican Children," *Sierra Educational News* 25 (December 1929): 37.

85.   Susan B. Dorsey, "Mrs. Pierce and Mrs. Dorsey Discuss Matters before the Principals Club," *Los Angeles School Journal* 6 no. 25 (March 1923): 59.

86.   Kluckhohn, "Cultural Factors," 41.

87.   Gilbert G. Gonzalez, *Chicano Education in the Era of Segregation* (Philadelphia: Associated University Press/Balch Institute Press, 1990); and *Labor and Community: Mexican Citrus Worker Villages in a Southern California County, 1900–1950* (Urbana: University of Illinois Press, 1994).

88.   Grace C. Stanley, "Special Schools for Mexicans," *Survey* 44 (September 14, 1920): 715.

89.   C. W. Barron, *The Mexican Problem* (Boston: Houghton Mifflin, 1917): 12–13.

90.   Robert N. McLean, *That Mexican!: As He Really Is North and South of the Rio Grande* (New York: Fleming H. Revell, 1928), 126.

IV
Agency, Gender, and Migration

Since the mid-1980s researchers have developed a substantial bibliography documenting the active role that Mexican immigrants have taken in constructing their everyday lives in the United States and the gendered character of a migration affected by a whole spectrum of individual, family, and group decisions. This important new literature sets out to identify what are called "micro" structures—immigrant networks, but even more important, the subjectivities, agency, or active roles taken by individuals as well as groups of immigrants within those networks. These studies seek to illustrate the ways in which migrants through the exercise of their own agency make choices and construct their lives against a backdrop of "macro" forces, which includes laws, institutions, and other large structures, even the state of the international political economy.[1]

In this chapter we attempt to extend the application of ideas about agency and the gendered nature of immigration from Mexico to the United States to the "macro" structures that frame this movement of people. This is feasible to the extent that the separation of "macro" and "micro" factors is not a rigid, impermeable barrier. The laws, policies, degrees of enforcement, and other "macro" structures are merely expressions of the "subjectivities" of U.S. legislators, officials of the Departments of Justice, Labor, Agriculture, and Treasury, the Border Patrol, and Mexican political leaders. These actors themselves respond to the active desires of other life economic actors, such as business leaders and associations of large agribusiness interests.

Because of the active intervention of these actors in the exercise of their own agency, federal and state laws in the United States, for example, have varied and shifted considerably over many decades to deal with a variety of changing economic conditions. The aggregate subjectivities of U.S. business and political interests—the agency of empire, so to say—gave us as their considered choices the 1942–64 Bracero Program, the maquila program in northern Mexico, various guest workers programs, as well as periodical decisions to allow the "forces of demand and supply"—misery—to do the job of channeling and regulating the flow of migrants to the United States.

When it comes to migratory policy, the gender consciousness of imperial agency appears most evident in the case of the Bracero Program and the promotion of maquila industry in northern Mexico. For more than twenty years the former program recruited and distributed a male working force. Mexican women could not choose to migrate under the Bracero Program. On the other hand, the maquila industry program in northern Mexico, which is very much part of the story of Mexican migration to the United States, has been for the most part confined to women. Programs such as these suggest that the gendered character of migration arises not merely from the "micro" choices and decisions made by the migrants themselves but more importantly from the choices and decisions laid out in advance by imperial agencies.

In the first part of this chapter we discuss a number of issues pertaining to the notions of agency or subjectivities when expanded to include the notion of imperial agency and the gendered impact of imperial choices regarding migration. Next we review in some detail the 1942–64 Bracero program, an immigration period of fundamental importance to the entire history of Mexican migration to the United States. The Bracero Program, besides revealing the importance of gender in the mind-set of the policymakers of empire, reflects most clearly the issue of power and domination of one country over the other. Whereas the impersonal macro "structures" of supply and demand are often sufficient to channel the needed number of migrant laborers, the conscious actors represented by the states of Mexico and the United States are ready to jump into the breach where market forces fail to do the job of providing cheap labor to the monopolies of imperialism. The Bracero Program by all accounts lays the foundations for other key programs and the development of subsequent migratory networks.[2] Within these networks later generations of workers can exercise some degree of autonomy, yet these networks principally function as structures of labor discipline and pipelines of labor flows for the benefit of imperial capital. We conclude with some thoughts on the utility of the notions of agency for the study of this migratory movement.

The "Subjectivity" of Empire and Migratory Choices

To provide an overall vision of the ways in which the deliberate actions of the agencies of empire establish the perimeters for migration and affect the parameters of migrants' "micro" negotiations, we need to look at the entire history of cheap labor migration to California and the Southwest. Whereas Mexican migration seems to have always been the rule, this was not always the case. In the last third of the nineteenth century, southwestern agribusiness began to grow simultaneous with the beginnings of U.S. intrusion into the Mexican economy to the south. With the growing of specialized fruit crops in the late 1860s and 1870s, large numbers of Chinese workers became indispensable in California agriculture. But a combination of labor and small farming interests, appealing to racism, succeeding in driving the Chinese from the California fields. The large California growers, in search of a new source of labor, promptly found one in the Japanese, who became a prime labor pool from the last few years of the nineteenth century to the beginning of World War I. But the Japanese were to meet the same opposition as the Chinese and eventually shared the same fate. In desperation, California agribusiness began to import East Indian and Filipino workers. Asian labor continued to provide the bulk of the labor needs of California agriculture until a better choice was found. Mexican migrants appeared to hold superior qualities: availability in larger numbers and, hopefully, disappearance in the off-season made possible through easy return to Mexico. From the point of view of agribusiness, the "illegal" Mexican worker might even be better: this type of worker could be accessed in large numbers when needed, and thrown to the mercy of immigration authorities when not wanted. Enormous benefits accrued to the employers. The costs of rearing, for example, were born by the sending country; thus the "illegal" worker did not require costly education, training, or sustenance (except for the portion of the year during which he or she worked). Moreover, because of the worker's precarious legal status, the Mexican could be expected to be a loyal and hardworking laborer, always in the sights of bosses and immigration officers.

The above underscores that Mexican labor became selected—the "choice" type of migration—by southwestern and California agribusiness much before the migrants themselves could begin to make choices about the micro aspects of their migratory lives.[3] Just as conveniently, the various governmental agencies serving monopoly businesses could turn around and deny many choices to the Mexican migrant, even the choice to remain in the United States. The example of repatriation drives interspersed with relaxed enforcement of border controls over the course of the twentieth century exemplifies the determination to manage Mexican migration, and as things have worked out, with relative success. When allowed the choice to migrate, perhaps the only choice available to many of Mexico's poor, the migrants faced other subjectivities at work, such as Americanization programs, racial segregation, and xenophobia. Thus, for example, the Bracero Program for more than twenty years recruited and distributed young, male workers forced to confront racialized stereotypes that circulated on a grand scale within government bureaucracies (and among the general public) in the United States.

Reflecting on the agency of empire may provide insight into how and why certain choices were made, from the initial selection of Mexican migration in the early twentieth century, to the 1917 contract worker program, the Bracero Program, the maquila program, and various guest worker proposals, to letting the market do the job of "automatically" regulating migration. In that light the Bracero Program, the maquila program, and other forms of stimulus and control are not isolated, discrete programs but merely temporal manifestations of a general pattern of active state involvement through its immigration laws, regulations, and enforcement. These various choices in turn reflect a deliberate effort to deal with the numerous vagaries that characterize monopolistic production: business cycles, wars, perceived shortages, relative surpluses, and foreign competition. Over time certain patterns appear. During periods of economic upturn, rising choruses of "Who will harvest our crops?" result in a relaxation of regulations; then follows recruitment, cycles of immigration, and integration of migrants into the economy. Then the inevitable economic downturn, bringing in its wake systematic denunciations and condemnations of migrant laborers, mass expulsions from the economy, deportation campaigns (under the guise of "repatriations"), and increased vigilance across the border.

Of course, not all policy is controlled or administered by U.S.-based interests. A compliant Mexican government representing Mexican elites' voices and subjectivities has worked hand in hand with U.S. immigration policymakers. Throughout the twentieth century the Mexican government also has been an agent of migration, providing the means to relocate available labor when called north.[4] Today Mexican border police wink at unauthorized recruiters who jostle migrants from dirt-poor southernmost states at border bus stations with offers to continue their migration *al norte* for an exorbitant fee.[5]

Gendering Migration

An informed state acting deliberately through its agencies conditioned the migrations and coerced return migrations over the course of the twentieth century. It was an important force to effect the movement of migrants from region to region and crop to crop, primarily to satisfy production requirements. U.S. immigration policy has served as a transnational social engineering force that never allows itself to be entrapped by the constraints of "one size fits all" programs. Immigration policy manifests an overarching flexibility to correspond with the vagaries of monopoly capitalism. The examples of contract labor programs, such as the 1917 contract program, which led to the importation of more than seventy thousand workers, and the better-known 1942–64 Bracero Program, which arranged nearly five million labor contracts for employer benefit, exemplify this active social engineering. Agricultural interests initiated both programs, and the legislation was U.S.-mandated, designed, implemented, and enforced, with Mexico's full cooperation. Each of these labor importation policies satisfied the expressed interests of large-scale capital and deliberately restricted labor contracts, and thereby migration, to men.

Immigration policy flexibility can be discerned in the periodic absence of border patrol vigilance to allow for easy entrance during times of labor scarcity. Alternatively, one observes the administrative relaxation of immigration restrictions. Variations in programs and the periodic flexible enforcement of policy are dovetailed to meet the evolving requirements of transnational capital dependent on managed flows of cheap labor. Over the first three decades of the century lax enforcement of immigration regulations coupled with opportunistic amendments of existing policy resulted in a virtual open border, allowing unlimited migration from Mexico. Labor-recruiting agencies based in the United States but active in Mexico (contrary to U.S. law) and at major border crossings signed weary travelers to work in sugar beets, cotton, vegetables, railroads, citrus, and mines. The Great Western Sugar Beet Company even produced a silent film to show in towns and villages in Mexico beseeching workers to travel north, appealing to them with promises of high wages and good housing.

Within a given agricultural sector, some lines of production preferred families; others, married men or families. For example, the Great Western executives had much to say about the makeup of the workforce. Sugar beet growers who signed contracts with Great Western were obligated by the terms to hire only Mexican labor and then only families. Subsequent to hiring Mexican families, Mexican colonias began to form in the Colorado beet fields.[6] Throughout the 1920s and into the 1940s the cotton industry in Texas, California, and Arizona actively recruited Mexican families, taking advantage of patriarchal gender relations (and preserving them in the bargain) to lower the cost of production through utilizing the unpaid labor of women and children. The citrus industry preferred married men (with families) for their picking force, believing that they were more dependable and pliable and less prone to radical ideas. Several industries favoring the employment of Mexican families organized housing programs, establishing communities for their workforce. But housing served also as a means to further control the workers by placing them into a strictly supervised environment. The geographic dispersion of these communities was determined by the location of economic activity, or as economist Paul S.

Taylor put it many years ago, "Irrigation means Mexicans." Migrants enjoyed little choice as to the community site and were forced to endure segregated social relations.[7]

At the point of production, within the fruit industries, women were employed nearly exclusively in the packinghouses, while men worked the fields. In the organized communities, women, following a gendered division of labor mandated from above, worked in a variety of occupations that included laundry work, garment factories, childcare, cooking meals, and housecleaning. Cut to the present, some eighty years later, and we find that women still provide the main workforce in the packinghouses; in upscale suburban centers women still perform domestic work, cleaning houses, caring for children, and cooking for variable under-the-table cash wages.

The state still performs its active role by managing the gendered migratory flows. Take the case of maids in El Paso, Texas. In the mid-1980s approximately twenty-six thousand Mexican women worked as domestics, many crossing the border illegally to their place of work. The policy of the INS was to ignore the daily mass movement of domestic workers, who prefer housework to the harsh discipline enforced in the maquila. One El Paso INS spokesperson told an investigator, "When you are working for the U.S. government, you have to prioritize your work, and maids are low-level priority."[8] From the perspective of imperial capital, gender and family do not play themselves out as independent variables (nor are they allowed to act independently). Rather, these form attributes of a subordinate society that renders its labor eminently attractive (and exploitable). Not all labor requirements are satisfied by one gender over the other or by solos rather than families. As the above examples illustrate, historically U.S. capital has modulated its labor recruitment based on needs that it weighs with its own subjective visions of gender into consideration. Thus, depending on specific conditions, U.S. capital in Mexico and in the United States has historically preferred hiring from among specific genders, from different age groups and family types.

At different periods and in distinct lines of production, men are favored and more heavily recruited, while simultaneously women might be favored in a distinct line of production or sections of the same line of production where men generally predominate. Deliberate choices of single men, because of the character of the occupations ("not ladies' work") or because they might more likely return to Mexico; married men, because they might be more "reliable"; and families organized into preconceived divisions of labor in company towns are some of the gendered ways in which imperial agency sought to organize migration *and* settlement.

Empire building affected men and women by organizing and reorganizing forms of production by gender and therefore affecting labor processes and migration. The operation utilized the dynamics of existing gender, age, and family relations in Mexico. Conversely, cultural patterns, whether religious, political, or gender, compatible with empire might be reinforced.

Pierrette Hondagneu-Sotelo offers a poignant example that can illustrate the ways in which imperial subjectivities can dovetail with the dynamics of Mexico's patriarchal peasant traditions. As mentioned before, U.S. agencies through guest worker programs recruited single males for decades. The preference for males reflected views on the type of work they would do, not considered "women's work," and the likelihood that they were more likely to return to Mexico. Hondagneu-Sotelo found out in her interviews that single males who traveled to the United States considered their main impulse neither necessity nor opportunity, but simply a desire for adventure. She discovered that over decades, a folklore of travel and adventure to the north has developed, which plays neatly into a traditional way in which Mexican men assert their independence and masculinity, by moving away and traveling. A gendered, patriarchal vision of migratory needs in the United States thus fits into the patriarchal, gendered dynamics of Mexico's countryside.[9]

Imperially designed, gendered patterns of migration and settlement are evident over a century-long exploitation of cheap, mobile, flexible, and available labor. Since the first decade of the twentieth century Mexican women and men have served in a wide variety of wage work for U.S. corporations in Mexico and the United States. Women were chosen to labor as housekeepers, laundry workers, agricultural workers, packinghouse workers, coffee sorters, mine ore sorters, nannies, cooks, tobacco workers, and factory workers.[10] Mexican men have worked in mining, railroads, agriculture, factories, manufacturing, power plants, petroleum, and more.

The 1942–64 Bracero Program and Sequels

The contract labor programs have nearly a century-long history in the United States, extending back to 1909.[11] The 1917 contract worker program, the infamous Bracero Agreements, and the more recent discussions in political venues regarding "guest worker" program initiatives, as well as the variation of the guest worker policy within the 1986 Immigration Reform and Control Act, have not been sufficiently appreciated for the gender patterns they called forth. The Bracero Program epitomizes the direct involvement of the agencies of empire in the direct gendering of migration, but also in the securing of stable flows of labor and the establishment of patterns of labor discipline and supply—"networks"—that ensure the labor needs of big capital.

The Bracero Agreements were essentially a binational program designed to remove men from one country and transport them to another to labor for a specified period of time and then be repatriated. In other words, the international labor market—demand—had failed to deliver and required the state to intervene to correct "market imbalances." Answering why men left their villages and towns, who left, and the consequences to their families are crucial to explaining the social effects of the agreements. After widespread advertising and after additional railcars and buses were pressed into service on routes to processing centers in Mexico, hundreds of thousands of men, many who went into debt to finance their travel to processing centers, responded to the promise of a good job and good pay. Cases have been recorded of men selling their unproductive *milpas* (small plots of farmland). They left their villages principally to escape poverty, and only young and strong males were allowed into the program. One former bracero vividly remembers that from his village in Guanajuato "the people who went were the younger men who were not eligible of land distribution, which really signified that the countryside had little available work, and this is why they left."[12] Diodoro Campos recalled that not all were accepted for work—there were inspections for size, illness, and eagerness to learn; all older and disabled men were automatically rejected. The selected men were sprayed with a lindane-based dust to ensure that they didn't infect their hosts with lice and other body pests. Those who failed to pass muster at the processing center in Mexico or at the U.S. border inspection station were left to be on their own, and then it "was a time of hunger, the boys would go door to door begging for food. . . ." One American physician, angered at the situation, offered a perspective on that "time of suffering": "They are simply dumped across the border, without even two bits for a meal. What do they do? Hell, what can they do? They scrounge the garbage cans of Mexicali. Go down any alley of the town and you'll see them."[13] Both the rejected men (overall some 10 percent of those applying, which amounted to five thousand annually trying to enter California alone) and the repatriated swelled the populations of Mexican border towns. Ciudad Juárez's population increased three times over the course of the Bracero Program, while Mexicali's population grew ten times. The centerpiece of the increase was "a huge floating population" of desperate men, many of whom eventually turned to illegal entry as *mojados* (labeled "wetbacks" in the United States) to survive.[14]

Living conditions seemed to grow worse rather than improve for the women left behind to care for the homestead. Maria de la Paz Vega, wife of a former bracero, recalled that she faced raising their children in the absence of her husband and asserts that hunger and poverty drove the men away. She recounted that in spite of the loneliness, the migration, although not willingly chosen, was necessary. "The poverty in which we lived was so great, that our men had no other choice but to go and leave us. When they returned they usually left another kid, born months later, and the second time, and the third, and so it went." Doña Olivia Villa recalled that woman like her had no choice but to assume the tasks normally taken by their departed husbands, parallel second shifts. Dona Olivia recollected that "one served as mother and father, with complete responsibility for the family. I cried every night over my situation, but by day I behaved very bravely so that my children would not see me as the coward that I was."[15] The Bracero Agreements and the illegal, but well received by employers, "wetback" flow stimulated by the agreements tore apart families, separated men from women, and separated children from their fathers. The agreements made villages dependent on an economy hundreds of miles away, and sent the ablest workers, the more highly educated in the village, to produce commodities for consumption in the United States. Unfortunately, for villages across Mexico, braceros never rescued their rural economy from economic stagnation.

Men who received contracts were often forced to display their ability to labor and endure arduous conditions by working without wages on large-scale farms in Mexico, many of which were owned by U.S. corporations. According to former bracero Agustín Gutierrez, workers were forced to pick eleven thousand pounds of cotton on farms in Empalme (two hundred miles from the U.S. border and the site of a Mexican processing center) as proof of their ability to work in the United States. Migrants were prepped for what they might expect in the north. Before he filled the cotton quota, Gutierrez worked under conditions that he marvels at today. "There would be these terrible storms and we were still out there picking cotton. . . . They had you sleeping under trees . . . so we would just throw a piece of cardboard on the ground and we would sleep on the ground. It was a sacrifice because you suffered before entering the United States."[16] After a waiting period that averaged two months, qualified braceros were then shipped in trucks, buses, and many by rail in boxcars that held up to 120 men. Felipe Macias vividly remembers feeling "like cattle . . . looked over as if we were their property . . . we ate sandwiches and drank Cokes until we arrived after many days on the road."[17]

Braceros found little protection from their government, which generally went along with the wages, treatment, and general conditions awaiting the laborers. Even when braceros complained to their consuls, word went out that the complainer was not dependable, and grievances were swept under the rug. Former braceros protested that even though their contracts stipulated good working conditions, housing, and mess fare, the guarantee proved worthless. Nevertheless, braceros' wages were deducted $1.75 per day for board, although the average cost for the daily fare for California's prison population was $0.60 and which was much superior to the food served braceros in the company mess halls.[18] "We worked hard," said Eustacio Perez, "with little rest and bad food. And recreation? Nothing."

Leonardo Guzmán worked sixteen-hour days seven days a week in the sweltering heat of California's Imperial Valley, and knowing that this was a violation of the contract, called for the consul. Few grievances were ever remedied. "[M]any times we called the consul . . . but he never came down to check on our complaints," recalled Guzmán.[19] Not even their wages, which were generally far below the local rates, were guaranteed. Moreover, the work periods were not always consistent; speedups and slowdowns were common. Still, all contracts stipulated that 10 percent of the wages would be placed in a savings account in the Mexican state-run bank and returned at the termination of the contract. Not one bracero received the back pay, which may have totaled as much as $150 million. The money, however, went into someone's pockets in Mexico, which could only have been a highly placed official or officials who shared in the stolen booty. A common complaint among returned braceros was that they had been cheated out of their wages; one former bracero complained that "the biggest check I ever got was $10. Mostly they were around $4. I won't even be able to pay the debt I got into to come to the United States. . . ."[20]

In the fields the laborers' traditional patriarchal baggage worked to little advantage, subjected as they were to the nearly complete authority of employers backed by the full power of the U.S. government and sustained by the Mexican government. The terms of the Bracero Agreements denied the migrant the right to organize or join a union, to bargain individually or in a group for wages, or even to complain to his employer of his treatment. The bracero was stripped of those democratic rights that workers in the United States generally take for granted, while Mexican government officials turned their backs on their countrymen. Like many, if not most, migrants, a bracero was legally deprived of any "agency" to thwart those conditions that motivated his decision to migrate or those that faced him as he was transported north. For two decades braceros typified the ideal wage labor force whose only task was to work according to orders assigned by the foremen. In the meantime, his individuality was forcibly reduced to arduous unskilled work and apolitical activities. The United States, with the cooperation of the Mexican government, ensured a controlled, flexible, cheap, willing, and easily deportable army of male laborers. Mexico acted as an international labor contractor, while the United States served as the employment agency.

The term "bracero," as well as the epithets "wetback," "*mojado*," and "wets," came to be masculine terms, popularly understood to apply narrowly to men and seldom, if ever, to women. Yet, these highly charged terms surfaced from within transnational immigration agreements and the flexible administration of policy responding to long-term labor requirements. Bracero and mojado, or its English equivalent, the "wet" or "wetback," were ideological spin-offs of the Bracero Agreements of the

1940s and 1950s and shaped the public image of agricultural labor and of the Mexican male as well.

The term "wetback," applied predominantly to the "illegal" but nonetheless prized and simultaneously dehumanized Mexican male, upped the advantage for employers. Racialized language strengthened the control over labor by evoking an image of an emasculated yet potentially dangerous lone alien male. Only the power of the employer and the state stood between the public and the potential monster. With such volatile images abounding in the media, legislatures, and the public, corporate agriculture found little legal or moral obstacle to the wholesale ignoring of contractual obligations while freely exploiting braceros. The state's commitment to support the growers and railroad corporations, and the knowledge that the Mexican government stood pat, only emboldened the corporations to use "their" labor as they pleased. Encouraged by the power of the state, officials overseeing the program routinely ignored what amounted to wholesale violations of the agreement.

Eventually, "Mexican" and "wetback" became synonymous and paralleled the older terms "peon" and "Oriental," which had fallen into disuse. "Wetbacks," like the discursive predecessor "peon," were said to eagerly toil for rock-bottom wages and to cheerfully endure the hardships of the fields and railroad work, and their wages amounted to what they rightfully earned. A farm placement supervisor's celebration of the endurance of the braceros was not an untypical claim: "[They] could scuttle down a row of sugar beets, crab-wise, faster than I could walk down a row behind them. They would have their short-handled hoe in one hand and swipe the loose plants and crud away with the other hand. And they could keep that up all day."[21] Such treatment bore heavily on the men, with few, if any, rights to redress grievances.

Private citizens who dared speak out publicly against the abuses were silenced. The case of Henry Anderson, who engaged a federally funded research on bracero health practices under the auspices of the University of California, Berkeley, exemplified the power of agricultural interests to throttle academic freedom and public scrutiny. While conducting research, Anderson wrote a scathing seven-page personal critique of the treatment of braceros that he observed. California agribusiness associations got wind of the critique and immediately set out to silence Anderson. The matter reached the Department of Labor, the state capitol, and eventually the university's office of the president. The project was shut down before it could be completed. Told that, as a concession, he may write up what amounted to a censured version of his findings, Anderson defiantly wrote an 850-page manuscript that described in great detail the deep wounds suffered by men laboring in "a system which humiliates them mercilessly." Anderson's

superiors complained that that his findings were unscholarly, "too contentious," "too controversial," and not worthy of publication. The university attempted to confiscate all copies of the manuscript. For his efforts,
Anderson was summarily fired and prevented from freely publishing his
research findings by University of California officials.[22]

Neither the violation of academic freedom nor the reprehensible state
system of labor importation and exploitation prevented politicians from
both sides of the aisle from lobbying for more than twenty years to maintain the Bracero Program. Legislators and their corporate patrons, agribusiness and railroads, often boasted that employers and workers shared
the benefits, each according to their just desserts, and comprised a perfect
organic unity. Of course, such boasts were to be expected from the nation's
politicians, who in fact privileged the interests of corporations dependent
on cheap bracero labor.[23]

The Bracero Program reached into the very heart of the villages and
towns that sent men, far beyond the lives of the men chosen to serve as
cheap labor. The women and children left behind were equally affected in a
variety of ways. Their lives were disrupted, families torn. If the best,
youngest, and strongest males departed for the north, the women who remained behind were also the best, youngest, and strongest women. Patterns of village economic activity were interrupted, some permanently. As
the mass migrations took shape and continued over several generations,
causing profound modification of village life, the initial causes propelling
relocation remained over the decades.

Thanks to the Bracero Program, a cycle of migrations nurtured by
migrants' family and friendship networks—which also are gendered—
continued a kind of informal labor recruitment process.[24] Corporate capitalism has always preferred to depend on the free employment services
provided by needy relatives and friends than to expend extra moneys in recruitment. Networks can and often do provide a steady supply of workers
and avoid the intensive use of recruiters. Connections among the workers
serve to gain migrants a job, but they also provide capital with a steady flow
of cheap labor. From the perspective of the employer, migrant networks
are welcome and effective means to a competitive operation; they provide
a kind of self-employed discipline that makes business easier and absenteeism nearly unknown—if a worker is ill, or suffers an accident, he or she
can be trusted to send a relative in his or her place. From the perspective of
the migrant, networks help facilitate migration, employment, and a host of
other needs.[25]

The Bracero Program of 1942–64 was one of three official contract
labor programs that have been in operation since 1908 and that continue
under various guises today. Bracero programs never terminated but inten-

sified and assumed a number of discursive forms, often as "guest worker" programs. The dislocation of Mexico's economy and the already established migratory networks never seem to quite do the job for empire as far as labor supplies are concerned. State intervention stimulates the supply.

Thus the H2 Program, passed in 1952, allows for the temporary importation of otherwise off-limits undocumented Mexican workers if it can be shown that there are insufficient workers at a given locale. In certain lines, southern poultry plants, southwestern agriculture, and Wyoming cattle ranches, as examples, have taken advantage of the law. In the 1990s, across the "chicken trail"—Arkansas, Mississippi, Georgia, and North Carolina—labor recruiters transported workers by the thousands from the Texas border to supply poultry processing plants with the scarce commodity. Orders are placed for a set number of workers, and the recruiters go about their business; contracts for as many as 450 at a time, at $175 per recruit, are not unusual. As the market in labor boomed, an official for one recruiting agency remarked, "By the time a company comes to us, they don't care what it costs. . . . They just want somebody there—a body." Bonuses are even offered to employees who can bring in more workers, motivating networking, and, of course, the use of smugglers for transporting that labor to the "new" South.[26]

In this connection it is worth noting another case of U.S. racialized and gendered subjectivities, that is, the differential treatment accorded in the media, and even in scholarly circles, to the occupation of labor recruiter. In the United States it is considered a legitimate business that provides a needed service for the clients. Never is the U.S. recruiter labeled a *coyote*, a notorious term of demonization for unauthorized Mexican labor recruiters. At best, Mexicans who bring workers across the line so the agencies can recruit them are called smugglers. *Coyotes* have few friends in the media or among academics and are universally condemned. Nonetheless, recruiters on both sides of the border acting in tandem brought new brigades of cheap labor by the thousands in the mid-1990s, reproducing the social images wrought by the earlier migrations of the 1920s and the bracero era.[27] One Florida farmworker's grievance could very well have been from the bracero era in California's Imperial Valley: "The rancheros don't give us water, they want us to work until we drop and they don't even let us raise our voice to complain."[28]

The continued policy intervention by the United States that protects undeterred flows of undocumented migrant labor into the agricultural centers across the United States serves as one example of active policies carried over from the bracero period. As in the 1920s, the company town continues as an introductory historical experience for newly arrived immigrants. Colonias sprout overnight in old motels and declining hotels on the "chicken trail." Company housing appears in some locales to shelter migrants. Hudson Foods, an employer of ten thousand workers, built company housing near one of its poultry plants in "the outskirts" (read "across the tracks") of Noel, Arkansas, to accommodate the "huge influx" of migrant laborers, some of whom brought their families. Suddenly Noel schools faced a new educational issue: more than a hundred Spanish-speaking youngsters upset traditional classroom teaching methods, a concern that had never impacted teachers there previously.[29]

Bracero programs (with a small "p") endure well past their supposed demise. Businesses that deal in the Mexican labor market are not uncommon. One agency, the North Carolina Grower's Association, imports an average of sixteen thousand men annually to the eleven hundred members of the association. The agency sends out to border sites *coy*—ahem!, recruiters—who charge the migrants $300 for the "privilege" of working for the association's clients, tending and harvesting tobacco for $6.54 per hour and a bunk in a company dormitory. The trade in workers that the association provides are legal, protected by the provisions of the 1952 H2 Program, which allows the temporary importation of agricultural labor to relieve shortages.[30] Convenient, albeit aging stereotypes are recycled in a region that had never experienced Mexican migration. The chaplain in charge of "company counseling" for Hudson Foods remarked that he did not "know why, but [Mexicans] are very good with their hands."[31]

Simultaneously, company towns abound in Mexico to house Mexican workers laboring in foreign-owned enterprises. The U.S.-inspired company town in Mexico, as in the era of late-nineteenth-century railroad construction, colors the country's landscape. In Ciudad Juárez the General Motors parts-making plant instituted a plan in 1996 to house their employees. GM arranged for seven thousand homes to be built for sale to its employees supported by a company mortgage program, a modern version of welfare capitalism. As in the past, the objective of company housing is to control labor by creating greater worker loyalty and cutting down on worker turnover, or as a Mexican government official described GM's motives, "rooting the people to the company."[32]

Migration as "illegals" has been widely practiced since the 1940s when, for all practical purposes, it became an appendage of the Bracero Agreements with the active support of federal and state authorities and amounts to de facto bracero programs. An important difference is that, by and large, women became an increasing proportion of the migration flows that developed after the close of the Bracero Program. Today, the number of illegals laboring in agriculture, urban manufacturing, and services is critical to the U.S. economy. Ironically, migrants often come to work for an industry that is ruining the farming economy of the region they left. Across

Mexico, the drastic decrease in the ability of farmers to remain economically viable collapsed with the open border to U.S. products mandated by NAFTA. One 1992 study by University of California researchers concluded that NAFTA would "force" roughly 850,000 small farmers off their lands.[33] The prediction appears to have rung true. In the state of Guanajuato alone, one fifth of the 250,000 farm families have left for cities, adding to the unemployment rolls, or migrated north in search of maquila employment.[34]

The depopulation of the countryside, caused by a combination of the effects of the transnational mode of U.S. domination described earlier, and the migration stream set in motion by other agencies of U.S. transnational capital, is happening all across Mexico. Recent reports indicate that it is not uncommon to find villages in Oaxaca where at least half the men have left for work in the United States, repeating the bracero era experiences not only among the men but also with the women. While their men are seeking a livelihood for themselves and their families, women shoulder raising children alone. A villager from Santiago Juxtlahuaca, in southern Mexico, remarked, "They [migrant men] come back for Christmas. The wife gets pregnant. They come back . . . the wife gets pregnant again. There's just more and more children without their fathers around."[35] Of course, as researchers have pointed out, more recent illegal migration may include about equal ratios of men and women, with the result that entire villages disappear.

In some locales it is still only the men who leave. Mexican psychologist Nelly Salgado de Snyder studied women from towns like Santiago Juxtlahuaca and observed, "It's a life of loneliness and worry, the life of the women. . . . These are single moms, witnessing the disintegration of solidity in the community and of unity in their families. These are women with kids growing up without fathers, and with an ingrained sense that their town is a way station, a place to leave." However, remittances and not much else confront the extreme want the villagers face daily. Paula Galindo Flores grows corn on a small plot of land, but her migrant husband's monthly mail orders of from $300 to $400 make the difference between hunger and satisfying basic needs. "Without that I don't know what we would do to survive" sums up her village's solution for endemic economic plight. With "few signs of progress" in Santiago Juxtlahuaca in the year 2000, villagers leave in droves; at least five full buses a week pass through and drive directly to the U.S. border.[36]

But the departure of both men and women has been generalized in the past thirty years, leading to the abandonment of villages. Deserted villages are now becoming all too common across Mexico, and many towns appear as virtual ghost towns. At one time Granjenal, Michoacán, like many towns in rural Mexico, survived on the remittances of its emigrants. Not so after

NAFTA opened the door to cheap corn imports that undercut local production; as the economy went into a tailspin, the people left by the busloads. Migration specialist Jorge Durand of the University of Guadalajara, in reference to the fate suffered by towns such as Granjenal, observed that in the past, migration "allowed many of these towns to survive. . . . But now you could say that they are dying because of that same migration."[37] One journalist reported that communities such as Santa Inés, in Tlaxcala State, "are being pushed to the brink of extinction, worsening the pressure to migrate north. Abandoned houses testify to the exodus of families to join husbands and fathers in California, and to the departure of young women, most often to find a mate but also to seek work for themselves."[38]

In the southern Mexican village of Chinantla, where migrations began half a century ago, the motivation to leave has varied little. As one observer noted, the "only way for a Chinantlecan to survive financially was to leave Chinantla." Elbia Cruz left many years ago, and like many of her family and fellow villagers, she eventually transplanted to New York. She claims, "Were it not for New York, Chinantla would be dead."[39] In some villages continuous migrations remove the able-bodied and leave only the old and the returnees who return for a vacation or to reestablish ties. Villages evolve not because of their economic development but due to the receipt of money orders sent by their departed villagers.

At the same time, the enforcement of immigration laws against contemporary undocumented workers betrays continuing gender impacts. Thus, for example, the Clinton administration's Operation Gatekeeper, intended to "secure the border" (in the words of INS commissioner Doris Meisner), has actually fostered a gender disparity (and escalating death tolls) among migrants. Professor Gary Huspek, California State University, San Marcos, argues that Gatekeeper "has changed the type of worker who succeeds in getting across the border. By directing border-crossers into the mountains, the Border Patrol weeds out older and weaker men, and most of the women and children. Young, physically fit males are the most likely to make [it] through the eastern wilds [of the southern California–Mexico border]."[40] Yet, on the main highways near southern Immigration Patrol checkpoints, motorists see warning signs profiling migrants running across the lanes, a family—a man, a woman, and a child—in flight! The farther one travels away from the larger border crossing points, the greater the concentration of male migrants; the reverse is true for female migrants. As in the Bracero Program, a selection process, albeit undeclared, within an immigration policy sponsored by the United States, and acquiesced to by the Mexican government, physically separates male from female laborers while continuing to administer to U.S. corporate interests with a steady flow of legally disenfranchised labor.

In the United States, in a pattern initially observed in the first decade of the twentieth century, immigrant community formation continues its historical trek. Older receiving communities expand, while new colonias are created and company towns emerge; meanwhile, their native communities slowly wither. As in the past, migrants find a variety of dead-end service and manufacturing jobs at *el mínimo*, the minimum wage, and all too often below the minimum. Guadalupe Flores left his Orizaba foothill village, San Isidro Tecomate, where folks live on subsistence crops and good jobs pay $5.00 a day. Flores works as a janitor at a southern California supermarket at $5.75 an hour. Networks among Flores' fellow villagers have made janitorial work common employment for them as they reach the United States. Harsh working conditions, long hours, and fifty- and sixty-hour weeks are not uncommon, leaving the fifty-six-year-old Flores with little time but to sleep in his unfurnished one-bedroom apartment, which he shares with seven other migrants. "Sure we're exploited," he laments, "We know that. But what can we do? What options do we have?" Even as the situation is extremely difficult, men continue to leave San Isidro, making the male something akin to an endangered species. According to Flores, whose wife and children remained in Mexico, every family sends at least one son to the United States. The Flores household sent two. Migrant networks help in settling and finding work for relatives and friends, but their motives for leaving remain the same as their bracero and *mojado* antecedents. Rather than subsist in a bare-bones economy, this village, in contrast to Granjenal, survives on the remittances from the foreign export of its laborers.[41]

For decades the U.S.–Mexico border had been a stopping point in the trek of dislocated Mexican workers. During the bracero era towns along the border began to suffer from unusually high male unemployment relative to other areas of Mexico due to the accumulation of those rejected and those hoping to recontract. The situation was exacerbated by the suspension of the Bracero Program as laborers continued to travel to northern Mexico hoping for a work opportunity. The U.S. Treasury Department and the Mexican government devised a solution of their own to the border unemployment crisis: the Border Industrial Program (BIP). In a previous chapter we detailed the magnitude and impact of the BIP, also known as the maquila industry program. The ways in which gender entered into the conception of the maquila solution was clear from the outset. The early rationales and program publicity focused on the benefits to be derived from the employment of a female labor force: "small hands," patience with monotonous routines of assembly, no tardiness or absenteeism, and absence of a culture of unionization.[42] Over a thirty-year period the maquila program maintained this gendered orientation. Today assembly plants employ well over a million workers, the vast majority of whom are overworked, underpaid, often underage (*and therefore illegal according to Mexican law*), women.[43]

Thus one clearly gendered employment policy edifice, a maquila program designed with women workers in mind, followed on the heels of a bracero program constructed on the back of male labor. What little effect thirty years of women's employment in the maquila has had on traditional gender relations in Mexico has been amply documented.[44] Indeed, a late 1990s report on the growth of the maquila industry in Yucatán points to the collaboration between two patriarchal gender regimes. In the 1990s, Yucatán hemp production wavered under the competition of synthetic fibers, and unemployment skyrocketed. Maquilas appeared in three towns that not only took up the unemployment slack but also began a cultural reformation. Formerly the Mayan peoples depended on hemp for their livelihood; now they depend on the production of Eddie Bauer, Gap, and Banana Republic garments for upscale mall stores in the United States. Production for foreign consumption now determines the economic and political fate of these communities. Women are such a large percentage of the employees and women earning a salary are such a new phenomenon that fathers are given tours of the plant to ease their paternal anxiety. Employees dare not form a union, or, as one maquila worker said, "If you do that, you'll lose your job," and a labor surplus makes the plant managers confident that their warnings will be taken seriously.[45] Across Mexico, the maquila plant women suffer yet another form of discrimination. According to a report by the American Friends Service Committee,

> The maquiladoras require them [women] to undergo pregnancy testing as a condition of employment and deny them work if they are pregnant; if a women becomes pregnant soon after gaining employment at a maquiladora, in some instances she may be mistreated or forced to resign because of her pregnancy. Maquiladora operators target women for discriminatory treatment, in violation of international human rights and labor right norms.[46]

The border maquila program was the forerunner of changes in the structure of U.S. industry—the notorious deindustrialization of America in the late 1970s—characterized by plant closings, the demise of the old industrial belt in the U.S. Northeast, and the growth of a whole set of industries in the Sunbelt to be constructed on the basis of cheap, imported, women's labor, principally electronic and garment work.[47] The imperial agency that makes sure this migration is gendered is summed up by a Silicon Valley assembly plant manager: "Just three things I look for in hiring [entry-level, high-tech manufacturing operations]: small, foreign, and female. You find those three things and you're pretty much automatically guaranteed the right kind of workforce. These little foreign gals are grateful to be hired—very grateful—no matter what."[48] And just as the lone Mexican male was vilified as a dangerous delinquent, the entrance of poor, hardworking women into the labor force has been met with gendered slurs that treat women immigrants as uncontrolled "breeders" whose children become a burden to society and/or as subjects subverting established norms of sexual morality.[49]

The Immigrant: Active Subject or Victim?

Immigration policies and programs, industrial development schemes, and major deliberate changes in industrial structure illustrate the ways in which gender constraints are not simply consequences of patriarchal peasant traditions and subjects of people's micro negotiations but also are part and parcel of the macro perimeters designed by imperialist "agency."

Perhaps the clearest view into the gendered nature of imperial decision making is a 1986 report by then President Reagan's Council of Economic Advisers, advising that undocumented men and women workers were indispensable to the international competitiveness of the national economy. One newspaper headline announced "Illegal Aliens Aid Economy, Report Says," which succinctly summarized the findings. The council's report praised the economic contributions of migrants and contended that their jobs were necessary to the nation's economic health. The report compared the relationship between the migrant and her or his employer to that of "[a] scientist [who] is more productive if there are assistants to wash the test tubes. . . ." The report also implicitly argued for the migration of women to serve as domestic labor, contending that "A worker with family responsibilities is more productive if there are others in the household to help with child care."[50] We can distinguish two familiar categories of labor filled by Mexican migrants identified in the report. In the case of braceros, men were chosen to "wash test tubes" and "do the menial work."On the other hand, women provided the "household . . . with child care."[51] Throughout the century women, men, families, and whole communities were central to the entire process of labor migration within Mexico and to the United States.

Where does all this leave the migrants themselves? Are they independent actors or victims of the system? The dichotomy of independent actors versus passive victims sets up a fallacious dilemma. If one looks solely at the subjectivities of the migrants, migration can easily become simply a study of what migrants do: the decisions they make, the networks they form while migrating, the communities they settle into, the adaptations to new forms of labor. In exercising their agency, migrants develop strategies to constrain, reshape, or modify the larger economic and political forces, thereby avoiding totalizing domination by outside forces. Migrants certainly exercise a degree of autonomy: migrant women, men, and families create community, construct and raise families, organize households, and act politically.

The fact remains that migrants do not freely and independently choose to uproot from a society they have known since birth to begin anew in a strange environment (or to begin a process of "circular migration"). Migrants (particularly undocumented) often go into substantial debt to smugglers; endure dangerous, life-threatening hardships to cross the border (one journalist described passage through the California border as "nightmarish"); settle with few legal protections; and then begin a life of poverty in the poorest communities. Even as they find employment, they are hired for the least secure positions and least desirable tasks with few benefits, at minimum wage, and all the while subjected to allegations of lawlessness, immoral conduct, or vagrancy.[52] No amounts of "social networks" and "social capital" can eliminate the precarious circumstances that greet migrants as they travel to the United States. Many migrants do not even survive the trek.

The history of Mexican migration is littered with instances of dangerous and deadly experiences. In 1956, eighty braceros died of various causes, mainly accidents, in California alone.[53] The number of "wetbacks" who died was not included in the statistics relating to the Bracero Program. Currently such statistics on "illegals" are recorded. With President Clinton's Operation Gatekeeper, the numbers of deaths has risen astronomically. Records show that from 1995 to 2002, twenty-two hundred migrants died crossing into the United States.[54] Consider that during the nine months that Elian González remained in the custody of the U.S. Justice Department, more than two hundred migrants lost their lives in attempting to cross into the United States in search of work. In the winter of 1997, thirteen migrants died in nine days while crossing mountains near San Diego, California. On a bitterly cold spring day in 2000, one rescue operation in eastern San Diego County could not save three migrants—two men and a woman—found dead from hypothermia but did manage to take twenty-eight "lost and disoriented" women and men to local hospitals.[55] In October 2002 eleven young men died hidden and locked in a grain car in Denison, Iowa. In the small rural town of Los Conos, Mexico, the local priest had buried "at least a dozen men" before the burial of two men from the village who died in the grain car.[56] Over the three-year span from June 1997 to June 2000, seven hundred migrants, threading their way on more or less established pathways, have lost their lives attempting to traverse the deceptive currents of the Rio Grande, deep irrigation ditches, icy mountainous terrain, and sweltering deserts. In two years, 1998 and 1999, INS rescue teams have rescued more than two thousand migrants facing life-threatening situations.[57] INS commissioner Doris Meisner piously explained that "it has been surprising to see how quickly that's happened and in the numbers that it's happened." Critic Michael Hudspek alleged, "The Clinton administration has entered into a dubious moral arithmetic—how many migrants' lives are we prepared to lose to keep the problem out of the national spotlight." We have no idea how many more simply languish on the Mexican side, never able to surmount the border patrolled by the Immigration and Naturalization Service and assisted by gun-toting vigilantes. Yet, as one headline put it, "For Migrants, Desperation Outweighs the Risks," so they come.[58]

While migrants achieve a substantial level of maneuverability within the confines of imperial capital, that independence is severely constrained. When it comes to issues of gender, the manner in which migrants shape and reshape their gender relations as individuals and families has been well documented. But this does not occur in a genderless vacuum: the agency of empire has, for the past century, methodically and systematically circumscribed, in a gendered way, choices with regard to migration, work employment, and settlement.

In an earlier chapter we documented the networks of domination dislocating the Mexican economy for more than a century that set in motion, and continue to propel, the growth of the Mexican-American population in the United States. Focusing on issues of "macro" subjectivies, or the agency of empire, allows a vision of how the networks of U.S. domination in Mexico are complemented by the direct intervention of state agencies in the United States. This focus also allows us to point out ways in which the subjectivities of empire deliberately set a highly gendered stage in which migrants manage to live out their lives.

Notes

1. Not surprisingly, gender will affect how responses to the option for migration will manifest. A rich bibliography has documented the active role of migrants and the gendered nature of their choices, in the midst of a situation the larger dimensions of which are beyond their control. From Vicki Ruiz to Pierrette Hondagneu-Sotelo we have an impressive array of empirical studies that document and honor the negotiations over the construction of the everyday lives of migrants.

   For an overall view of current research on the gendering of migration: *American Behavioral Scientist* 42, no. 4 (January 1999), a special issue devoted to gender and contemporary U.S. immigration, and edited by Pierrette Hondagneu-Sotelo.

   On the increasing participation of women in U.S. immigration: M. F. Houstoun, R. G. Kramer, and J. M. Barrett, "Female Predominance of Immigrants to the United States since 1930: A First Look," *International Migration Review* 18 (1984): 908–63. K. M. Donato, "Understanding U.S. Immigration: Why Some Countries Send Women and Others Send Men," in *Seeking Common Ground: Multidisciplinary Studies of Immigrant Women in the United States*, edited by Donna Gabaccia (Westport, Conn.: Praeger, 1992), 159–84.

For an overall presentation on history of Mexican undocumented settlement and the increased representation of women over time: Pierrette Hondagneu-Sotelo, "The History of Mexican Undocumented Settlement in the United States," in *Challenging Fronteras: Structuring Latina and Latino Lives in the U.S.*, edited by Mary Romero, Pierrette Hondagneu-Sotelo, and Vilma Ortiz (New York: Routledge, 1997), 115–34.

On the process of "restructuring," which leads to the increased employment of women in particular industries: Saskia Sassen, *The Mobility of Labor and Capital: A Study on International Investment and Labor Flow* (New York: Cambridge University Press, 1988); also M. Patricia Fernandez-Kelly, "Broadening the Scope: Gender and International Development" in *Comparative National Development,* edited by A. Douglas Kincaid and Alejandro Portes, (Chapel Hill: University of North Carolina Press, 1994), 143–68; Edna Bonacich, "Asian and Latino Immigrants in the Los Angeles Garment Industry: An Exploration of the Relationship between Capitalism and Racial Oppression," *Working Papers in the Social Sciences* 5, 13 (Los Angeles: UCLA, Institute for Social Science Research, 1990); Karen J. Hossfeld, " 'Their Logic against Them': Contradictions in Sex, Race, and Class in the Silicon Valley" *Women and Workers and Global Restructuring,* edited by Kathryn Ward (Ithaca, N.Y.: Cornell University Press, 1990), 149–78; Maria Angelina Soldatenko, "Organizing Latina Garment Workers in Los Angeles," *Aztlan: Journal of Chicano Studies Research* 20, nos. 1–2 (1991) 73–96.

On women in domestic service: Rebecca Morales and Paul Ong, "Immigrant Women in Los Angeles," *Working Papers in the Social Sciences* 5 (Los Angeles: UCLA, Institute for Social Science Research, 1990); and Mary Romero, *Maid in the U.S.A.* (New York: Routledge, 1992).

On networks of migration: Douglas S. Massey, Rafael Alarcón, Jorge Durand, and Humberto González, *Return to Aztlan: The Social Process of International Migration from Western Mexico* (Berkeley: University of California Press, 1987).

On the development of women-to-women networks: S. Kossoudji and S. Ranney, "The Labor Market Experience of Female Migrants: The Case of Temporary Mexican Migration to the U.S." *International Migration Review* 18, no. 4 (1984): 120–43.

2. Douglas S. Massey, "The Social Organization of Mexican Migration to the United States," in *The Immigration Reader: America in Multidisciplinary Perspective,* edited by David Jacobsen (Malden, Mass.: Blackwell, 1998); Nestor Rodriguez, "The Battle for the Border: Notes on Autonomous Migration, Transnational Communities, and the State," in *Immigration: A Civil Rights Issue for the Americas,* edited by Suzanne Jonas and Suzie Dod Thomas (Wilmington, Del.: Scholarly Books, 1999); also Douglas S. Massey, Rafael Alarcon, Jorge Durand, and Humberto Gonzalez, *Return to Aztlan* (Berkeley: University of California Press, 1987).

3. Mexico contains a highly varied and therefore rich (and easily available) labor pool. Throughout the twentieth century, Mexico's population was sufficiently well educated/skilled, mature, employable, politically controlled, and composed of relatively young men and women, many without permanent employment and living precariously in difficult circumstances. A seemingly inexhaustible, varied, and flexible supply of labor meeting a wide spectrum of labor requirements has historically satisfied U.S. capital's requirements. Conveniently placed by history next door to a country administered by an acquiescent ruling elite governing an easily accessible mix of natural and human resources, the United States opportunistically exploits a treasure trove that other industrialized countries lack.

4. See Gilbert G. Gonzalez, *Mexican Consuls and Labor Organizing: Imperial Politics in the American Southwest.* (Austin: University of Texas Press, 1999).

5. One recent migrant testified that in Tijuana "It's totally open. . . . There are police and they see what's going on but what do they care?" He claimed that the police and smugglers worked together. (Mark Fineman, "For Migrants, Desperation Still Outweighs Risks," *Los Angeles Times,* April 28, 1996.)

6. See Sara A. Brown, assisted by Robie O. Sargent and Clara B. Armentrout, *Children Working in the Sugar Beet Districts of the South Platte Valley, Colorado* (New York: National Child Labor Committee, 1925), 69; also Bertram H. Mautner and W. Lewis Abbot, "Child Labor in Agriculture and Farm Life in the Arkansas Valley of Colorado," *Colorado College Publication* 164 (December 1929). Mautner and Abbot write: "The general practice is for the sugar companies to send out in the spring of each year their labor recruiting agents, who go into Texas, New Mexico, and to the Mexican border, where through local employment agencies

they recruit sufficient number of families, especially those with large numbers of children, for the prospective needs of the beet farmers," 29. See also Jeffrey Marcos Garcilazo, "Traqueros: Mexican Railroad Workers in the United States, 1970–1930" (manuscript, Department of History, University of California, Irvine, 1998). Garcilazo cites examples of railroad companies fostering family migration, particularly the migration of women (as wives), and of companies encouraging employees to act as informal recruiters, initiating what sociologists would later define as "chain migration." Garcilazo documents that "the Santa Fe Railroad provided an institutional framework for chain migration," 85. One company official claimed that "to obtain a better trained and steadier class of laborers, efforts are made to locate men with families on each location," 239.

7. Although the conditions were difficult, to say the least, there is abundant evidence that demonstrates the communities' resolve to overcome oppressive political and economic restrictions. The Chicano community fought numerous battles against segregation and for the right to organize unions. The literature on Chicano history is replete with examples. See Gilbert G. Gonzalez, *Labor and Community: Mexican Citrus Workers Villages in a Southern California County* (Champaign: University of Illinois Press, 1994); Devra Weber, *White Gold, Dark Sweat: California Farmworkers, Cotton, and the New Deal* (Berkeley: University of California Press, 1994); and José Alamillo, "Bittersweet Communities: The Mexican Workers and Citrus Growers on the California Landscape, 1880–1841," Ph.D. diss., University of California, Irvine, 2000.

8. Rosalia Solarzano Torres, "Women, Labor, and the U.S.–Mexico Border: Mexican Maids in El Paso, Texas," in *Mexicanas at Work in the United States*, edited by Margarita Melville (Houston: University of Houston, Mexican-American Studies, 1988), 7.

9. Pierrette Hondagneu-Sotelo, *Gendered Transitions: Mexican Experiences of Immigration* (Berkeley: University of California Press, 1994).

10. Gender considerations were part of the policy and practices of U.S. immigration authorities before migration from Mexico became the norm. With regard to migration of Asian women to the United States in the nineteenth century, sociologist Yen Le Espiritu argues that "labor recruiting patterns and immigration exclusion policies were the most significant factors in restricting the immigration of Asian women." See Yen Le Espiritu, *Asian-American Women and Men: Labor, Laws, and Love* (Beverly Hills, Calif.: Sage, 1997), 17.

11. Manuel Garcia y Griego, *The Importation of Mexican Contract Laborers to the United States, 1942–1964*," in *Between Two Worlds: Mexican Immigrants in the United States*, edited by David Gutierrez (Wilmington, Del.: Scholarly Books, 1996), 47; Mark Reisler, *By the Sweat of Their Brow: Mexican Immigrant Labor in the United States, 1900–1940* (Westport, Conn.: Greenwood Press, 1976).

12. Francisco Robles, "Braceros Reclaman Justicia," *La Opinión* (August 22, 1999). A study carried out in Mexico on 160 returned braceros in 1954 found that 117 "lacked sufficient land, which produced small yields." Another study, in 1946, found that only 12 percent left Mexico out a spirit of adventure; the majority left for economic reasons within the rural agrarian context. Moíses González Navarro, *Los Extranjeros en Mexico y Los Mexicanos en el Extranjero, 1821–1970* (Mexico City: El Colegio de Mexico, 1994), 199.

13. Henry P. Anderson, *The Bracero Program in California* (New York: Arno Press, 1976), 39. Originally copyrighted by the author in 1961.

14. Ibid., 112.

15. Robles, "Braceros Reclaman Justicia."

16. Yvette Cabrera, "Braceros Hold Little Hope on Missing Pay," *Orange County Register*, October 31, 1999.

17. Robles, "Braceros Raclaman Justicia." See also Anderson, *The Bracero Program in California*. One Mexicali official testified, "It is not good when men come in freight cars. Many times they have no drinking water. There is no heat in the cars, and the trip lasts all night. There are no toilets in the freight cars. . . . There have been many times when we got trains with two or three men missing because they had fallen on the way [relieving themselves]," 110.

18. Anderson, *The Bracero Program in California*, 89–90. In his "Fields of Bondage" Anderson noted that even if consuls had responded (which was a rarity), the overwhelming and widespread problems faced by braceros would never have been remedied through the handful of consulates in the areas saturated with bracero laborers. In addition, braceros distrusted Mexican government officials, were reluctant to call for assistance, and preferred to suffer

the indignities. Finally, for the most part consuls were a class-conscious group and uninterested in braceros; many preferred the lifestyle of a foreign official hoping for a promotion. See Henry P. Anderson, "Fields of Bondage: The Mexican Contract Labor System in Industrialized Agriculture" (mimeo, 1963), 46.

19. Robles, "Braceros Reclaman Justicia"; also Gonzalez, *Mexican Consuls and Labor Organizing.*

20. Anderson, *The Bracero Program,* 137.

21. Ibid., 138.

22. Henry P. Anderson, *A Harvest of Loneliness: An Inquiry into a Social Problem.* (Berkeley: Citizens for Farm Labor, 1964), 9–12. Fortunately for students of Mexican migration, Anderson kept the ditto masters and printed two clandestine copies, one of which he kept; the second was eventually archived at the Bancroft Library of the same university that tried to keep the information from the public.

23. See Ernesto Galarza, *Merchants of Labor: The Mexican Bracero Story* (Santa Barbara, Calif.: McNally & Loftin, 1964), chap. 20. Every now and then frank admissions by central figures in U.S. immigration policy offer honest, albeit unintended, insights into U.S.–Mexico economic and political relations. At a congressional hearing held during the bracero era, several "patricians of industrial agriculture," in explaining the necessity of maintaining the Bracero Program, hit upon a historical parallel: "The same thing was true even in the Roman Empire," they contended. "When they reached a stage of civilization they had to reach out to other areas where there was a lesser standard of living to bring in those people to do the menial tasks."

24. Massey, "The Social Organization of Mexican Migration to the United States," 205–6, 214.

25. On network theory see Massey, "The Social Organization of Mexican Migration to the United States"; Hondagneu-Sotelo, *Gendered Transitions;* and Wayne Cornelius and Philip L. Martin, *The Uncertain Tradition* (San Diego, Calif.: Center for U.S.–Mexican Studies, 1993).

26. Jesse Katz, "New Migrant Trails Take Latinos to Remote Towns," *Los Angeles Times,* November 12, 1996; Esther Schrader, "Seeking to Widen Field of U.S. Farm Workers," *Los Angeles Times,* August 26, 1999; Stephanie Simon, "Latinos Take Root in Midwest," *Los Angeles Times,* October 13, 2002. Simon writes of Mexican migrants surging into midwestern states from Kansas to Minnesota, largely illegals, and many recruited at the border by meatpacking companies. Simon found an open recruiting system operating in the region she studied: "Desperate for employees, meatpackers sent buses to recruit workers in Texas, along the U.S.–Mexico border. By the mid-eighties, many plants in Colorado, Nebraska and Kansas were staffed mostly with Latinos."

27. In testimony before the President's Commission on Immigration, Ernesto Galarza made reference to the linkage between the coyotes and his across-the-border partners the growers: "The Immigration Service is not able to cope with this flood of illegals. . . . The Service is up against organized rings of dealers in illegals who transport these men out of the border areas and into the San Joaquin Valley for sums up to $200 per head. A statewide grapevine keeps contact for this racket. The routes of the underground railway leading northward are well known and heavily traveled. Growers provide trucks for the convenience of the 'wetbacks.' " Ernesto Galarza, "American and Foreign Farm Workers in California," statement to the President's Commission on Migratory Labor (mimeo), August 12, 1950, 7. The documentary films *Año Nuevo,* produced and directed by Todd Darling (Cinema Films, 1981) and *The Golden Cage,* produced and directed by Susan Ferris (Filmmakers Library, 1990) demonstrate persuasively the informal but critical, business relationship between the U.S. recruiter and the Mexican coyote. In *Año Nuevo,* ranch foremen recruited workers in Oaxaca and recommended coyotes at the border for transport to a northern California ranch. *The Golden Cage* also provided solid evidence of linkages between coyotes and employers in the United States.

28. Hector Tobar, "A Growing Voice for Fla. Farm Workers," *Los Angeles Times,* March 28, 2000.

29. Katz, "New Migrant Trails Take Latinos to Remote Towns." Reports surfaced of squatter camps along border towns and skirting agricultural locales. In San Diego County, California, on the border, Mexican migrants set up makeshift camps from discarded materials, plastic sheets, cardboard, two-by-fours, and flattened cans. In the early 1990s, studies found that approximately ten thousand migrants inhabited similar camps across Califor-

nia. See Patrick McDonnell, "Survival Tactics: Ingenuity Turns Discarded Materials into Homes for Migrant Laborers," *Los Angeles Times*, April 25, 1991; Gonzalez, *Labor and Community*, 187–88; and the films *Año Nuevo; The Golden Cage;* and *Uneasy Neighbors,* produced and directed by Paul Espinosa, University of California Extension, 1990. The latter films demonstrate widespread squatter camps in suburban and rural areas formed by migrants working in agriculture and urban unskilled labor.

30. Schrader, "Seeking to Widen Field of U.S. Farm Workers."
31. Katz, "New Migrant Trails Take Latinos to Remote Towns."
32. Chris Kraul, "Mortgaging the Future, Firms Help Employees at Mexico's Border Factories Buy Homes," *Los Angeles Times*, December 21, 1996.
33. Juanita Darling, "Fearing a Bitter Harvest," *Los Angeles Times*, March 16, 1992.
34. Chris Kraul, "Growing Troubles in Mexico," *Los Angeles Times*, January 17, 2000. According to Kraul, "NAFTA gave U.S. farmers the right to export 2.5 million tons of corn annually duty-free to Mexico starting in 1994, with the ceiling being lifted until 2008, when U.S. farmers will be able to send all the corn here [Mexico] they want duty-free." NAFTA has ruined thousands of poor peasants throughout Mexico, forcing them to migrate to cities or the north to seek employment in the "booming maquiladoras."
35. Mark Shaffer, "Migrant Mom's Death: A Desperate Prologue," *Los Angeles Times*, July 9, 2000.
36. Ibid.
37. Nancy Cleeland, "Mexican Town Left Behind," *Los Angeles Times*, August 3, 1997. On the emptying of towns within the scope of internal migration, see Douglas Stanley Butterworth, "Factors in Out-Migration from a Rural Mexican Community," Ph.D. diss., University of Illinois, 1969, chap. 11.
38. Esther Schrader, "Growing Exodus Turns Mexican Towns Glum," *Orange County Register*, August 24, 1993.
39. Deborah Sontag, "A Mexican Town That Transcends All Borders," *New York Times*, July 21, 1998.
40. Robert Kahn, "Keeping Illegal Workers Male, Young, and Fit," *Los Angeles Times*, July 6, 1997.
41. Nancy Cleeland, "Heartaches on Aisle 3: Sweatshop for Janitors," *Los Angeles Times*, July 2, 2000.
42. *The Global Assembly Line,* produced and directed by Lorraine Gray (New Day Films, 1986). In response to the question "Why are women favored as maquila workers?" a representative of the El Paso, Texas, Chamber of Commerce answered, with a note of satisfaction, "They're just damned good with their hands."
43. Chris Kraul, "Boom Times in Tijuana Draw Flood of Workers," *Los Angeles Times*, September 24, 1996; Frank Clifford and Mary Beth Sheridan, "Borderline Efforts on Pollution," *Los Angeles Times*, June 30, 1997; "U.S., Mexico Face Border Problems, New Report Warns," *Orange County Register*, May 10, 1999; Laurie Goering, "Mexico's Poverty a Growing Concern," *Orange County Register*, September 7, 2000; Mark Shaffer, "Migrant Mom's Death." The articles describe a nation drowning in poverty (at least 60 to 70 percent of its people living in poverty). This in turn propels a "crushing population increase" at the border as internal migrants seek work at maquiladoras; many will attempt to cross into the United States.
44. Fernandez-Kelly, "Broadening the Scope," 143–68; Massey, "The Social Organization of Mexican Migration to the United States," 205–6, 214; Mercedes Pedrero Nieto, "The Economically Active Population in the Northern Region of Mexico," in *Demographic Dynamics of the U.S.–Mexico Border*, edited by John R. Weeks and Roberto Ham-Chande (El Paso, Tex.: Texas Western Press, 1992), and Sassen, *The Mobility of Labor and Capital.*
45. Mary Beth Sheridan, "Riding the Ripples of a Border Boom Town," *Los Angeles Times*, June 9, 1997. CEOs and managers of the maquilas currently enjoy some of the highest salaries in history, possibly due to a shortage of qualified personnel (Kathy Kristoff, "Executive Compensation Climbs into Stratosphere," *Los Angeles Times*, July 5, 2000). In the rapidly expanding assembly plants, companies experience difficulty in filling top-level positions. Companies operating maquilas contract with recruiting agencies whose only business is the search for experienced middle-level and higher managers. One service relocates about four hundred executives every year with enticing salary packages. The maquila "perks" are impressive and include car, housing, six-figure salaries, travel, and even weekend recreation budgets and unlimited-vacation compensation packages (Joel Millman, "Mexico Is Perk

Paradise to U.S. Middle Managers," *Orange County Register*, May 24, 2000). Managed migration moves in two directions simultaneously. Just as in the first decade of the twentieth century, laborers from Mexico moving north and corporate managers going south passed each other on their journeys, oblivious of the irony that a transnational corporate hierarchy was in the process of construction.

46. See Women's Rights Project of Human Rights Watch, "No Guarantees: Sex Discrimination in Mexico's Maquiladora Sector," in *The Maquiladora Reader: Cross-Border Organizing since NAFTA,* edited by Rachel Kamel and Anya Hoffman, (1996; reprint, Philadelphia: American Friends Service Committee, 1999), 31.

47. Hondagneu-Sotelo, "The History of Mexican Undocumented Settlement in the United States," 115–34; Morales and Ong, "Immigrant Women in Los Angeles"; and Romero, *Maid in the U.S.A.*

48. Patricia R. Pessar, "Engendering Migration Studies: The Case of New Immigrants in the United States," *American Behavioral Scientist* 42, no. 4 (January 1999): 581.

49. See Grace Chang, *Disposable Domestics: Immigrant Women Workers in the Global Economy* (Cambridge, Mass.: South End Press, 2000). Chang documents the widespread popular representation of women migrants as, among other things, "idle, welfare-dependent mothers and inordinate breeders of dependents."

50. Robert Pear, "Illegal Aliens Aid Economy, Report Says," *Orange County Register*, January 23, 1986.

51. Benefits for the two-parent and single-parent households on the U.S. side from the availability of Mexican women are significant. Mexican maids (and in southern California, Central American *and* Mexican maids) allow for a greater participation of women in the workforce. Employers are generally in the professional classes that depend on the services of their maids for childcare, housecleaning, and cooking. Mary Romero, *Maid in the U.S.A.*; Vicki Ruiz, ed., *Las Obreras: Chicana Politics of Work and Family* (Los Angeles: UCLA, Chicano Studies Research Center, 2001); Fernandez-Kelly, "Broadening the Scope"; and Edna Bonacich, *Asian and Latino Immigrants in the Los Angeles Garment Industry.* Many works mention the widespread use of *mozos,* or servants, by foreigners, mainly Americans in Mexico during the early twentieth century. See, e.g., Ralph McA. Ingersoll, *In and under Mexico* (New York: Century, 1924); Mrs. Alec Tweedie, *Mexico As I Saw It* (London: Hurst & Blackett, 1901); and Grant Shepherd, *The Silver Magnet* (New York: E. P. Dutton, 1938).

52. See, e.g., Charles LeDuff, "Immigrant Workers Tell of Being Lured and Beaten," *New York Times*, September 20, 2000.

53. Anderson, *The Bracero Program in California,* 232.

54. Richard Boudreaux, "Frustration Marks Fox, Bush Talks," *Los Angeles Times*, October 27, 2002; "Another Day of the Dead: Another 140 Dead Migrants at the California Border," *U.S.-Mexico Border Program,* October 31, 2000; see also Ken Ellingwood, "INS Chief Targets Risky Rural Crossings," *Los Angeles Times,* September 7, 2000; and Joseph Nevins, "How High Must Gatekeeper's Death Count Go?" *Los Angeles Times,* November 19, 2000. Nevins writes, "[I]t is clear that the expensive operation has accomplished little other than to create an image of boundary control and to cause large numbers of deaths. . . . By knowingly 'forcing' people to cross such terrain, the INS has contributed to the resulting deaths." However, Nevins adds that the INS refuses to accept responsibility. But why would the United States claim responsibility for the 603 deaths in southern California alone in the six years after Operation Gatekeeper's 1994 inception? It seems that the INS places blinders on the consequences of its policies.

55. Ken Ellingwood, "3 Suspected Illegal Immigrants Die, 28 Rescued in Freezing Mountains," *Los Angeles Times*, March 7, 2000.

56. See Will Weisbert, "11 Train Deaths Don't Deter," *Orange County Register*, October 21, 2002; also Richard Boudreaux, "Father's Modest Dream Leads to Tragic Journey," *Los Angeles Times*, October 23, 2002.

57. Ken Ellingwood, "INS Intensifies Campaign to Lessen Migrant Death Toll, *Los Angeles Times*, June 27, 2000.

58. Mark Fineman, "For Migrants, Desperation Still Outweighs the Risks"; Boudreaux, "Father's Modest Dream Leads to Tragic Journey"; see also Michael Huspek, "Violations of Human and Civil Rights on the U.S.–Mexico Border, 1995–1997: A Report," *Social Justice* 25, no. 2 (Summer 1998).

V
The Integration of Mexican Workers into the U.S. Economy

It is commonly said that the Mexican immigrant, and second-generation Mexican Americans, Chicanos, or more generally ethnic Mexicans, have been and remain in a position of segregation and marginalization in American society. That terminology refers to a wide variety of factors, ranging from education, political participation, and income to occupation and residential location. However, when one looks at the economy and its functioning, what is striking is the central role, the perfect integration of the Mexican ethnic into the workings of the U.S. monopolistic economy.

A cultural, racial approach pervades the discussion about the marginalization of the Mexican immigrant and the ethnic Mexican, and it implies that these "problems" may be open to "policy" solutions. Policy solutions that hint at the possibility of Mexican immigrants and ethnic Mexicans moving from the margins to the "mainstream," eligible to compete for the prized "American Dream," insulate the social and political sphere from the economic.

This cultural approach misses some essential characteristics of the social organization of production in capitalist societies. As capitalism reached its maturity in the early nineteenth century, it required for its maintenance the development of a working, propertyless class that was "marginal" in terms of the usual attributes the term implies: low levels of education, poor housing, political disenfranchisement, low income levels, and so on. Most members of this new working class possessed a new characteristic, a historical product of industrial capitalism: they were *unskilled laborers*. But, in addition, there was a fraction of the working class whose

123

living conditions were even worse. It was made up of those whose employment was particularly precarious, whose terms of employment were largely temporary, seasonal, forever at the mercy of cyclical fluctuations, who were the last to be hired and the first to be fired. Those workers were maintained by capitalism, Marx argued, in reserve, a *reserve army of labor* to be pressed into service at special times and/or places and to be cast off as surplus, unwanted labor when demand dwindled.

It should be clear that in any developed capitalist society a large proportion of its population will make up the working class, within which some fractions, while extremely deprived socially and even legally segregated in residence and education, are fundamentally integrated and necessary for the smooth functioning of the system as a whole. In many ways the above description of classical capitalism points to the characteristics of many Mexican workers of both sexes in the United States—in great demand during some periods, persecuted and deported at other times.

Whenever and wherever this antithesis did not obtain historically, marginal versus central, or better, worker versus capitalist, capitalism could not thrive. This is why an economic thinker of the nineteenth century, Edward Gibbon Wakefield, was quite critical of the early development path taken by the United States. In his opinion, the ability of a potential wage worker who arrived as an immigrant on the East Coast of the United States to migrate into the interior of the United States and become a self-employed farmer was the gravest obstacle to the development of capitalism. Wrote Wakefield: "Where land is very cheap and all men are free, where everyone who so pleases can easily obtain a piece of land for himself, not only is labour very dear . . . but the difficulty is to obtain labour at any price."[1] In other words, abundant, elastic, and cost-efficient wage labor is fundamental to capitalism.

The entrance of significant numbers of Mexican workers into the United States early in the twentieth century occurred when capitalism had undergone a substantial transformation, which we pointed to in the second chapter. In brief, capitalism had entered a new phase in its development. Its general aspects consisted of the loss of importance, at the national level, of the small, competitive firm, and its replacement by monopolistic industrial corporations that eventually produce a surplus of capital. This in turn leads to the growing impact of financial institutions and the development, based on those changes, of massive foreign investments and a transnational mode of economic domination. The ability of U.S.-based corporations to have their way in weaker countries such as Mexico, and to reap superprofits from their operations, empowers them to provide for an overall improvement in working-class conditions in the United States. Thus, historically, Mexican workers begin to come to the

U.S. Southwest and into the bottom layers of the U.S. labor force at a time of generally rising standards for the rest of the working class.

Social and living conditions bordering on deprivation—that is, "marginalization"—is merely one aspect of the existence of a working class under either "classic" or contemporary monopoly capitalism, a class indispensable for the functioning of the system. Workers form a constituent part of an economic *system* built on the foundation of their ability to perform wage labor. In the last analysis, under capitalism the propertyless are always marginal, which nonetheless translates into an active centrality within the process of production. To occupy the "center" and bask in the "mainstream," one has to be a property owner—a capitalist—or belong to a privileged stratum of workers whose well-being is inseparable from the abject poverty of the many.

A number of other factors, some social in nature, others of a physical and geographic nature, impinged on the character of the historical integration of the Mexican worker into the fabric of U.S. society. Five factors were key: first, the monopolistic nature of land ownership in the U.S. Southwest; second, the low population density of the region; third, the vast extension of the area; fourth, the general aridity and soil fertility in the region; and finally, the development of gigantic irrigation projects and agribusiness in the Southwest.

In the second half of the nineteenth century the characteristic land monopolies that had prevailed in the Southwest during Spanish and Mexican times changed hands, but they remained largely intact in the transition from Mexico to the United States. The feudal land monopolies that dominated the economy in Spanish times were transformed by the early twentieth century into another monopoly, albeit a capitalist one, of the same land. The concentration that already existed by way of the Spanish land grants of old was continued and reinforced through a series of policies and events, such as railroad grants and land speculation, that eventually transformed the Southwest, especially California, into an empire of large farms. Thus, from the very outset, whoever was not an owner of a portion of this "empire," as Carey McWilliams called it, was a landless peasant and potential wage worker.

The development of capitalist agriculture in these farms faced the obstacle that concerned economist Wakefield, namely, the absence of large numbers of free laborers. The Southwest was a region with a very small population. That is why, from the beginnings of agriculture in California and elsewhere in the West, agribusiness has looked to pools of foreign, cheap labor to meet their production needs. Chinese, Japanese, Filipino, and East Indian workers were imported to work in California fields during the last part of the nineteenth century and the early decades of the twentieth.

Meanwhile, U.S. investments in Mexico were wreaking havoc in the traditional Mexican countryside, something we explored in some detail in the second chapter. After working on the building of the railroads in their own country, Mexican labor was recruited to work in the building and maintenance of railroads in the U.S. Southwest and Midwest. As we shall see later in this chapter, the building of the railroads did not offer a passport to freedom or better opportunities for the former peasants. Railroads were, however, instrumental in bringing these peasants to the labor markets; first, to the American-operated mines of northern Mexico, then to mining districts in the Southwest, and eventually to a variety of other sites where labor was needed in the Southwest. Thus the first major occupation in which Mexican workers become integrated into the U.S. economic system is as railroad workers.

The integration was not limited to the workplace connection, but in the early years included a lifelong attachment to a railroad life—"life in boxcar," McWilliams called it. Workers and their families followed the building of new tracks throughout the countryside, sometimes staying and dotting the landscaping with colonia settlements by the railroad tracks. Given the enormous extension of the southwestern territory, the building of the railroads became a preeminent need for the large U.S. industrial and commercial firms concerned with the shortening delivery times for their products. But it also became a way of transporting needed labor from point A to point B throughout the Southwest as needed. Thus the railroads made possible, then fostered, the importation of Mexican laborers that allowed the development of large-scale cotton farming in Texas.

We hasten to point out that the new migration phenomenon was not unique to the contiguity of Mexico and the United States. The development of monopoly capitalism in Europe at the same time also was marked by the appearance of new migratory flows. Early analysts of Mexican migration to the United States were aware of it. Thus, as Max Handman insightfully observed:

> Germany . . . presents an analogy with the agricultural labor situation of the Mexican in America. . . . Germany, in particular in the East, had large landed estates which needed additional seasonal labor in order to produce for a growing market. In proportion, however, as the cities and industrial life made calls on the working forces of the country, the large landowners and producers began to call in seasonal labor from (other) regions . . . the result was that Germany before the War [World War I] imported annually more than four hundred thousand agricultural laborers to harvest her crops.[2]

The circumstances of land monopolization and labor scarcity were compounded by the development of large-scale irrigation in the Southwest as a whole. Beginning at the turn of the twentieth century, a grand alliance of industrial corporations, bank financiers, agribusiness, and federal and state governments in the Southwest launched this ambitious plan. In 1902 the Southwest, an area larger in size than the original American thirteen colonies, was largely an unpopulated, desertic area. In 1902 the Reclamation Act, which made possible the use of federal funds for the construction of large irrigation projects, was passed, marking the beginning of modern, corporate development of the Southwest. The multiple damming of the Colorado, beginning with mammoth Hoover Dam, the California Water Project, and other similar endeavors were carried out in the first seventy years of that century. Irrigation allowed the reclamation of millions of previously arid and unproductive acres and helped turn large portions of desert brush into fertile farms and orchards.

As Paul S. Taylor pointed out in the 1930s, the employment of Mexican labor was proportional to the expansion of irrigation projects. Such an expansion of acreage and the ability to grow cotton and truck produce—now profitable, given the development of the refrigerated railcar—in previously uncultivated areas necessitated increased numbers of laborers. Large-scale irrigation meant, additionally, new and increased overcapitalization of the land. Heavy capital investments, in addition to creating "agribusiness" by bringing banking capital into the agricultural enterprise, meant a persistent demand for elastic pools of cheap labor. The convergence of large monopoly capital and large supplies of labor, while perhaps paradoxical—one usually assumes that great amounts of capital are synonymous with mechanization and labor saving—is a general characteristic of capitalism in agriculture.

To be sure, the development and application of science and technology to agriculture historically occurred with the expansion of capitalism to rural areas. But this expansion took place sporadically in most Western nations and usually lagged behind developments in urban, commercial, and industrial capitalism. Why? Because in the development of capitalism as a system of production, the application of machinery to agriculture has had to overcome more technical obstacles than in urban industry. In the latter, the workplace—the factory—can be molded to the physical requirements of the machinery; in agriculture the physical setting is given, and the machinery has to be adapted, not always a simple, or even possible, task. In urban industry, machinery represents a larger saving in the use of labor, since machines can be run on a 24-hour, 365-day schedule; in agriculture, their utilization is limited to a seasonal basis. In terms of human requirements, typical urban industry under capitalism strives and gets by with the utilization of "unskilled labor."

With agricultural machinery, the problem is not so straightforward, since considerable training is necessary for the operation and maintenance of harvesters, pickers, and other instruments. This obstacle—the intrinsic contradiction between endless capitalist profit seeking and the natural, seasonal character of agriculture—made the use of large amounts of cheap Mexican labor unusually attractive for southwestern agribusiness. The dependence of the arid Southwest on vast supplies of water to develop its agriculture led to the creation of a complex web of dams, reservoirs, and canals, and to a vast technocracy to manage it. It has been referred to as a modern hydraulic society.[3] Several authors have noticed its nefarious ecological by-products.[4] In terms of the way in which the resulting agribusiness empire exploited the immigrant Mexican worker, "Occidental Despotism," to paraphrase Karl Wittfogel, may be a more apt description.[5]

So far we have suggested the ways in which the labor of Mexican-American migrants is central to the development of capitalism in the U.S. Southwest. Now we wish to follow the previous abstract discussion with an empirical, historical, and many-sided look at the way in which the economic integration of the Mexican American into the U.S. economy took place. We look at representative examples from the sectors of transportation, agriculture, service, processing, and industry. In the area of transportation we focus on Mexican labor in the construction of railroads. The building of the U.S. railway network unified the whole national economy, in particular California agriculture, to eastern markets. In agriculture we look at the citrus industry and the production of lettuce. In these two very different crops, we observe how different kinds of Mexican labor—legal or illegal, long-term or contract bracero, male or female—were linked by employers in the organization of production. In terms of service, we survey recent work on the impact of Mexican domestic workers in the economy. We also touch on the kinds of settlement and living that emerged from different kinds of work patterns. The chapter closes with a brief overview of the economic region we call the Pacific corridor, a zone encompassing southern California and northern Baja California.

Railroads

Shortly after the end of the Civil War, the U.S. economy underwent a dramatic shift from one based on small-scale production to that governed by industrial and financial monopolies and oligopolies. An economy of small manufacturing gave way relatively quickly to huge industrial forms of production. Statistics taken at the turn of the nineteenth century bear out the significance of economies of scale at the core of the emerging imperial powerhouse. In 1904, 0.9 percent of all industrial enterprises produced nearly 40 percent of all industrial output. These in turn employed more than a quarter of the total workforce, 1.5 million workers. The trend continued its dizzying pace, so that in 1909 slightly more than 1 percent of all industrial enterprises produced 44 percent of all industrial output and employed nearly 2 million workers, more than 30 percent of all industrial labor.[6] As small-scale production declined in importance, eclipsed by behemoths such as Standard Oil; U.S. Steel; Atchison, Topeka, & Santa Fe; Southern Pacific; American Smelting & Refining; House of Morgan, and linked to names such as Guggenheim, Gould, and Carnegie, the modern working class assumed center stage in the new industrial order.

The appearance of large-scale capital is nearly simultaneous with the development of the nation's railroad corporations. The railroads broke down regional economic exclusiveness and in no small measure helped to construct a nationalized and centralized economy. In their wake manufacturing, mining, livestock, and agricultural production ascended with the opening of national markets. Production, expansion, and maintenance of the railroad system alone demanded continually increasing amounts of steel, timber, coal, and oil. As U.S. corporations began construction of Mexican railroads in 1880, 93,000 miles of railroads girded the northern nation, a labor-intensive operation that required more than 1 million workers in 1900, and by 1925 that labor force numbered nearly 2 million.[7]

Upon crossing the border, Mexican immigrants were recruited without hesitation by agents working for labor-hungry railroads, then transported into the core of that economic hierarchy. From 1900 to 1930 El Paso served as the point of entry for labor moving north and as a central rail connection for the Santa Fe, the Texas & Pacific, the Southern Pacific, and the Mexican Railway. These and other economic giants reached unobstructed, via labor agencies, into the Mexican labor pool to move labor across the Southwest and Midwest. A measure of centralization of Mexican immigrant labor is nowhere more visible than in the case of their massive employment by railroads. Victor Clark noted this common border scenario:

> The immigrants arrive at the border practically without funds, but with the moral certainty of securing immediate employment. Here they are met by the representatives of large authorized labor contracting companies, who regularly supply an entire railway system, or many of its divisions, with all the labor needed, and by private agents looking for smaller bodies of men for some special section, or simply speculating in labor; that is, holding it at their headquarters on subsistence until they can secure a good commission by delivering it to some enterprise badly in need of workers.[8]

Clark further reported that "more Mexicans are employed in the United States as railway laborers than in any other occupation."[9] A contemporary of Clark, Stanford economist Samuel Bryan, writing in 1908, found that six employment agencies "operating in El Paso supplied 16,479 Mexicans to the various railroad companies, or an average of 2,060 per month." A practice so widespread, observed Bryan, that "[m]ost of the Mexican immigrants have at one time or another been employed as railroad laborers."[10] Mexican labor replaced native and European immigrant workers to such an extent, noted the late historian Jeffrey Garcilazo, that "Mexican workers constituted two-thirds of the track labor forces of the Southwest" between 1900 and 1930. Not surprisingly, more Mexican immigrants entered the United States via the railroads than through any other economic branch. According to a 1926 study commissioned by the state of California, nearly 40 percent of all employed Mexican immigrants in California worked for the railroads, followed by 24 percent working in agriculture, 26 percent as common labor, and the rest scattered in service, construction, and industry. The study also reported that on the southwestern railroads, 33,000 to 48,000 Mexican track workers, or 75 percent of section gang labor, worked seasonally.[11] Naturally, Mexican labor was considered ideal for the type of work: cheap, manageable, eager, flexible, and expendable.

However, securing labor required more than collecting a gang of able bodies. Railway officials worried about the tendency of workers to defect into other lines of employment and sought methods to keep labor dependable and tied to one place. One method that seemed to accomplish the goal was to hire married men with families and transport the entire family to the work site. An engineer on the El Paso & Southwestern, reflecting on a general policy among railroads employing Mexican labor, commented, "Mexicans with families are preferred to the single men as the latter will not stay and work as well."[12]

The development of rent-free company housing—boxcars for married men and adobe huts or flimsy wood cabins for the solos—at central rail points appeared across the Southwest and into the Midwest. A colonia system sprouted along the rail lines, prompting one railroader to note that "groups of houses dot the desert from here [El Paso] to Los Angeles." One interurban rail system in southern California established twenty-two boxcar camps across four counties.[13] The degree of consideration for the quality of housing for track workers can be gleaned from the statement of the general manager for Holmes Supply Company, a labor-recruiting agency in Los Angeles. He commented, "As a rule, the average Mexican laborer and family are satisfied with the most primitive arrangements so far as comfort goes . . . he makes no demand for conveniences, facilities, or arrangements for his well-being, accepting a box car with wooden bunks and no windows with the same readiness that he would a modern bunk car. . . ."[14]

More than company housing proved profitable for railroads; officials also used the family to encourage chain migrations. According to Jeffrey Garcilazo, "Foremen instructed traqueros [track workers] to invite family and friends to work on specific lines, divisions, or sections. These workers wrote of jobs, housing, and free transportation from the border to specific destination."[15] Writing paper, pens, envelopes, and stamps were distributed by a number of railroads to facilitate and encourage networks and thereby use the family as an inexpensive labor recruiter. Other means were employed to hold labor at a work site for the duration of a specified task. Return transportation could depend on whether the worker remained until the job was completed. The practice was not unique; rather, it appears as a variation of the bonus system that obtained in other lines of work employing Mexican labor. Other benefits obtained as well. Samuel Bryan noted that even though Mexican labor was the cheapest available, the bonus system "enables the railroad companies to hold their employes of this race at lower wages than are customary in other industries of the same locality."[16] In other words, the system was set up to discourage workers, at least temporarily, from migrating to another branch of the economy. Yet, in the long run, many chose to skip to other jobs.

The Mexican immigrant's experience in the first three decades of the twentieth century, while seemingly colored by regional or even racial factors, on deeper analysis demonstrated his or her integration into the heart of the U.S. corporate order: the railroads. However, while railroads served as the entry point for thousands of Mexican immigrants, they also distributed labor in ways that assisted other industries seeking cheap labor, including agriculture, mining, and urban industries of various sorts. As Victor Clark noted, "It is from this occupation [trackwork] that they drift into other lines of work."[17]

The Citrus Industry

Mexican laborers eventually moved from railroad maintenance and construction into the emerging labor markets. The development of refrigerated cars in the mid-1880s and federally funded irrigation projects late in the nineteenth century stimulated ancillary economic developments across the Southwest. Labor-intensive agriculture swelled in what appeared to be a seamless upward spiral. In California's heralded agricultural expanse, one that produced hundreds of products from nuts and berries to avocados and cotton, citriculture assumed superstar status. All other products stood in the shadow of the citrus industry. No other product competed with the citrus industry's finely cultured mythical romance nor matched its dominant position as the most profitable branch of California's agriculture. From the turn of the century to the post–World War II era, citrus reigned supreme across southern and central California.

Not even the fabled "Gold Rush" of 1848, the symbolic historical event signifying California's origins, produced as much wealth as did citrus from 1890 to 1960. Only the oil industry outmuscled oranges, lemons, grapefruit, and tangerines. In 1936, for example, citrus garnered $97 million in profit, while the state's petroleum industry amassed $159.6 million. The Great Depression seemed not to topple the citrus industry from its dominance; citrus growers garnered no less than 10 percent of the state's total farm income in 1938, or $51 million. During the peak of the citrus production, California produced 60 percent of the nation's supply and 21 percent of the world's supply.[18] From small and scattered citrus ranches producing for a small and regional market in the 1880s, the industry grew into the state's chief agricultural product within a generation. Abreast of the steadily enlarging acreage devoted to citrus, communities tied to the industry "sprang like wildflowers" along the interior of the southern California coastline, from Santa Barbara to San Diego. At the center of Valencia orange production, Orange County, citrus expanded from 40 acres in 1870, to 5,000 in 1900 and reached more than 75,000 in 1945. In that year nearly 300,000 acres were planted with citrus trees across the state and produced more than 90,000 boxcars of fruit for regional, national, and international markets.

That the industry basked in success from its very beginnings must be explained in light of the hierarchical structure of the industry. Nearly 250 packinghouses at the local level were organized into two main associations, the California Fruit Growers Exchange (Sunkist) and the Mutual Orange Distributors. The former controlled the lion's share of the industry, but also about three-quarters of the citrus output. Not only did Sunkist and Mutual supervise the overall policies governing the industry, but also the central exchanges determined labor policies and housing programs and stepped into such areas as Americanization aimed at Mexican children and adults. However, the larger growers determined the overall policies governing the associations. Upon examination, the inequalities in the industry become readily apparent. In 1940 less than 3 percent of growers controlled more than 40 percent of total acreage (usually the most productive and therefore most expensive groves). On the other hand, nearly 63 percent of all growers owned less than a quarter of total citrus acreage. Observed noted social critic Carey McWilliams, "The center of power in the industry [is] in the offices of the California Fruit Growers Exchange in Los Angeles," and added that it was the commercial (large-scale) growers "who dominate the exchange and its local and district offices."[19]

The political power at the top evolved from a voting arrangement based on shares equal to the quality *and* quantity of the individual grower's harvest. Each share garnered one vote. The larger the grower, the more productive the harvests, the larger the voting shares. Although voted in by popular vote, the president and boards of directors of the central exchanges truly represented the unequaled power held by the larger and more successful growers. A U.S. Senate report issued in 1938 affirmed the pyramidal structure of the industry: "[N]ot only do the larger growers have a controlling voice in the direction of the local associations but, through them, they control the district and central exchanges."[20]

Nature limited production to six counties of the southern region, which contained 90 percent of the state's citrus acreage, the bulk of the industry's productive activities, and corresponding social relations. Citrus differed in many respects from other branches of agricultural production, which in turn dictated the need for a permanent settlement pattern for labor. The two main types of oranges—Valencias and navels—were picked in nonoverlapping six-month seasons—summer and winter, respectively—requiring a largely permanent labor force able to move within neighboring districts in the citrus belt. In large packinghouses, which dominated a town's activities, packers, usually women, prepared citrus for shipment. Picking and packing during the season and pruning, fumigating, and spraying in the off-season were labor-intensive operations that required no fewer than 50,000 workers. At the local level, a large force able to assemble at a moment's notice when orders came in or when ripening dictated picking was essential. No sooner did picking commence that packing operations swung into full tilt. Citrus workers settled into an environment characterized by paternalistic employee policies and strict patterns of social and economic segregation. Within this labor-intensive economic context, one that demanded a year-round labor force, the mass of Mexican colonias in southern California mushroomed in the late 1910s and 1920s.

After Mexican immigrants had taken over track crew labor in southwestern railroads, that labor appeared in increasing numbers during the second decade in citrus. Eventually Mexican workers supplanted the Japanese, who had monopolized the workforce at the turn of the century and had become a liability by organizing unionlike associations. In addition, anti-Japanese legislation cut into the availability of experienced citrus labor. Consequently, growers began to look toward Mexican labor in about 1910, and by 1920 Mexican workers constituted 30 percent of the workforce but by 1930 comprised the backbone of the industry, about 90 percent of the labor force in the groves and packinghouses. As one grower vehemently stated, "If no Mexican pickers were available, it would be impossible for us to move our crops." The industry opposed all measures to tighten immigration restrictions, successfully lobbied for the 1917 "guest worker" legislation, and vehemently opposed quotas on Mexico under the infamous 1924 immigration act. A virtual open border solved any labor shortages that may have affected the industry from 1910 to 1930.

Similarly to railroad labor policy, citrus growers hit upon family labor as a means to root their workers to the immediate area. Worried that single men were prone to move on to higher-wage work or even dabble in radical or socialist practices, growers began to sponsor housing projects aimed at attracting men with families. Soon company and privately sponsored housing projects sprouted throughout the region. Whereas Mexican communities in Watts (Los Angeles) and San Gabriel were established to house railroad workers, other communities—La Jolla, Campo Colorado, Atwood, La Puente, Jim Town, and many more—were created to supply the citrus industry with a steady, readily available, and dependable supply of low-wage labor.

No fewer than twenty-four association-owned housing projects were founded throughout the southern region specifically to house Mexican laborers and their families. In the interests of growers, many privately owned residential tracts were set aside specifically for sale or rent exclusively to Mexican citrus workers. Thus, as the citrus industry expanded, the number of Mexican communities in the region rose in corresponding fashion. Although substandard housing set the physical conditions of the citrus worker communities, workers and their families created a vital and dynamic community life. Originally the communities were designed to shelter men (pickers) and their families; however, over time women were recruited to pack oranges and lemons and eventually dominated packinghouse crews. A colonia complex formed by the deliberate strategy of the citrus industry to seek Mexican labor sprinkled the citrus belt, intentionally segregated and set apart from the larger community but indispensable to the varied processes of citrus production.

The interests of the industry colored public policies affecting the Mexican community. School boards regularly consulted with industry officials regarding public school curriculum and adult programs for the Mexican community. Segregated schooling, Americanization for children and adults, industrial training for boys and girls based on Mexican "aptitudes" for manual labor, and a "glass ceiling" together acted to dissuade aspirations beyond picking and packing and to ensure the reproduction of the labor force over generations. However, that segregation and overt discriminatory policy complemented a more important characteristic of the Mexican immigrant labor: their integration into the production of California's primary agricultural product. To be sure, the citrus industry's enormous expansion to become the center of the nation and the world's supply (and ensuing immense profitability) cannot be explained apart from this integration.

By 1940, immigrant Mexicans were the primary source of labor supply for every major fruit and vegetable crop in California. Migrant workers shuttled to and fro across the state to provide ample and able labor in suffi-cient amounts at the peak harvest time of many highly perishable crops. The growth of cotton production in Texas, Arizona, and California de-pended on Mexican immigrant labor, as did the mining industry in Ari-zona, and the production of sugar beets in Colorado and the Midwest. Mexican agricultural workers also could be found in Oregon, Washington, Nevada, New Mexico, Utah, and Idaho. By the 1920s Mexican immigrant workers had joined industrial work. Thousands labored in Pennsylvania steel mills and in auto plants in Detroit, Flint, and Saginaw.[21]

Meanwhile, agricultural products needed to be packed and/or processed. Not surprisingly, California was the center of the packing and canning com-plex. "During the period from 1939 to 1950, California produced more canned fruits and vegetables than any other state. . . . In 1946, the state's share in the U.S. fruit pack was approximately 50 percent."[22] Vicki Ruiz has docu-mented the central role of Mexican immigrant women workers in packing and canning. This labor force worked in the packing of walnuts, almonds, grapefruit, oranges, and lettuce; in the processing of apricots, peaches, black-berries, pears, figs, apples, plums, cherries, dried fruit, fruit cocktail, and salad fruits; and in the canning of asparagus, green beans, wax beans, beets, carrots, corn, lima beans, spinach, peas, pimentos, tomatoes, and pumpkin.[23]

As we noted in the second chapter, the Great Depression of the 1930s and World War II slowed down the mass migration of the early part of the century. But as it picked up steam again beginning in the 1950s, Mexican immigrant workers continued not only to provide the bulk of agricultural labor in the West and the Southwest, but they also moved into every kind of urban employment available in these regions: in manufacturing, con-struction, services (especially restaurant and hotel work), maintenance, gardening and landscaping, electronics, as day laborers, as street vendors, and so on. Mexican immigrant women, joined by other Latinas, especially from Central America, and Asian women, provided the backbone of the garment industry in Los Angeles. As the century drew to an end, Mexican immigrants worked in agriculture and food processing throughout the en-tire United States. The search for work in agricultural crops such as to-bacco and sugar cane, as well as the processing and service branches in poultry-processing plants, meatpacking, and restaurants made Mexican workers a ubiquitous presence in the United States. In some counties in North Carolina, Georgia, Iowa, Arkansas, Minnesota, and Nebraska, Mexi-cans made up, by century's end, almost a quarter of the population.[24]

"The Vegetable Crop par Excellence"

The organization of Mexican labor may comprise men, women, men and women, families, legal immigrants, illegal immigrants, contract workers,

U.S. citizens, and Mexican citizens. All of these categories enter into the deliberations of growers as they consider the specifications of an ideal labor force—yet another way in which Mexican labor is deeply woven into the fabric of U.S. agribusiness. One of the areas of agriculture in which Mexican labor currently predominates is lettuce production, a staple in the daily diet and nutritional culture of the nation. In lettuce production one observes a deliberate manipulation of legal status and gender in the deployment of laborers.

Between 1960 and 1990, California's fruit and vegetable acreage doubled, and vegetable crops such as lettuce, broccoli, and cauliflower assumed a central place in that state's agriculture and required a 22 percent increase of seasonal workers. None of this expansion could have occurred without the availability of a large reservoir of cheap, skilled labor. Mexican labor's importance grew dramatically between 1970 and 2000, so that by the last decade of the twentieth century, approximately eight hundred thousand to nine hundred thousand farm workers, nearly all Mexican immigrants or descendants of immigrants, worked the fields of the vast expanses of California's valleys. The large-scale increase in acreage met by unfettered flows of immigrants has led to an increase in the production of labor-intensive crops and a decrease in the impetus to mechanize production. Moreover, the largest "10 percent of all farms account for 80 percent of total production and employment," meaning the vast majority of immigrant Mexican labor works for the largest entities in corporate agribusiness.[25] As in the case of citrus, lettuce production centers, largely in California (and in the contiguous valleys of Arizona), served as effective media for advancing a national mythology regarding California lifestyles.

By the 1930s lettuce had earned (or, better, allocated) the title "Nature's Concentrated Sunshine," and by the 1970s had become the "vegetable crop par excellence."[26] Both citrus and lettuce production have been central to the agriculture sector, both highly profitable, and both exhibited centralized forms of management. Data collected by Robert Thomas demonstrate the pyramidal large-scale proportions of the industry within which a noteworthy imbalance among all the producers predominated. Figures taken from the late 1970s demonstrate that of ninety-three firms engaged in lettuce production only three, or 3.2 percent, contributed more than one-third of all production; meanwhile, seven firms, constituting 4.3 percent of all firms, garnered 53 percent of total lettuce production. These seven firms stand within the top 2 percent of California's agricultural enterprises and, moreover, combine with larger conglomerates (the two largest lettuce firms are subsidiaries of corporations listed among the *Forbes* 500).

On the other hand, seventy-three firms comprising 80 percent of all firms produced but one-quarter of all lettuce for the market. The seventy-three fell within the economic shadow of nineteen companies, 20 percent of all firms, that produced 75 percent of the lettuce crop. Another way of appreciating this economic pyramid: the top-rank firms farmed an average of twenty-three thousand acres, and, through a system of contracting with smaller, often family-run firms, the larger companies actually influenced, if not dominated, far into the industry's periphery.[27] Although firms produced and sold lettuce nationally and internationally, the top three (noted above) controlled $275 million in annual sales in the early 1980s, the lion's share of the $500 million in total industry receipts.

These giants in turn depended heavily on the availability of low-wage Mexican immigrant labor, women, men, undocumented immigrants, documented immigrants, and, to a far lesser extent, U.S. citizens. Noncitizens of the United States form about 80 percent of the labor force, and today the number who are undocumented is reported to be 40 to 50 percent (and growing) of the labor supply.[28] The concentration of production and sales by a handful of enterprises translated into the central role played by these firms in setting industrywide labor practices and is critical for explaining the form that the economic integration of Mexican and Mexican-American labor has assumed in lettuce production. Qualities according to the categories of gender, legal status, and citizenship bestow a special role and place in the organization of labor. Each classification is assigned a separate function in the corporate-dominated production of a single commodity, "Nature's Concentrated Sunshine."

Two forms of harvesting and packing appear in lettuce production. The first is a less-mechanized method in which cutters, who sever the lettuce from the ground; packers, who also work on the ground; and lifters, who place packed boxes on a moving truck, form a crew. The second, a mechanized, tractorlike harvesting system, differs in that it resembles an industrial process, with cutters on the ground while the remaining crew works on a moving machine aboveground. Accompanying the cutters are wrappers (who wrap the lettuce in plastic wrap), packers, box closers, and a driver, all working on a large, tractorlike machine that moves through the rows of lettuce.

The bulk of lettuce production, about 80 percent, stems from the first method and requires more skilled labor. However, it is in this method that the use of undocumented workers is primarily found; in the second, the majority of U.S. citizens, primarily women, and documented workers are found. Why is this the case? Robert Thomas has presented persuasive evidence arguing that the less-mechanized system required more skilled labor and greater cooperation in the work process, and it was in seeking to control that labor and keep costs down that growers specifically searched for the more malleable undocumented over documented labor. The reasons were simple: the undocumented are politically vulnerable and hold less potential to either challenge orders, leave, or seek redress for grievances.[29] Documented workers and U.S. citizens, on the other hand, have degrees of legal protection and a consequent greater propensity to organize and challenge company policies. Documented males and female citizens were favored to work on the moving machine, while undocumented worked as cutters on the ground. Again, the work was more repetitive, unskilled, tied to the motion of the machine, and more costly. In splitting workers into documented and undocumented, men from women, and citizens from noncitizens, the work crews were tied politically to those least protected in the crews, and work stability could be more or less ensured. In applying this system of hiring and deployment of labor, the potential for shared camaraderie was correspondingly lessened, given the separate functions and varying political rights accorded to each category of worker. This is especially evident in the case of women who were concentrated in the wrapping section of the process and the least remunerated of all the workers. Here again, the definition of "women's work" and the status assigned to such a category aligned them closest to the undocumented workers in the perceptions of the growers. Taken together, growers survey the needs of the enterprise and create an artificial workplace hierarchy to discipline and control labor.

In step with the growing concentration of Mexican immigrants within the agricultural economy, a widespread rural segregated residential pattern has emerged. Between 1960 and roughly 1990 the Mexican presence in agricultural sectors of the California economy mirrored the concentration of Mexican immigrants in inner cities. Perceptions of lettuce workers, like those of agricultural workers, tend to imply that they reside out of the main political and social "streams." In fact, their assimilation into the corporate structure translates into discrete residential patterns. The research of Juan Vicente Palerm demonstrates the growing ruralization of the Mexican immigrant community over the last two decades of the twentieth century, inseparable from its economic role in the region. Rural California, like inner cities, serves as an economic entry point for Mexican immigrants, a social process interconnected with an increasing demand for agricultural labor, albeit cheap labor, *within a state boasting the sixth-largest economy in the world.* Palerm notes that in the late 1980s Mexicans and to a lesser degree Mexican Americans constituted at least 65 percent of the residents in sixty-one agricultural communities.[30] In no less than fourteen of these communities, the Spanish-surnamed, overwhelmingly Mexican immigrants and Mexican Americans comprised 80 percent or more of its residents. Another sixty-one communities counted at least one-third of its population as Mexican or Mexican American, and in another twenty-four communities at least 17 percent of the residents were so identified. In all of these examples, the vast majority of Mexican and Mexican-American residents live in segregated *and impoverished* quarters, although they are indispensable to and consequently integrated into the agricultural economy.[31]

As in the case of railroad and citrus workers earlier in the twentieth century, the economic life and social experience of lettuce workers cannot be separated into spheres isolated from the larger social and economic processes. Nor can the success of each economic branch bear explanation without recognizing the critical importance of free access to Mexican immigrant labor, a labor pool marked by the state with qualities that privately owned agribusinesses seize upon, measure, and incorporate into a preferred organization of "industrial relations."

Domestic Service

The employment of Mexican immigrant workers and their descendants has never been solely the province of large firms and businesses. Domestic work constitutes a telling example that also shows the ways in which Mexican labor—in this case the labor of women—has become deeply imbedded into the everyday life of urban middle-class America.[32] This is especially the case in major urban centers in the U.S. Southwest. U.S.–born Mexican-American women, immigrant women holding green cards, women commuters who live in Mexico and travel to work in the United States, and undocumented women all work in domestic service in the cities near the border and in the Southwest as a whole. As Mary Romero points out in her book on domestic work, "domestic service remains undesirable work, and only women with no other options enter the occupation."[33] Romero points to the conscious role of the state in the regulation and gendering of labor flows from Mexico. In El Paso, she states, "[t]he hiring of maids from Mexico was so common that locals referred to Monday as the border patrol's day off because the agents ignored the women crossing the border to return to their employers' homes after their weekend off."[34]

The importance of domestic work remains imponderable and, in a way, "invisible," as most of the employer/employee transactions are carried out on an informal basis. Thus, aside from a few outstanding case studies, there are no firm aggregate estimates of the size of the domestic service workforce in the United States. The underground character of the domestic service economy is more pronounced in the case of undocumented workers, who have a vested interested in hiding their status. But a few high-profile cases—for example, President Bill Clinton's early candidates for the post of attorney general, Zoe Baird and Kimba Wood; President George W. Bush's proposed candidate for secretary of labor, Linda Chavez; opposing candidates in the 1994 California senate race, Michael Huffington and Diane Feinstein; and then mayor of San Diego and future governor of California

Pete Wilson—showed that the hiring of undocumented Mexican and/or Latina women to perform household chores reaches into every corner of the U.S. economy, not only in the Southwest.[35] Given the number of publicized cases of illegal employment of undocumented workers, we should not be surprised at the extent of their employment beyond the confines of the political elite. Romero refers to an indirect estimate of the number of domestic service workers in El Paso in the mid-1980s: "Half of the 28,300 daily trips taken on the city buses are maids."[36]

A number of factors led to an explosion in the number of domestic workers in the United States in the last three decades of the twentieth century. During those three decades, a decline in the purchasing power of the one-salary home, the increase in the number of college and professionally trained U.S. women, as well as the rise of middle-class women's feminist ideology, which privileged working outside the home, coincided with changes in immigration policy, such as family reunification programs and amnesty programs under the 1986 Immigration Reform and Control Act. These, in turn, encouraged the increase in migration of, first, Mexican women, and from the early 1980s on, Salvadoran, Guatemalan, and Nicaraguan women and families. Other statistics complete the scenario. A report by the U.S. Department of Labor showed that in 1997 46 percent of married women were employed in full-time jobs, up from 22 percent in 1969. Not only are married women entering the labor force in greater numbers, they are also doing so when the average workweek is steadily increasing. A study conducted by the International Labor Organization found that U.S. workers increased their annual working hours from 1,883 in 1980 to 1,966 in 1997. These factors were critical to an exhaustive study of nannies and maids in Orange County, California, conducted by San Diego State University political scientist Kristine Hill Maher. She found that a continually increasing demand for nannies and housekeepers led to the development of a thriving formal market in recruiting agencies. However, the increasing numbers of Latinas overmatches the demand such that domestic help is affordable for some in the middle class as well.[37] No wonder that the number of agencies placing nannies and housekeepers servicing the upper- and upper-middle-class areas of Orange County rose from four in 1990 to twenty in 2000. One agency alone placed eleven hundred nannies before it was shut down, allegedly for urging undocumented workers to acquire false papers with a conspiring partner.[38] One observer noted, "These agencies . . . are a clearinghouse for harried mothers who need help at home and for new immigrants eager to find work."[39] However, agency fees as large as 85 percent of the first month's salary encourage a system of informal networks for finding employment. Family and social networks can and often do bypass the agencies, and it is not uncommon for potential employers to take advantage of these networks, particularly for swapping nannies from one employer to another as children grow older and are able to care for themselves.

In her study of domestic work in Los Angeles, Pierrette Hondagneu-Sotelo illustrates the many ways in which the abundant presence of domestic servants in Los Angeles (as well as day workers, gardeners, tree trimmers, house painters, hotel chamber maids, etc.) is part of the fabric of that urban center, making life easier and cheaper for those who can afford the services. She cites a study that indicates that twice as many domestic workers were working in Los Angeles in 1990 as in 1980.[40] In her eleven-month investigation on domestics in Orange County, Los Angeles County's next-door neighbor, Maher also found a dramatic increase in the percentage of Latinas in the domestic workforce. In 1970 Latinas comprised 19 percent of women employed as domestics; twenty years later the percentage of Latinas in the domestic force rose to 70 percent and continues on the upswing.[41] In aggregate figures the number of Latinas in Orange County working in households rose from 703 in 1970 to more than 5,000 in 1990. The increase in Los Angeles County was equally dramatic. In 1970 the figure stood at 5,283 but rose to an astounding 33,770 in 1990.[42]

After the nanny (or, more accurately, "private household worker") has found work (or perhaps after she has been "found" by an employer), she now begins another vital search. Transportation from the residence of the domestic to the workplace is always a troublesome matter. Most women have no car or other means of private transport, and if not working as a live-in must rely on public transportation—the "nanny express"—to ferry them to and from work. Usually such trips are two and often two and half hours of riding on up to three different bus routes to reach their destination. But the daily journey is not finished; she must then walk some distance, frequently a half hour to an hour, to the employer's residence.[43] Valeria Godines reported on one women's first day at work, an experience commonly encountered on a daily basis by *niñeras:* "Shortly after dawn on a rainy Monday morning, [Josefina] Macias set out for her first day of work. . . . Clutching her lunch, she took two buses to get somewhat near the neighborhood. Then she marched under the pearl-gray sky for about an hour before arriving at the community."[44] Some bus routes, such as bus 57 from Santa Ana, California, begins its daily run to affluent southern Orange County areas at 4:57 A.M. Nannies, maids, and housecleaners ride to neighborhoods guarded by gated entrances and others with impressive flower-decked entries that set them worlds apart from the communities and everyday lives of the nannies and housekeepers.

Earnings on average are barely enough to maintain the women. In 1997 Maher found that the average weekly wage for live-ins was slightly more than $150.00 while live-outs earned slightly less than $180.00 per week. The hourly average for the former stood at $2.30, while the latter's wages averaged $3.80 per hour. Not surprisingly, most of the women are undocumented, seldom are their papers required by the employers, and few pay payroll taxes or withhold Social Security and Medicare taxes. Indeed, the nanny industry is largely underground in an economic sense, yet knitted into the fabric of American society. And it is out in the open—no one tries to hide his or her nanny or maid from friends or neighbors. If a language problem exists, local supermarkets often carry small books of common English expressions (e.g., "sweep the floor") translated into "easy" Spanish for assisting employers to guide the nanny on her chores. Everyone knows and no one cares, so maids seldom have reason to hide their "profile," that is, no need to worry that their appearance may betray their legal status. But this is only the case while working. In Newport Beach or Beverly Hills they are off-limits to the Immigration and Naturalization Service.

Well-manicured neighborhood association parks with swings and sandboxes (cared for by Mexican men contracted by gardening agencies who knowingly hire the undocumented) provide social gathering places for the women as they bring in baby carriages or strollers filled with snacks, diapers, and, of course, the infant or toddler. Here they may celebrate a cohort's birthday, discuss job openings, voice personal family matters, and complain about their employers. Employing nannies and housekeepers (as in the case of the gardeners) has become an aboveboard, albeit illegal, practice that authorities deliberately overlook, even by those who stridently denounce illegal immigration. Nannies, maids, and housecleaners exemplify the historical centrality of cheap, mobile, reliable, skilled, and manageable Mexican labor to the U.S. economy. The benefits are clear and openly embraced, or as one syndicated journalist wrote, "The readiness of off-the-books workers who care for children . . . and perform other duties maximizes employment and frees those with greater skills— mainly women—for higher-paying jobs."[45]

The Pacific Corridor

No case exemplifies better the full and complete integration of Mexican labor into the U.S. economy than the economy of the Pacific Corridor. That is the name given to a subregion composed of northern Baja California and southern California. The subregion contains three of the largest cities along the North American Pacific Rim: Los Angeles and San Diego (the second- and sixth-largest U.S. cities), and the estimated 2-million city of Tijuana. The 225-mile stretch between Santa Barbara in the north to Ensenada in the south contains nearly 30 million people. This urban megalopolis differs from previously described urban complexes in one important sense. The original megalopolis—the eastern seaboard of the United States studied by Jean Gottman three decades ago—and locations in Japan, China, and elsewhere are situated within the borders of a single nation.[46] *The Pacific Corridor is the only binational megalopolis of its kind in the world, a global city of a new type.* It constitutes an economic network that transcends the U.S.–Mexico boundary and is built on Mexican labor of every possible description.

The Mexico side of the corridor is the home of the maquila industry. Total maquiladora employment on the Mexican border hovers at about 700,000 workers, the vast majority being women. Approximately 1,081 maquilas—one-quarter of all maquilas in Mexico—and more than 215,000 workers—about 20 percent of the total maquila workforce in Mexico—labor in "strategically located" plants in four Baja California cities not far from the U.S.–Mexico border: Tijuana, Tecate, Mexicali, and Ensenada.[47] The maquiladoras, most of which are operated by large U.S. corporations belonging to the exclusive *Fortune* 1,000, have been operating in that region for more than three decades. During that time Tijuana, which has more than 700 maquilas (more maquilas than any other city in Mexico) has become the center for the world's production of televisions—for the American consumer.

The relationship between employment and manufacturing in southern California and maquiladora production is complementary rather than competitive. Over the past twenty years, whenever manufacturing employment declines or grows in southern California, it also declines or grows in northern Baja California. The industrial economy of southern California and the maquiladoras are linked simply because maquiladora production is usually no more than one face in the production cycle of one commodity—the one requiring the largest labor component. As a result, the whole industrial economy of the region oscillates simultaneously. A recent example is telling: in the first three months of 2001, as the economy of southern California began to slide, maquiladora employment took a massive dive. In the first months of 2001 more than 250,000 maquila workers throughout Mexico received dismissal notices; along the border area 100,000 joined the ranks of the unemployed.[48] An already impoverished population fell deeper into difficulty. Even during periods of high employment in the maquilas, poverty associated with the worst of conditions in the Third World marked the Mexican—that is, the maquila—side of the border. In Tijuana, hundreds of maquilas employing nearly 150,000 crowd the landscape, yet half of the city's population lives under the poverty level as measured by Mexican standards. Meanwhile, "only 5 percent of all families are able to meet their basic needs without difficulty."[49] Thus a truth was expressed in a newspaper headline that read, "*Maquiladoras* Offer Work but Not Prosperity . . . Many laborers . . . still find themselves living in squalor."[50] Studies have shown that of Mexico's border cities, Tijuana exhibits the "highest morbidity and mortality rates."[51] While living standards were deplorable, maquila start-up agencies on the U.S. side advertised a "plentiful labor supply" and the wage disparity between the United States and Mexico as "attractive options" that offered an average savings of $17,000 annually per worker. In other words, squalor and ill health in Tijuana, and all along the border, are integral functions of a "free trade" formula that touts "high productivity and low cost of labor."[52]

Not all labor resident on the Mexican side of the border is employed in manufacturing, nor is it all female labor. Part of the corridor is made up of a lesser known agricultural "hinterland," as it were, which a simple example will illustrate. In the fall of 1989, Los Angeles newspapers announced that a white poinsettia fly infestation had hit Imperial Valley. Why might this be important? The massive infestation affected the production of cantaloupe, melon, and other fruits. Within one week three things had happened: Farmers in Imperial Valley were losing money, what with the ruin of their crops. Consumers in Los Angeles found a decline in the quality, and a rise in the price, of fruit products. And the agricultural workers of Imperial Valley found themselves without employment. Who are these agricultural workers? Roughly 90 percent of the laborers, approximately 30,000, who work the vast fields of Imperial Valley are *commuters*. These are workers who live in Mexico–in Mexicali or surrounding areas—but work north of the border. Every day nearly thirty thousand workers— mostly males—walk or drive from Mexico to the United States to work in Imperial County, which provides many agricultural products for consumption in southern California and the nation.[53]

Thus we have Mexican women working in industrial production in Mexico proper, and Mexican men working in agriculture in the United States. North of the border, in the remaining counties that comprise southern California—San Diego, Riverside, San Bernardino, Orange, Los Angeles, Ventura, and Santa Barbara—we find Mexican men and women, legal or undocumented, working in agricultural production, services, and industry. Throughout southern California homes are cleaned, babies cared for, lawns manicured, trees trimmed, garbage put out, houses painted, and cars washed by cheap labor, men and women, legal and undocumented, contract workers or day laborers. The same kinds of laborers produce garments; do janitorial work; provide the backbone of the enormous hotel, recreational, and restaurant industry, one the pillars of the corridor's economy; clean business offices; and work in large numbers in construction and manufacturing. While estimates of the number of undocumented Mexican laborers in the United States vary between 8 million and 12 million, it is safe to say that a significant proportion, numbering in the millions, are employed in the southern California sector of the Pacific Corridor economy. Virtually all work available to the undocumented and documented cited here falls into the category of "dead end" jobs—jobs that offer little opportunity for "mobility" to a higher skilled position.

Historically, the cities of southern California and northern Baja California, from Santa Barbara to Ensenada, grew in tandem throughout the twentieth century. Agriculture growth, water development, and urbanization along the entire corridor, north and south of the border, occurred simultaneously, on the basis of the enormous supply of cheap Mexican labor of every legal, gender, occupational, or skill description. Thus the dense integration we describe today is not a recent phenomenon; it was a constant throughout the twentieth century. It has only grown in sheer magnitude in the past three decades.

The 2000 U.S. census returns verified that a century of migration continued into the next century. Traditional trends survived, such as the concentration of migrant settlements in two states, California and Texas; however, the vast majority are settling into California, and primarily the southern region contiguous with Baja California. Between 1990 and 2000 the Latino population of the state nearly doubled, but it is in the southern part of the state where the growth was most telling. In Los Angeles County alone, more than 4 million Latinos make their home, and in Los Angeles, nearly 47 percent of its 3.6 million residents are Latinos. Southern California contains at least ten urban cities that are predominantly populated by Mexican immigrants and their descendants. Four of these are among the ten communities across the United States with a population of at least 100,000 containing the highest concentrations of Latinos. East Los Angeles leads in this respect, where nearly 98 percent of its residents are Latino; followed by Santa Ana, 76 percent; El Monte, 72 percent; and Oxnard, 66 percent.

However, these statistics are matched by the population explosion on the Mexican side of the border. The *New York Times* reported, "Lured by jobs in American-owned plants, more than 1 million people in the last five years [1995–2000] have migrated from Mexico's impoverished south to cities along the northern border."[54] Tijuana's population swelled from 341,000 in 1970 to an estimated 2 million in 2000. According to the San Diego State University Institute for Regional Studies of the Californias, Tijuana's population increased at an annual rate of 7 percent between 1990 and 1995, the years of the largest maquila increase spurred by the passage of NAFTA. However, the border town's upsurge derived from sources other than natural increase, given that nearly 60 percent of the city's population migrated from elsewhere in Mexico. With its "twin city," San Diego, the two form "the largest international border community in the world."[55] But an important distinction remains: Tijuana maquila workers assemble a variety of commodities, including televisions, for sale in the United States; San Diego firms (among others in the United States) finance, design the research, and otherwise control the production of those goods.

Sociological studies that look only at the U.S. side of the Mexican labor question, and focus on what is sometimes called Greater Mexico, tend to emphasize issues familiar with students of U.S. society, such as questions of the potential "integration" of ethnic Mexicans into the mythical U.S. "mainstream." Not all authors see a Greater Mexico from the U.S. side; a few adopt it while narrating Mexico's history. Whether applied by Mexican specialists or Chicano studies specialists, the concept remains a kind of unquestioned conventional wisdom and is essentially identical regardless of which side of the border the concept is employed.[56] For such U.S.-centric approaches, history and sociology stop at the border's edge. By looking at the Pacific Corridor, by examining how the powerful U.S. economy extends into Mexico as a kind of "Greater U.S.A.," one is able to look beyond the cultural issues so prevalent in the Chicano-related literature in the United States, going beyond cultural and racial questions to lay bare the thick and deep integration between Mexican labor and U.S. monopoly capitalism.

Notes

1. Cited in Karl Marx, *Capital*, 3 vols. (New York: International Publishers, 1967), I: 768.
2. Max S. Handman, "Economic Reason for the Coming of the Mexican Immigrant," *American Journal of Sociology* 35 (January 1930): 601–11.
3. Donald Worster, *Rivers of Empire: Water, Aridity, and the Growth of the American West* (New York: Pantheon, 1985), passim.
4. Daniel J. Pisani, *From the Family Farm to Agribusiness: The Irrigation Crusade in California and the West, 1850–1931* (Berkeley: University of California Press, 1984).
5. Karl Wittfogel, *Oriental Despotism: A Comparative Study of Total Power* (New Haven, Conn.: Yale University Press, 1952).
6. Gilbert G. Gonzalez, *Progressive Education: A Marxist Critique* (Minneapolis: Marxist Educational Press, 1982), 21.
7. Jeffrey Marcos Garcilazo, "Traqueros: Mexican Railroad Workers in the United States, 1870–1930" (typescript, 1998), 27.
8. Victor Clark, *Mexican Labor in the United States*, U. S. Department of Commerce and Labor, Bureau of Labor Bulletin 78 (Washington, D.C.: U.S. Government Printing Office, 1908), 475.
9. Ibid., 477.
10. Samuel Bryan, "Mexican Immigrants in the United States," *Survey* 28 (September 1912): 728.
11. Garcilazo, "Traqueros," 103–4.
12. Ibid., 240.
13. Ibid., 229, 264.
14. Ibid., 241.
15. Ibid., 88.
16. Bryan, "Mexican Immigrants," 728.
17. Clark, *Mexican Labor*, 477.
18. Hebert John Webber, "The Commercial Citrus Regions of the World: Their Physiographic, Climatic, and Economic Characters," in *The Citrus Industry*, edited by Herbert John Webber and Leon Dexter Batchelor (Berkeley: University of California Press, 1943), 71.

19. Carey McWilliams, *Southern California Country: An Island on the Land* (New York: Duell, Sloan, & Pearce, 1946), 212.

20. U.S. Senate Committee on Education and Labor, *Violations of Free Speech and Rights of Labor*, Report of the Committee on Education and Labor (Washington, D.C.: U.S. Government Printing Office, 1942), 539.

21. Mark Reisler, *By the Sweat of Their Brow: Mexican Immigrant Labor in the United States, 1900–1940*, 100–101.

22. Vicki L. Ruiz, *Cannery Women, Cannery Lives: Mexican Women, Unionization, and the California Food Processing Industry, 1930–1950* (Albuquerque: University of New Mexico Press, 1987).

23. Ibid., 23.

24. *Los Angeles Times*, May 10, 2001.

25. See Kathleen Reynolds and George Kourous, "Farmworkers: An Overview of Health, Safety, and Wage Issues," *Borderlines* 6, no. 8 (October 1998); Philip L. Martin and J. Edward Taylor, "For California Farmworkers, Future Holds Little Prospect for Change," *California Agriculture* (January–February 2000): 19–20; Philip Martin, "Poverty Amid Prosperity," Report of the Summary of a Conference on Immigration and the Changing Face of Rural California, University of California, Davis, October 9, 1997; and Alicia Bugarin and Elias S. Lopez, "Farmworkers in California," California Research Bureau, California State Library, July 1998.

26. Juan Vicente Palerm, "Farm Labor Needs and Farm Workers in California, 1970 to 1989," report, California State Development Department, California Agricultural Studies. Labor Market Information Division, April 1991, 67.

27. Robert J. Thomas, *Citizenship, Gender, and Work: Social Organization of Industrial Agriculture* (Berkeley: University of California Press, 1985), 41.

28. Harry Bernstein, "Growers Addicted to Foreign Workers," *Los Angeles Times*, October 2, 1985; Martha Groves, "Window of Opportunity?" *Los Angeles Times*, October 2, 1997; Martin and Taylor, "For California's Farmworkers, Future Holds Little Prospect for Change," 21; and Reynolds and Kourous, "Farmworkers: An Overview," 2.

29. Thomas, *Citizenship, Gender, and Work*, 105. Thomas writes: "Citizenship is a key variable in the allocation of individuals to the positions in the labor process and, subsequently, in the allocation of rewards associated with those positions. The critical dimension informing the citizenship variable is political vulnerability. Each level of citizenship—citizen, documented, and undocumented—represents a different level of vulnerability or susceptibility to external influence based on the formal legal mechanisms for controlling and legitimating claims on the polity."

30. Palerm, "Farm Labor Needs," ii.

31. See J. Edward Taylor and Philip L. Martin, "Central Valley Evolving into Patchwork of Poverty and Prosperity," *California Agriculture* 54, no. 1 (2000): 1.

32. Latina and Mexican women have occupied the forefront of domestic employment to such a degree that they now fill the acting roles for housekeepers, nannies, and the like in television and films. In a career spanning 25 years, actress Lupe Ontiveros has acted in at least 150 roles as a maid in commercial films such as *As Good as It Gets* and in sitcoms such as *Veronica's Closet*. As Ontiveros commented, "It's their [the film industry's] continued perspective of who we are. . . . When I go in there and speak perfect English, I don't get the part." Noted TV and film historian J. Fred McDonald commented, "The baton has passed from Black actors to Hispanic actors to play this kind of stereotypical role." Mireya Navarro, "Trying to Get Beyond the Role of Maid," *New York Times*, May 16, 2002.

33. Mary Romero, *Maid in the U.S.A.* (New York: Routledge, 1992), 66.

34. Ibid., 1. See also Michael Quintanilla and Peter Copeland, "Mexican Maids: El Paso's Worst Kept Secret," in *U.S.–Mexico Borderlands: Historical and Contemporary Perspectives*, edited by Oscar Martinez (Wilmington, Del.: Scholarly Resources, 1997), 213–21.

35. In the early seventies it was discovered that at President Richard Nixon's San Clemente presidential retreat, undocumented Mexicans worked among the gardeners tending the grounds.

36. Mary Romero, *Maid in the U.S.A.*, 92.

37. Valeria Godines, "Statistics on Servants Aren't Easily Documented," *Orange County Register*, April 8, 2001; Valeria Godines, "Foreign and Domestic," *Orange County Register*, April 8, 2001.

38. Don Lee, "Trust Built and Broken," *Los Angeles Times*, January 14, 1997.

39. Godines, "Foreign and Domestic."
40. Pierrette Hondagneu-Sotelo, *Doméstica: Immigrant Workers Cleaning and Caring in the Shadows of Affluence* (Berkeley: University of California Press, 2001), 7.
41. Godines, "Foreign and Domestic."
42. Kristine Hill Maher, "A Stranger in the House: American Ambivalence about Immigrant Labor," Ph.D. diss., University of California, Irvine, 1999, 5. Maher points out that whereas in 1980 "Hispanic Origin" women comprised 4 percent of the total employed in households, by 1990 the figure had increased to 6 percent, 8.
43. Godines, "Foreign and Domestic."
44. Ibid.
45. Daniel Akst, "Our Economy Is Anchored Underground," *Los Angeles Times*, June 18, 1991; An estimated 20,000 day workers in southern California stand on street corners, parking lots, and other gathering spaces waiting for temporary manual labor assignments. These men work in gardening crews, construction, house painting, and other lines. See Raul Anorve and Torie Osborn, "*Jornaleros* Deserve Dignity," *Los Angeles Times*, July 27, 2001.
46. Jean Gottman, *Megalopolis: The Urbanized Northeastern Seaboard of the United States* (New York: Twentieth Century Fund, 1961). See also Brian Hook, ed., *Beijing and Tiajin: Towards a Millennial Megalopolis* (New York: Oxford University Press, 1998).
47. Manufacturing and Economic Information. *http://www.tijuana-edc.com/html/man_info. html.*
48. Graham Gori, "Goodyear Cuts Jobs in Mexico," *New York Times*, May 1, 2001.
49. Evelyn Iritani, Chris Kraul, and Tyler Marshall, "Global Showdown Will Hit Home," *Los Angeles Times*, March 26, 2001.
50. Patrick McDonnell, "Maquiladoras Offer Work but Not Prosperity," *Los Angeles Times*, June 17, 1991.
51. Regional Pediatric Information. *http://www.usfcc.org/3b_regionalinfo.html.*
52. Maquiladora Subcontract Manufacturing in Mexico. VerTek. About Maquilas. *http://www. mexicomfg.com/maquiladora.html.;* and Mexico Maquiladora Manufacturing. About the Maquiladora Industry. *http://www.maquila.com.insider.html.*
53. For a detailed analysis of the economic integration of the economy of Imperial Valley with Mexico see Raul Fernandez, "The Economic Evolution of the Imperial (U.S.A.) and Mexicali (Mexico) Valleys," *Journal of Borderlands Studies* 6, no. 2 (1987).
54. The *New York Times. http://www.nytimes.com/ima . . . d/010211_for_MEXICOch.html.*
55. San Diego State University, Institute for Regional Studies of the Californias. Tijuana, Basic Information. *http://www.usfcc.org/3b_regionllinfo.html;* Regional Pediatric Information. *http://www.usfcc.org/3b_regionalinfo.html.*
56. See, e.g., the work of Mexican history specialists William H. Beezely and Colin M. MacLachlan, *El Gran Pueblo: A History of Greater Mexico, 1911 to the Present*, vol. 2 (Englewood Cliffs, N.J.: Prentice Hall, 1994), 441–46.

VI

Denying Empire
The Journal of American History on the Ideological Warpath

The business of rationalizing, explaining away, or obfuscating the realities of imperialisms and empire building is not the exclusive province of the nonacademic world of travelers, missionaries, journalists, and other molders of popular opinion. As the United States intensified tenfold its stranglehold over the Mexican economy with the enactment of NAFTA, no less an august and presumably "objective" scholarly publication as the *Journal of American History,* the official organ of the Organization of American Historians, threw its weight behind this new phase of domination over its southern neighbor.

Declaring, "Challenges to the nation-state challenge history to its core," editor David Thelen set the stage for a wide-ranging special issue of the *Journal of American History* (1999) titled "Rethinking History and the Nation-State: Mexico and the United States as a Case Study." Nation-states, argues Thelen, are "less self-evidently necessary or desirable, and more fragile and constructed" and this is reflected in the increase in Mexico–U.S. border crossings, which, among other things, "challenge traditional claims of both nation-states."[1] Consequently, historians need to reassess conventional thought regarding the nation-state. Toward this goal, nine invited articles and interviews of five prominent Mexican personages implore readers to "explore and rethink connections between history and the nation-state." The authors and five interviewees elaborate on that objective on a variety of subjects, including the movement toward democracy in Mexico, the rule of the market in U.S.–Mexico relations, U.S.–Mexico economic integration, the primacy of the transnational corporation in the contemporary nation-state, migration, and the "third space," or the communities that migrants form in the United States. The journal editor professes that the "articles prepared for this special issue . . . present a fresh sense of what may be at stake in doing history amid transnational realities."

In this chapter we interrogate that conclusion by critically reviewing representative articles, with particular attention to the virtual negation of empire that courses throughout the issue. Through the medium of challenging history and the nation-state the special volume of the *Journal of American History* silences the history of the U.S. empire. Rather than forging a "fresh sense" of "transnational realities," that silencing sustains an institutionalized practice in U.S. political and academic thought. The first portion of this chapter focuses on two areas: the central presence of Mexican government representatives as contributors to the special issues and their analysis of the activities of Mexican consuls within the expatriate community; and the discussion of U.S. intellectuals within U.S.–Mexico relations. The second section of the chapter briefly examines some common themes that appear throughout the special issue.[2] Those themes suggest the most traditional, top-down, and well-worn paths in U.S. and Chicano historiography. Here we find the conventional periodization of Mexican-American history, the push-pull treatment of Mexican migration to the United States, and a deafening gender silence that permeates the material. We also explore the contradictory treatment of the notion of the "weakening of the nation," and finally the *JAH* authors' musings about NAFTA, economic integration, and the current process of democratization in Mexico.

The Consulates and Mexicanidad

Three of the invited contributors are high-level officials of the Mexican foreign service. The consuls of Boston and Houston, and the director of the Division of Hispanic Affairs in the Mexican embassy in Washington, D.C., were cordially invited to present their views on an allegedly self-modifying nation-state system increasingly at the mercy of the transnational market. That the leading journal in the field provided ample space for presentations that "explore" and "rethink" the nation-state from several foreign ministry officials seems rather unusual. The positions these men hold in Mexico's foreign office, and therefore within the Partido Revolucionario Institucional (PRI), the ruling party over seventy years, strongly suggest that they express the voice of Mexico's elite. The foreign office dignitaries, all career diplomats, made it abundantly clear that they were not advancing their personal views but were expressing official policy of their home government. (That the three were introduced in the biographical sketches as officers of the Mexican government made explicit that they represented Mexico's official position on foreign relations.) We expect, then, that the officials speaking in the special issue were voicing the PRI position on foreign relations.

Two diplomatic officers elaborated on programs aimed at the Mexican immigrant community in the United States and administered by Mexico's Secretariat of Foreign Relations. The consul general in Houston, Rudolfo Figueroa Aramoni, former ambassador to Colombia and ex-director of the Program for Mexican Communities Abroad, detailed the activities of the program, which he described as a "key instrument of Mexico's foreign policy."[3] According to issue contributor Carlos González Gutiérrez, then head of the Division of Hispanic Affairs (who later joined President-elect Vicente Fox Quezada's transition team as adviser and speechwriter on Hispanic affairs—that is, on emigrants in the United States), the program aims at nothing less than a "close, long-term relationship with the people of Mexican ancestry in the United States."[4] That relationship comes with the expectation by the Mexican state of raising the "awareness of belonging to the Mexican nation," a cultural landscape that "extends beyond the territory contained by its borders."[5]

The Mexican government, through the medium of its forty-two consular offices in the United States, sponsors a variety of activities via the program intended to develop Mexicanidad, a sense of Mexicanness, or loyalty to, and pride in, the homeland, the Mexican nation-state. (There are other stated reasons, too, including ensuring the flow of remittances, supposedly a defense of migrants' human rights, and promoting Chicanos as a pressure group regarding issues of interest to the Mexican nation-state.) González Gutiérrez describes the state's role as creating a "diasporic consciousness" among the migrant community. (Mexican migration translates into "diaspora.") The program sponsors, among other things, six thousand sports leagues, urban cultural centers, bilingual teachers for U.S. public schools, and a guest speaker program that features state governors invited to speak to, and meet with, expatriates from those states. (We can assume that previous to President Vicente Fox, these guest speakers were either members of the Partido Revolucionario Institucional or were in accord with its foreign policies.) These several activities are expected to elicit cultural solidarity across borders. In raising the consciousness of a transnational Mexicanidad, the border supposedly loses its power to divide and separate two sovereign nations and cultures.

Several questions arise in relation to the historical record that these officials submit in connection to Mexico's northern policy. Mexico's representatives contend that these activities promoted by the Mexican state among their emigrants in the United States originate from a relatively new guiding principle within the Secretariat of Foreign Relations. González Gutiérrez, for example, declares, "Until recently Mexico did not cultivate the consciousness of a 'dispersed people' among its emigrants." Further, he alleges that in the past Mexico "forgot our emigrants, with the shameful attitude of a mother who has abandoned her children and does not want to know about them."[6] Here, either González Gutiérrez's historical knowledge and/or his veracity can be called into question.

Contrary to González Gutiérrez's contentions, the PRI (and its antecedents formed after the 1910 Revolution) and thus the Mexican state exhibits a long history of interventions into the political affairs of the expatriate community through the consulate system. After the massive migrations and settlement during the 1910s and 1920s, the postrevolutionary Mexican state assumed a high political profile within the rapidly growing emigrant community, or *Mexico de afuera*, as the "diaspora" was then called. Moreover, the record shows that Mexico sought nothing less than to orchestrate and dominate the political culture of the expatriate community and subordinate *Mexico de afuera* to the governing party.

That presence by the Mexican state via its consulates within the incipient Mexican migrant communities, like the consuls in the late twentieth century, emphasized a nationalist cultural program within the Americanizing environment. At its core, the early examples of Mexicanidad always corresponded with postrevolutionary politics. (Late-twentieth-century versions of Mexicanidad display a parallel political correspondence with the main contours of contemporary domestic and foreign policies.) The underlying objectives, shrouded within a strident nationalistic rhetoric of cultural preservation, aimed to incorporate the Mexican community into the political ideology and institutions of the Mexican nation-state. Beginning in the early 1920s the fifty Mexican consulates across the United States engaged in a high-priority strategy for organizing the Mexican emigrant community and launched activities that promoted political allegiance to the state. Across the United States, wherever a sizable Mexican community formed, consuls energetically engaged the task of organizing consulate-directed groups in the Mexican community.[7]

One major undertaking involved instituting *comisiones honoríficas* (honorary commissions) and honorary consuls to act as political extensions of the consulate within the expatriate community. According to the Secretariat of Foreign Relations' statements from the 1920s, three tasks occupied the consulate-controlled comisiones. First, to "maintain alive and constant the memory and love of Mexico"; second, to "remind Mexicans of the duty to their fatherland"; and third, to "serve as a connector between Mexicans . . . and the consulate."[8] Consuls dominated the activities of each comision. For example, the regulations governing comisiones stipulated that the local consul appoint the president of the comision and supervise their activities. In areas of large migrant concentrations, numerous comisiones could be found operating to preserve Mexicanidad and to extend the influence of the consulate. In 1940 the southern California region alone contained forty comisiones operating under the administrative eye of the consulate.

Comisiones managed the Independence Day celebrations, took annual censuses of the community, organized funeral societies, established evening schools to impart Mexicanidad, rallied to support the official candidate for the presidency, and, when called on by the Mexican state, organized conservative labor unions under consulate supervision. The Los Angeles version of the comision, the Confederación de Sociedades Mexicanas, was directed in 1927 by President Calles to form a labor union, an order that the organization complied with immediately. But as the then consul, Ignacio Pesquiera, pointed out in local newspapers, the first Mexican union in California also comprised the first branch of the Mexican labor central, Confederación Regional Obrera Mexicana (CROM), in the United States.[9] CROM served as a ruling-party-controlled and patronage-plagued union. (More on CROM later in this chapter.)

Consulates were charged with extending the influence of the Mexican government into every important Mexican settlement and emerged as the principal organizing force in the Mexican communities. For sure, that organizing steered clear of intervening into "sensitive" areas. From the early years of the century Mexican children attended segregated public schools, yet not once did the consulates become centers of protest against school segregation. Nor were consulates critical of the aggressive Americanization and, on the basis of "intelligence" tests based on the pseudo-scientific racism of the period, of the heavy tracking into vocational education that public schools forced on the "diaspora." More often than not, the consuls found much to recommend in the American educational system of the 1920s and 1930s and even sponsored tours for Mexican educators to these segregated facilities.[10]

A seeming contradiction, Americanization and Mexicanization actually worked in tandem. Both programs aimed at creating class harmony, a functional political solidarity between classes that preserved the social and economic status quo. That mutual political objective made possible the cooperation between the two governments during the infamous repatriation drives and the workers' militancy of the 1930s. In the former instance, Mexico assisted U.S. authorities by urging Mexican immigrants to return; in the latter, the Mexican government sided with agribusiness to break independent unions, undermine strikes, and form company unions.

That presence was seldom more significant than during the Great Depression, when the Mexican government, through its consulates, cooperated with U.S. authorities to deport massive numbers of Mexican citizens and their U.S.-born dependents to Mexico. Under the pressure of U.S. county and state authorities eager to cut social expenditures, the Mexican government, in a not-so-subtle change in policy, turned from Mexicanidad to repatriation.[11] The 450,000 women, men, and children who supposedly returned voluntarily to Mexico, but did so only under threats and pressures of various kinds, constituted one of the largest mass national deportations in history. (Here it should be pointed out that the Mexican "diaspora" has never been a one-way flow. During the periodic state-directed repatriation drives, the migratory flow moves in the opposite direction, from the United States to Mexico. During the 1930s repatriation campaign, the majority of returnees were permanent residents rooted in the United States, and many were U.S. citizens; the greater part chose to return to the United States rather than remain permanently in Mexico.) However, without the steady cooperation of the Mexican consulates, that repatriation, intended primarily to serve U.S. economic interests, would never have been carried out so efficiently or effectively. On the other hand, when agribusiness, railroad, or mining corporations required labor, the Mexican government responded in splendid fashion. Throughout the 1900 to 1930 period the Mexican nation-state presented no obstacle to migration; moreover, they fostered it when possible.[12]

The presence of the consuls in the California farm worker labor movement of the 1930s also illustrates the significant political responsibilities, and their reactionary character, fulfilled by the consuls. Numerous examples of consulates cooperating fully with employers during the 1930s to break strikes, organize company unions, and stop radical and independent union movements dot the historical landscape. A number of studies have presented incontrovertible evidence of overt and covert consular actions to subvert independent and leftist union organizing and strikes.[13] The cases of the Los Angeles County farm worker strike and the San Joaquin Valley cotton pickers strike of 1933, the Imperial Valley farm worker strikes of 1933 and 1934, and the Orange County citrus picker strike of 1936 all demonstrated a decisive role by the consuls in the eventual outcomes of the strikes. In the instance of the Imperial Valley strike, the consul, at the behest of growers, became an organizer for a company union that undermined a leftist-led organization. In the San Joaquin Valley, the consul was called on to perform the same role but failed to break through worker solidarity. In the 1936 strike the consul, working under cover of police protection, operated behind the scenes to exclude radicals and hard-liners from the negotiating table. In the latter case, President Lazáro Cardenas rewarded the consul personally with a sinecure, a seat in the Mexican Congress.[14]

The role of consuls in breaking farm worker unions extended into the entire Southwest and Midwest with the advent of the binational Bracero Agreements. With the approval of the consular authorities, braceros not only were used as cheap farm labor but also served as unwitting strikebreakers when called on.[15] Agribusiness interests were well served by the consuls in several other ways. The agreements stipulated that the Mexican consular corps assume the responsibility for ensuring the observance of the worker protections cited in the agreements. However, as we documented in an earlier chapter, the consuls were notorious for their absence rather than for monitoring and enforcing bracero protections. The blatantly substandard working and living conditions experienced by braceros were rarely rectified, even when braceros forwarded formal complaints. Not only were the braceros denied proper living conditions, but also costs for health care and room and board were taken out of meager wages. Systematic gouging of the powerless laborers by contractors and local businesses was common, yet the consuls who were charged with ensuring that their nationals were guaranteed their rights were seldom to be heard. Consequently, the agreement protections were seldom implemented.[16]

Consular intervention, such as it was, did not end with the termination of the Bracero Agreements in 1964. The civil rights era brought renewed interest by the Mexican government in the Chicano movement of the 1960s and 1970s, and that government began to inject itself into the various organizations. Subsequent to these early ventures into that political era, the consuls broadened their responsibilities and renewed some of the practices of an earlier period. In the early 1970s the Mexican government founded the Office of Mexicans Living Abroad, housed within the Secretariat of Foreign Relations, with the responsibility of developing interactions and ties with the Chicano leadership and organizations. That office evolved into the Program of Mexicans Living Abroad, a "key instrument of Mexico's foreign policy," as mentioned earlier. Into the 1980s the consular presence rose dramatically, as they were called into action on an increased scale. President-elect Miguel de la Madrid Hurtado appointed a Chicano to serve as an adviser on Chicano affairs during his presidential campaign, and a series of meetings were called with the leadership of several Chicano organizations, including the Mexican-American Legal Defense Fund, the National Council of La Raza, and the League of United Latin-American Citizens. At one meeting de la Madrid committed the PRI "to fortify, expand, and systematize these linkages that, having their base history and sentiment, can evolve into forms of cooperation even more dynamic and positive."[17]

None of the suggestions for eliciting ties was controversial; the activities were of a conservative and nonthreatening character. President-elect de la Madrid offered, "One manner of defending the rights of these communities is to affirm their cultural identity and solidarity."[18] Affirming a shared "identity" and common interests across the border seemed the order of the day. However, while de la Madrid spoke of the late-twentieth-century version of Mexicanidad, the Mexican nation-state would enter a long economic depression with disastrous consequences for the middle and working classes and the peasantry. Undocumented migration rose steeply.

With the unabated economic crisis, the Mexican state under the leadership of the staunch neoliberal, Yale-educated president Salinas de Gortari, expanded the role of the consulates. Salinas de Gortari, like his presidential predecessors going back to Obregon in the early 1920s, proclaimed that the "linkages [with emigrants] should be actively promoted and strengthened."[19] However, the effort can only be explained by way of two important events: first, the context of the NAFTA debates in the U.S. Congress; and second, the election of 1988, pitting the Partido Revolucionario Democrático, led by PRI defector Cuauhtemoc Cárdenas, against the PRI. Like the election of 1929, the 1988 version brought Mexican domestic politics into the heart of *Mexico de afuera.*

The election of 1988 would not see the first north-of-the-border strategy for a Mexican presidential candidate. José Vasconcelos announced his run for the 1929 election in Chicago, and his followers campaigned energetically throughout the Southwest. The ruling party at the time, the Partido Nacional Revolucionario, founded by President Calles, responded in kind. The consulates and the comisiones honorificas crusaded determinedly, particularly in Los Angeles and Chicago. However, the PNR had access to comisiones, and that placed Vasconcelos at a disadvantage. The comisiones served as the campaign vehicle for Calles's handpicked candidate, Pascual Ortiz Rubio, who won the election by way of vote fraud. Similarly, the 1988 version brought the consulates into the fray and extended Mexican electoral politics north. The consulates became the medium to thwart the PRD's northern strategy to cultivate supporters and possibly voters and its moderate opposition to the emerging "fast track" on moving a free-trade agreement forward. The PRI responded with, among other plans, establishing fifty pro-PRI organizations from Los Angeles to Chicago. Although it appears that the old-guard PRI was caught off guard by the PRD strategy, the fraud-tainted election nonetheless went to the PRI and Salinas de Gortari. The northern strategy then shifted to lobbying for NAFTA in the United States.

NAFTA and its predecessor, GATT, derived from the free-market theories formulated by and for the dominant nation-states seeking regional economic advantages and a competitive "edge." With no alternative in sight, Mexico accepted the terms dictated by the northern world power and bought into the latest version of the open-door policy stipulated by the trade agreements. However, the treaty's passage through the U.S. House of Representatives was not a done deal; opposition arose from labor, and consequently politicians representing heavy working-class districts (which included many Mexican Americans) began to waver. The Hispanic Caucus in the House of Representatives, with a large contingent of Mexican Americans, emerged as the swing vote that could move NAFTA up or down. And to ensure that vote, the Mexican government, in close cooperation with the Clinton agenda, launched a $10 million lobbying effort largely focused on the Chicano legislators and the Chicano community. Mexican sociologist Arturo Santamaría Gómez reported that at that time regarding the Los Angeles consulate the "frequency of political functions attended by . . . powerful Mexican-American leaders from southern California is astonishing. Similarly, the ties between Los Angeles Mexican clubs, associations, and fraternities and the consulate [have] been greater under Salinas de Gortari than during the previous six decades."[20] A variety of cultural activities aimed at promoting NAFTA, from taped radio presentations, pre-Columbian art exhibits, book donations, and visits to Mexican communities by prominent Mexicans to special state medals for important Mexican Americans entered into the growing endeavor.

The actions of the Mexican nation-state within the Mexican communities throughout the twentieth century carry the policies, ideology, and politics of the ruling party of Mexico into the emigrant community. That presence is not disinterested or primarily concerned with questions of identity and Mexicanidad, as the consuls allege in the special issue of the *JAH*. The historical presence of the Mexican government via its consulates is steeped in Mexican state politics and is more of an example of a conventional nation-state than of an evolving nation-state. We cannot make the facile assumption that the PRI (or its more conservative and proneoliberal successor, the Partido de Acción Nacional [PAN]) operates with a more distinct political character north of the border than it does within its borders. Mexican state politics in the expatriate communities is an old practice, and in the *JAH* issue this history has been conveniently forgotten or overlooked. More important, the consular practices seldom if ever conflicted with international real politik: Mexico knows well the level of activities the United States finds acceptable and safely remains within those borders. The evidence does not indicate that the Mexican state is transforming (at least in regard to its north-of-the-border strategy); rather it appears that the state continues a long history of interventionist politics within the expatriate community, but an interventionist politics consonant with its economic subordination to the United States.

Unfortunately, the *JAH* special issue never undertook a critical examination of the views that the diplomats presented. The absence of critical review is all the more surprising when we consider the well-known history of corruption, bribery, and police oppression by the PRI against those who would challenge the ruling elites. However, giving voice to that political apparatus in the leading journal in the field without so much as questioning the premises and evidence that these authors/officials submit is highly questionable. The very first responsibility of serious scholarship is the incorporation of a spectrum of critical perspectives and the fair reviewing of the quality of the contributions, their arguments, evidence, and sources. Yet, none of this was evident. We question why a scholarly journal invited officials representing a nation ruled by a "corrupt and bloated" state party to present "cutting edge" perspectives on history and the nation-state. One might have done just as well by visiting the party's headquarters (or PAN's, for that matter) in Mexico City to request contributions to the special issue. At least we would have been spared the pretense of scholarship.

Transnational American Intellectuals

American writers of various stripes, novelists, academics, travelers, diplomats, scientists, and politicos have long held a romantic fascination about Mexico and "things Mexican."[21] Jesús Velasco, assistant professor of international relations at the Centro de Investigaciones y Docencia Economicas (CIDE) in Mexico City, undertook a major task in writing about American intellectuals active in Mexico from the 1920s to the 1990s. (Due to a printing error the section on 1990s intellectuals was inadvertently omitted in the hard-copy volume.) His ambitious study brings a number of important themes to the attention of those interested in people-to-people relations linking Mexico and the United States. Velasco opens his narrative by summarizing U.S.–Mexico relations that, in his view, are "full of events, images, bargains, anecdotes, and problems. . . . It has its ups and downs, although there have been more downs than ups." And in this imaginative nutshell Velasco bundles the history of U.S.–Mexico relations over the course of two centuries. However, Velasco's historical account, like the diplomats' contributions, contains numerous highly questionable arguments and assertions. We analyze several representative samples.

Velasco examines eleven transnational intellectuals who supposedly worked in an unofficial capacity during the 1920s to alter and ultimately shape U.S.–Mexico relations. The subjects chosen by Velasco are ostensibly examples of "transnational actors linking Mexico and the United States" who represented the Mexican agenda in the United States and helped shape U.S. policy to fit Mexican interests. In so doing, argues Velasco, "these intellectuals . . . nullified national boundaries and emerged as the central vehicles of communication between the two countries . . . a lobby for the Mexican government to promote its interests in the United States."[22] Throughout the somewhat rambling piece there is no mention of the dynamic American corporate presence in Mexico or of the U.S. foreign policy that advanced the corporate agenda and labored to keep the open door for U.S. capital. Velasco expresses little interest in economic relations in his study of persons he portrays as "transnational American intellectuals." Here we only need to examine the case of the 1920 cohort to understand the deeply flawed construction of the article purported by the issue editor to set a new agenda for understanding the nation-state.

A number of individuals from the 1920s who, in Velasco's account, acted as bridges between the two countries are represented as intellectuals with wide-ranging (and never fully defined) political orientations, from liberal to radical to leftist. However, several of the intellectuals simply cannot be defined as intellectuals or as radicals, which suggests that Velasco applied a very loose interpretation of the terms. For example, Velasco positions Samuel Gompers, then president of the American Federation of Labor, and Robert Haberman, representative of the AFL in Mexico, a sometime spy for J. Edgar Hoover and a member of Grupo Acción, the highly secretive CROM central committee, alongside Carlton Beals, John Dewey, Katherine Anne Porter, and Frank Tannenbaum. Not only is the representation of men such as Gompers and Haberman as "transnational American intellectuals" extremely problematic (as is the presence of the novelist Katherine Anne Porter, whom Velasco labels a "journalist"), but also the roles the intellectuals are alleged to have engaged to advance Mexico's interests are open to criticism as well.

The economic transnational context within which these actors are alleged to have lobbied for Mexican interests is unfortunately ignored, which helps to obfuscate the meaning of the actions taken by these actors. For example, at the end of the 1920s, U.S. corporations controlled 98 percent of Mexico's mining, 94 percent of oil production, 100 percent of bananas and other fruits, two-thirds of coffee production, 84 percent of cotton production, 95 percent of refined sugar, and large sectors of Mexico's cattle and agricultural lands.[23] Yet, the actions of the transnational actors are seldom placed within this all-important imperial context, which may very well help explain their actions. In failing to raise this economic "transnational relation," Velasco ignores the significance of this factor on these transnational actors. We simply do not know whether Beals, Ernest Gruening, or the nonintellectual Gompers, for that matter, opposed the overwhelming U.S. presence in the Mexican economy or whether they had anything to say about the rising tide of Mexican emigration. On this, only silence. Yet according to Velasco, they represented Mexico's interests to U.S. authorities and the American public. However, that ostensible defense of Mexico's interests never appears to threaten the political and economic dominance of the United States and implies by default that the national interests of the two nations coincided. But what was this all-important Mexican national interest that these transnational actors defended and pressed for? Velasco asserts that these individuals fought for U.S. diplomatic recognition and opposed the U.S. military intervention that many in the United States favored. These assertions are true, but their significance differs considerably from what Velasco attributes to them.

First, the suggestion that by opposing military intervention, this earned the "transnationals" a central place among the defenders of "Mexico's interest" is groundless. We must keep in mind that there were two possible approaches to Mexican policy discussed in the U.S. State Department as far back as the 1870s. One faction favored outright territorial colonization, commonly referred to as "annexation," which many favored even in the 1920s, while the second faction counseled economic conquest. The latter "model" emerged as the favored policy toward Mexico that the administrations of Wilson through Harding and Coolidge implemented. Velasco correctly depicts the transnational actors as opponents to military intervention, yet they never uttered a word against economic domination. This strongly suggests that by opposing intervention and possible annexation, the American intervenors were in fact lobbyists for the preferred foreign policy chosen by U.S. policymakers. These early-twentieth-century "internationalists" appear to have more in common with the likes of mid-nineteenth-century filibusterers—William Walker in Central America, for example—than with defenders of national sovereignty.

Unfortunately, rendering adherents of the U.S. open-door foreign policy such as Haberman and Gompers as the American voices of Mexico's interests stretches the historical record beyond recognition. This requires a closer look at Gompers and Haberman, Velasco's American defenders of Mexico's sovereignty. Gompers headed the AFL during the Mexican Revolution; in response to the rise of the IWW in the United States and anarchism in Mexico, the AFL became actively interested in Mexican politics. Gompers advocated nonintervention and diplomatic recognition as early as 1915 (Wilson extended de facto recognition by 1916). In his study of the AFL and CROM, historian Gregg Andrews carefully analyzes the heart of the AFL's political stand. He writes, "Gompers carefully manipulated the anti-interventionist tendencies within the AFL in a way that did not challenge the fundamental tenets of Wilsonian policy." Andrews adds that Gompers was committed to "U.S. hegemony" over Mexico and "refused to commit the AFL to an anti-imperialist policy."[24] Norman Caulfield's study of Mexican labor and the state in the twentieth century corroborates Andrews. Caulfield writes, "The AFL had always advocated the protection of American business interests in Mexico and Latin America."[25] Gompers advocated the elimination of anarchistic and leftist sympathies (particularly anti-U.S. sympathies) from the Mexican labor movement. Looked at from anther angle, Gompers promoted a labor movement synchronized with the open-door investment policy he avidly supported.

In time Gompers allied with reactionary labor leaders in Mexico, one of them Luis Morones, and with Morones and blueprints borrowed from the AFL, helped found the Confederación Regional Obrera Mexicana in 1918. CROM and the AFL established an alliance that lasted throughout the 1920s, each leader attending the other's annual conventions celebrated with speeches professing fraternal unity across borders. CROM served the Obregon and Calles administrations, and indirectly U.S. foreign policy, by "keeping labor on the leash."[26] As the dominant labor central in Mexico, CROM acted as a government agency, which prompted Frank Tannenbaum to comment that in Mexico the "labor movement and labor unions are essentially creatures and instruments of the government." As an "instrument of the government" CROM acted as a police force when necessary, to enforce a cooperative working class and thus prevent Mexican labor from opposing the open door to U.S. capital. (Recall that the Mexican union Confederación de Uniones Obreras Mexicanas, formed in Los Angeles in 1927, served as the branch of CROM in that region.) Unfortunately, author Velasco either ignores or overlooks this important piece of the historical transnational picture.

The second "transnational intellectual" analyzed here, Robert Haberman, a self-proclaimed socialist, emerges as a rather strange fellow. During the Obregon administration Haberman represented the AFL to assist Obregon to outmaneuver leftist labor organizations. Somewhere along the line he surfaced as a member of Grupo Acción, the highly secretive and nonelected central committee of CROM (a point that Velasco also fails to mention). Here Haberman, known as Roberto to his associates, participated wholeheartedly in an authoritarian body that occasionally found it necessary to assassinate challengers to CROM's absolute power or to stifle a strike it did not approve. No local held power to act independently, and no labor organization held legal authority to represent labor apart from CROM. It was either CROM or nothing, and if CROM decided to "organize" a local, workers either joined or searched for another job. Haberman wore other hats as well. He served as an informant for the U.S. Department of Justice, relaying information about Mexican politics to American authorities, and he "worked with AFL leaders to defeat radicalism in Mexico."[27] Historian Norman Caulfield concludes (like other historians before him) that Haberman demonstrated a "long history of collaboration with corrupt labor leaders," reflected in his close collaboration with Morones from the late 1910s to the end of the Depression.[28]

Running contrary to the historical record, Velasco sympathetically portrays Haberman as a "transnational American intellectual" with leftist and radical tendencies. However, the evidence demonstrates that Haberman's principal role was that of a political operator working to maintain the existing economic ties between the United States and Mexico. Not only is Haberman fitted with the mantle of defender of Mexico's interests, but also the governments of Obregón and Calles are given equal praise for having the political sense to form this critical alliance with the likes of Haberman and Gompers.

But more is awry here, for not all of Velasco's American intellectuals were consistent supporters of Mexican politics. Carlton Beals, who is pictured alongside Haberman, Gompers, Tannenbaum, and others, grew increasingly dissatisfied with the regimes of the 1920s and found it necessary to critique the leaders he once praised (Velasco paints a harmonious relationship among the transnationals and Mexican officials). In Beals's opinion, President Obregón was an opportunist "without any particular love for the people."[29] In a 1931 *New Republic* article, Beals wrote a stunning rebuke of Mexican politics, noting that after 1926 the "old economic doctrines of Europe and Diáz had triumphed."[30] But none of this finds mention in the article.

A salient feature of Velasco's study is the absence of "transnational American intellectual" opposition to the economic relations between Mexico and the United States. The "transnationals" operated within existing transnational relations and set out to further develop U.S.–Mexican relations on it. Haberman, for example, in one of his informational reports on Mexican politics during a tense diplomacy, confidently assured anxious "American officials that adequate guarantees would be given to foreign capital."[31] At best these individuals opposed the annexationists, but on the other hand they admired U.S. foreign policy when represented by men such as the U.S. ambassador to Mexico, Dwight Morrow, and his staged displays of support for Mexican arts and culture. Ultimately Velasco finds these transnational intellectuals a remarkable cohort, primarily because their ideas and actions allegedly coincided with the design of Mexico's national interests chosen by the postrevolutionary regimes. What Velasco does not mention (and this is crucial), that these "intellectuals" were first and foremost supporters of U.S. economic hegemony in the region, undermines the entire purpose of the article. Finally, the "transnationals" advocated a functionalist political solidarity between the United States and Mexico, an international version of the theory of the organic society developed by Edward A. Ross and other sociologists of the period. In functionalist theory, unequals live harmoniously (or should live harmoniously) with each other because their self-interests demand it. That inequality, however, emanates inexorably from the division of labor that undergirds every society. In the case of Mexico and the United States, the transnational division of labor obtained.

Finally, Velasco dismisses the voluminous materials written about Mexico by Americans that reached the American public before and during the 1920s (discussed in the third chapter). The architects of an ideology of empire fit the general definition of "transnational American intellectuals." Given that they wrote candidly about an in-process economic annexation of Mexico and championed the interests of U.S. investors in Mexico, they are extremely important to a fuller understanding of the transnational discourse and activity. In rendering a developed portrayal of "transnational American intellectuals," the likes of Frederick Starr and Wallace Thompson deserve a place alongside Robert Haberman and Samuel Gompers. Then the broader transnational significance of American intellectuals and others investigating Mexico and relaying information to American officials and the public would have been forthcoming.

The Nation-State or the "Third Space"?

Taken as a whole, the various articles written by academics, consular officers, civic activists, and others raise many issues, in a variety of ways, creating the impression of multiple voices and views, verging on incongruency. Yet there are a number of general themes and approaches that hold the articles together. For one, the contributors assume the existing relations between the United States and Mexico as optimal relations and thus appear to celebrate rather than critique those economic and political linkages.

To be fair, the articles are not presented as necessarily based on research and substantial evidence, but rather as "think" pieces that might point to new ways of theorizing about the histories of the United States and Mexico. This approach presents the readers with some difficulties. For example, Thelen grounds much of his approach to recent changes in Mexican history on the analysis he found in a novel (!) by the well-known Mexican writer Carlos Fuentes. Thelen, furthermore, injects confusion into his argument by counterposing what he calls the U.S. model of capitalism, as opposed to Mexico's "model of nationalism," as if the United States model was not a nationalist as well as a capitalist one, and the same for Mexico. For his part, David Gutiérrez initiates his discussion of what he calls the "third space" on a couple of glimpses of social behavior. One is a description of the pro-Mexico atmosphere at an international soccer match between the national teams of the United States and Mexico in Los Angeles. The other is an account of a demonstration, a largely Latino gathering, that took place in 1994 in Los Angeles in protest of the anti-immigrant Proposition 187. Each of these activities, according to Gutiérrez, suggests evidence of a "third space." It is difficult to critique arguments based on subjective and anecdotal evidence.

In general the articles in the special issue of the *JAH* engage in a rhetorical disparaging of nation-states that is *au courant* in the historical discourse. The increasing uselessness of the nation-states is emphasized: the nation-state becomes progressively irrelevant as intellectuals "nullify borders," apparently and simply, by crossing them (!), and migrants continually "defy and ignore" the two nation-states by establishing their own "third space." Mexico and the United States are presented as losing importance as organizers of history. Insofar as they exist and relate to each other, however, they are viewed as independent and sovereign. Relations of domination, or of empire, are dismissed. Thus the relationship between the United States and Mexico is described as one like "any relationship." The United States and Mexico are said to have relinquished "to the invisible hand of the market the issues of trade between the two countries," and this provides the foundation for their close but reciprocal and equal status.[32]

While these two nation-states may be equal and on the path toward irrelevancy, the United States is generally described in benevolent terms. The words "marginality," "mainstream," and "upward mobility," classic terms from the pluralist, liberal credo—the most commonplace of American political science textbook rhetoric and the stuff of American exceptionalism—are utilized throughout as measures for gauging social relations. Mexico, on the other hand, is presented as a nation moving away from its "authoritarian" and "protectionist" moorings. Otherwise, the presumed equality between these two countries is driven home by other examples. Editor Thelen speaks of law enforcement officials of both countries crossing borders in pursuit of criminals. The reality, of course, is quite different: there are dozens of U.S. law enforcement officers active in Mexico, mostly from the Drug Enforcement Agency (DEA) and the Federal Bureau of Investigations (FBI), and cases of U.S. officials who have carried out kidnappings of Mexican citizens on Mexican territory. There are no such Mexican officers or actions permitted by the United States within its own borders.

In keeping with the issue's main thesis, the decline of the nation-state, the notion of a "third space" emerges as a central theme. This notion addresses the development of the Mexican-American community in the Southwest, which, over the years, developed a particular consciousness, stemming from its second-class status, much like the African-American community. We have no quarrel with this notion per se. In a sense, there is nothing new here: in the past Chicano historians have attempted to deal with this issue with former popular "paradigms" such as the "internal colony," the "oppressed nation," or "Aztlan."[33] What all these constructs have in common is their failure to discern more than one hundred years of economic dismemberment of Mexico and the consequent demographic transformation that is at the origins of that community. It is as if, in a thorough discussion of African-American history, one would focus only on the contemporary consciousness and self-construction of the community but leave out three hundred years of the trade in African slaves and of its effects on Africa. And yet, there was something positive about the earlier notions of "internal colony," "oppressed nation," and "Aztlan." At least they presumed to be in opposition and a challenge to the status quo. It is not clear whether the "third space" issues a political challenge or whether it is a descriptive representation of the contemporary ethnic Mexican community. Certainly it does not purport to explain the origins of this community or identify the factors that have led to a century of its development. The focus on the third space, furthermore, avoids a discussion of what one space, the United States, has inflicted and continues to inflict on another space, Mexico. Indeed, there is, throughout the special issue, a soothing feeling about that relationship, which is portrayed as harmonious, reciprocal, and inevitable.

The critical rhetoric against the nation-state notwithstanding, the special issue provides ample forum, and support, for the voices representing the elites of the Mexican nation-state. There is speculation about a "third space," or Greater Mexico, the cultural extension of Mexico via migrants into the United States (but not of the United States into Mexico, so the theorists of the declining state propose no "Greater United States"), where Mexican immigrants construct a new life and civic meaning. Yet the *JAH* devotes substantial space to the confident voices to the Mexican nation-state, via their consuls. Never mind that nation-states are presumed to be irrelevant. The spokespeople for the Mexican nation are provided ample forum, their many voices are so strong that they become a deafening roar—which receives standing ovations by the editors—and consular activities are treated in the most reverent tones.[34] However, the overwhelming evidence confirms that consulates collaborated in the exploitation of its citizens abroad and offered meager protection.

In regard to the development of consciousness in the "third space," articles in the special issue contradict each other. To begin with, those consuls writing about the Mexican government's intervention into the cultural affairs of the "diasporic" community (diasporas are imagined communities) are describing a conventional practice of nation-states. The director of the Program of Mexican Communities Abroad, Carlos Gonzalez Gutiérrez, for example, defends the role of the Mexican state in designing a policy intending to orchestrate a "diasporic" consciousness among their emigrants to the United States. This appears to be a contradiction to the general theme of the book—that the role of the nation-state has changed, that borders no longer divide as before, and that national consciousness is no longer territorial. Again, González Gutiérrez falls short of presenting evidence for a withering of the nation-state. He concedes that the expatriate and Mexican-American community will be more strongly rooted in the nation-state that absorbed them than in the country they left regardless of the transnational intervention. Mexico then comes in second to the United States for the construction of an ethnic consciousness among the immigrant community despite the interventions of the Mexican nation-state to channel that consciousness. This also contradicts the notion of a "Greater Mexico," given that the ethnic Mexican community views itself as a U.S. community, with secondary ties over time with Mexico.

In connection with the overwhelming significance of U.S. political culture for understanding the politics of the Chicano community, we need only revisit the Mexican-American political movement of the 1940s and the Chicano movement of the 1960s and 1970s. These actions resonated with the major national political issues of their eras—segregation and local control, respectively—which were not hotly contested issues in Mexico. For example, the matter of education and educational equality assumed importance in both eras, but the issues were framed from within the political conventions of the United States—that is, that racism played a key role in maintaining inequality and that education was a "ladder" for "upward mobility" and hence social change. Taken to another level, the Chicano movement of the 1960s and 1970s appropriated political themes (racism, inequality, educational reform, etc.) that resonated with those of other minority communities, namely the African-American community. Mexican national politics was peripheral at best. For those born and raised in the United States, American-style ethnic politics supersedes by far the politics of Mexico.

Two other issues that have been a basic staple of traditional Chicano historiography are given new vigor in this special issue. One is the dating of the beginning of Mexican-American history to the War of 1848. Carlos González Gutiérrez contends that the first Mexican diaspora originated from the Mexican-American War. And what constitutes this imagined grouping? He answers in much the same way that his predecessors in the diplomatic corps answered when doling Mexicanidad to *Mexico de afuera*. Diasporas are formed by way of "sentimental or material links with its land of origin." Given this definition, we need to question whether the Mexican-American War did indeed create an "imagined community" across borders. The conquered Spanish/Mexican population found themselves as a real, material, subjected people who were forced into a new society, which cost them dearly, but this never led to a transnational consciousness—that is, a diaspora. In the absence of a national administration governing the province, the sparse and dispersed population of the Old Southwest experienced a negligible national consciousness instead of a heightened regionalism. González Gutiérrez, like at least a generation of scholars of the Chicano experience, mixes two distinct periods in the history of Spanish-speaking populations (as is the case with virtually every Chicano history text) and in so doing unwittingly leaves no space for applying the "diasporic" argument to the periodization of Chicano history that he cites.

For most Mexicans living in the United States today, the Southwest of 1835 or 1848 has little "sentimental" meaning. The Treaty of Guadalupe Hidalgo in 1848 constitutes a historical fact of a once-upon-a-time Mexican territory, but that historical fact does not harbor a "sentimental or material" link between that once-Mexican territory and the present (or past) Mexican immigrant community. Chicano cultural nationalists, Chicano historians, and now theorists of the descent of the nation-state refer to 1848 continually, but for most migrants an "imagined link" to 1848 is beyond their consciousness and therefore rather far-fetched. Sometimes it appears that not only are nations, "diasporas," and "third spaces" imagined, but that history, too, is subjected to the same protocol. Thus David Gutiérrez backdates the immigrant colonias, which literally covered the Southwest landscape in the twentieth century, into the nineteenth century, obliterating any distinctions between the nineteenth and twentieth centuries. The periodization used by Gutiérrez—the established wisdom among many Chicano historians—obfuscates the imperial role of the United States and the trend to minimize the importance of a century of migration.

The second issue is the reiteration of the sociological push-pull explanation for Mexican migration to the United States. This matter is not treated in detail. Gutiérrez suggests that a combination of factors, such as unemployment in Mexico and demand for low-wage labor in the United States, led to the recent intensification of northward migration. The article by sociologist Massey adds the notion of chains of migration to explain, for example, why Chiapanecos chose to revolt, instead of being pushed, as people from other regions were, into migrating to the United States. What is telling about the treatment of migration is that in both cases the "push" and "pull" factors are treated as separate and independent of each other. As we pointed out in the second chapter, a historico-economic analysis demonstrates that economic domination by the United States lies at the root of both "push" and "pull" factors.

In general, an absence of economic-historic analysis mars the special issue, which utilizes the most traditional of political history. Let us take two examples. The discussion of Mexico's presumed move toward democracy focuses on politics, not economics. There is no discussion of the imposition on Mexico, by the United States, of entry into GATT in the 1980s and into NAFTA in the 1990s. There isn't the slightest hint that the so-called movement toward democracy—meaning a U.S.-inspired two-party system—has been accompanied by a host of drastic economic measures. In the past fifteen years, but especially since NAFTA, Mexico has been obligated to dismantle government programs of all kinds, weaken labor protections and legislation, and privatize public enterprises. The results have been the ruination of tens of thousands of small firms, massive unemployment, demographic dislocation, deepening poverty, and increased migration.[35]

There is no discussion in the articles about the economic substratum of the Mexican transition to democracy where the choice, between the PRI and the PAN, was how far and how fast to deepen the economic policies put into effect in the years since Salinas de Gortari (1988–94). With the taking over of power by the conservative, neoliberal PAN, the meaning of the change toward democracy in Mexico became clear: the new president, Vicente Fox, to the cheers of Wall Street and the international community of financiers, appointed a cabinet made up of the heads of U.S.-based multinational corporations operating in Mexico. To administer Mexico's state-run oil industry, PEMEX, he named the chief executive of Dupont of Mexico. Chief executives of Mexican subsidiaries of other international consortiums, such as WorldCom, Gillette, and veteran officers of the World Bank and the International Monetary Fund, were designated to fill the most important economic and financial ministries in the new governmental hierarchy.

The abject, obsequious attitude of the new government toward the global economic warlords was exemplified by the manner in which some of the early candidates for positions were hastily withdrawn after meeting with public objections from international economic chieftains. Thus when neoliberal guru Rudiger Dornbush from MIT questioned the possible appointment of Luis Ernesto Derbez and Eduardo Sojo to leading economic posts, the president-elect promptly came up with more suitable candidates. Derbez himself was no neoliberal slouch: a Ph.D. from Iowa State University, with a lengthy tenure as a World Bank economist. In fact, he helped "restructure" the Chilean economy under Augusto Pinochet. Sojo, another dyed-in-the-wool neoliberal, hailed from the University of Pennsylvania. After Dornbush publicly scorned the potential cabinet members, perhaps because the U.S. universities that granted them Ph.D.s did not inspire confidence, Fox moved quickly to make University of Chicago Ph.D. Federico Gil Díaz his minister of finance. Meanwhile, Derbez was shifted to a lesser post, the newly fashioned ministry to promote medium to small businesses. Gil Díaz cut his neoliberal teeth first as the deputy treasury minister during the administration of Salinas de Gortari and later as chief executive of Avantel, a subsidiary of U.S.-based WorldCom. During the Salinas de Gortari administration the current "open door" model of U.S. domination over Mexico was set into motion. Fox, who has often referred to the previous governments led by the PRI as "dictatorships" and "corrupt," rushed to appoint a pillar of a famously corrupt PRI administration when called to task by his international mentors.

The slightest attention paid to economic matters reveals that beneath the fanfare of democratic change in Mexico—presumably one of the forces providing impetus for the *JAH*'s attempt at "rethinking"—there is no change on the horizon vis-à-vis the economic policies carried out by the two previous administrations. Besides Salinas's Gil Díaz in the Ministry of Finance, the new administration reappointed Guillermo Ortiz, Zedillo's Central Bank president, to assure anyone concerned that the new administration would not deviate a millimeter from the ideological paths established by its PRI predecessors. Indeed, the electoral promise, and its early enactment by the Fox administration, shows an acceleration along that path: "deepening" of NAFTA, more "integration" with the United States, increasing U.S. investments in Mexico, a new guest worker program, and increasing Mexico's exports—read: using cheap Mexican labor for the multinationals' benefit—were the mantras of the new Mexican democrats. The new leadership heartened international investors; the head of the Latin American arm of Goldman, Sachs found the appointments "extremely reassuring."[36]

The *JAH* might have pointed to an upcoming change, in degree if not in kind, in the relations between the United States and Mexico. Under Fox, the United States would no longer bother with granting its Mexican underlings the appearance of being junior partners. Instead it would have the executives of American corporations run its business in Mexico directly from the executive offices of the government.[37]

Then-candidate Fox's political genuflection before the United States shone in his visit to Washington to show voters back home that "he's presidential material." According to one journalist, Fox needed "to shake hands with administration officials . . . to convince the millions expected to cast ballots back home that he is taken seriously where it counts: the United States."[38] (Can anyone seriously contemplate then-candidates Al Gore or George W. Bush journeying to Mexico City to prove his mettle?) What is also most interesting is that González Gutiérrez, who directed the Office of Mexicans Living Abroad in the Mexican embassy under the PRI, joined with the Fox transition team and wrote President-elect Fox's speeches delivered to emigrant audiences in the United States. But this was not an aberration; reports from the Mexican embassy confirmed that the entire embassy jumped onto the Fox bandwagon immediately after the election. One diplomat was quoted as saying, "Everyone at the embassy is suddenly calling themselves a PANista now." Electing either candidate meant so little to the Mexican diplomatic corps, including the consular officials, that they could work equally well for either the PRI or the PAN. And since President Fox has promised to continue the "diasporic" outreach, the program of the Office of Mexicans Living Abroad will continue undisturbed, although leaning farther to the neoliberal far right.[39]

Within the past thirty years, Mexican immigrants as a percentage of the total Chicano population have increased dramatically and today comprise about 40 percent of that grouping. With the return of a social landscape similar to the 1920s and 1930s marked by large numbers of immigrants, the consular politics of the 1930s described above has reemerged. The significant and growing Mexican immigrant population has been partly organized (recall the six thousand soccer leagues and numerous state organizations) under the banner of the Mexican government. These organizations, like the comisiones honorificas of the 1920s and 1930s, provide avenues for overt Mexican government intervention into the political processes of the larger Mexican and Mexican-American community. Using the same Mexicanidad and other nationalistic overtures that the consulates utilized to intervene into the union struggles of the 1930s, the Mexican government through its representatives will attempt to steer the politics of its expatriates into correspondence with neoliberal social and economic policies. In implementing this variation of a transnational political "enforcer," the Mexican government expects to calm the political storms within the Mexican community before they arise. In seeking this advantage, Fox has obliged his administration to assume a proimmigrant stance, personified in his greeting a contingent of Mexican Americans at his inauguration and further demonstrated by visiting the U.S.–Mexico border and demanding that Mexican border guards treat migrants fairly and with respect. If the Fox agenda succeeds, political divisions will surface within the expatriate *and* Mexican-American community, generated by a government that celebrates an economic model that carries forward a century of social dislocation, massive poverty, and escalating migration. Unfortunately, the *JAH* also celebrates this same model, and minus interrogation, proposes it as an explanation for the erosion of the nation-state.

The avoidance of economic matters seems to be the *JAH*'s order of the day and relates particularly to the discussion about the "third space." That ethnic Mexicans live in marginal, unstable, interstitial communities, as David Gutiérrez describes, sidesteps the unity of integration and marginalization. In the fifth chapter we explained that it is precisely through this marginality that economic integration of ethnic Mexicans into the monopoly capitalist economy is effected. Barrios and colonias are stable, permanent examples not only of poverty, discrimination, segregation, and second-class citizenship but also of the economic integration of ethnic Mexicans into the fabric of U.S. monopoly capitalism. To assume otherwise is to argue that the United States, its economy and society, develops in a historical vacuum. In such an analysis, the standard of living in the United States, which occasionally allows for "mainstream" living for a large proportion of its "middle class"—to use a term that the editor of the *JAH* might feel comfortable with—had nothing to do with its economic, political, and military role in the world. Great corporate profits obtained from the exploitation of Mexico and many other countries, and the exploitation of migrant groups living in "unstable, interstitial spaces," are inseparable from "mainstream" living and "upward mobility"—that is, the "American Dream"—for other segments of U.S. society.[40]

Gutiérrez is aware of the limited and uneven manner in which ethnic Mexicans have been able historically to emerge from the barrios and colonias. He argues that recent increases in migration might put the much-vaunted myth of the American Dream beyond the reach of larger numbers of ethnic Mexicans. We find it perplexing that standard national narrative myths about the U.S. nation-state, namely, "upward mobility" and "mainstream" (elements of the "American Dream"), still appear as ideals. These terms, along with a few others, have constituted for two centuries the foundation of American exceptionalism, the most nationalist of all national discourses. Their utilization seems to belie the ostensible goal of the special issue, to redefine the significance of the nation-state on the world historical stage.

Reaffirming Traditional Narratives

The deafening roar of support for the official voices of the Mexican nation is matched by a nearly equally deafening silence when it comes to questions of gender. It would have been relatively easy for the editors of the *JAH* to include a discussion of the gendered aspects of migration involved in the bracero and maquiladora programs, or of the housekeeping, garment, and janitorial industries. The gendered aspects of community construction in the "third space" are vital for our understanding of the political dynamics at work in Mexican working-class communities.[41] Unquestionably, the manner in which U.S. monopoly capital depends on Mexican families in Mexico for the reproduction and maintenance of fresh supplies of labor-power that, as soon as they are able to travel, become new migrants to the

United States, is integral to the history of Mexican migration. The only possible exception—the article on migration by Massey et al.—points to an unintended gender impact of the Immigration Control and Reform Act. It suggests that the strictures of ICRA shifted what had been a largely male, seasonal labor force into a more stable, permanent, family-based migration and settlement. And there the matter of gender went no farther.

Lip service to the critique of the nation-state as presented in the special issue evidently cannot, and does not, alter the fundamental explanations (or conventions) for migration and is less able to explain the continuities marking the Chicano experience in the twentieth century. Moreover, in the process of constructing arguments for the diminishment of the nation-state, "mainstream" interpretations of Chicano history and of U.S.–Mexico economic and political relations seep through every paragraph of the issue. The reconstruction of the nation-state does not carry with it a reconfiguration of the predominant explanations for Mexican migration, Chicano history, U.S.–Mexico relations, or the presence of the Mexican government in the affairs of the Mexican expatriate community. These critical themes that surface within the Chicano experience are conventionally treated. In other words, there is nothing new here other than the terminology.

In an unusual approach to the claim of rigorous scholarship generally adhered to by the *JAH*'s editors over the course of its history, the "voices" of Mexico's elites via their consular representatives are privileged over the voices of a cross section of Mexico's scholarly community. Although Thelen makes a determined effort to go beyond the national borders that traditionally structure narratives, the borders of traditional scholarly investigation are kept intact, so that migrants are spoken about but they never appear except in the abstract. We are not apprised as to the reality of migrant experiences, the workers in maquiladora plants, or of life in a squatter colonia in a Mexican border town. Thus, in the assessment of the role of the state, only those in charge of the role of the state, or those charged with carrying out the policies of the state, are given voice, so the reality of migrant life is safely cloistered, the national image protected.

The "voices" of the Mexican elites via their consular representatives never conflict with existing or past U.S. foreign policy, thus ignoring the historical relationship between Mexico and the United States extending back to the Porfiriato. That such an identity of interests extending back to the late nineteenth century is not only espoused but also never subjected to questioning represent the failure of the special issue to accomplish anything beyond the ordinary. Indeed, the case may be made that the entire issue capitulated to the domestic and international status quo, in particular conventional interpretations of Chicano history and U.S.–Mexico relations. Although it proclaims to find new terrain for historical understanding, by working within the status quo the issue carries a commitment to actively work within existing explanatory models rather than provoke new approaches to historical understanding. In fact, the consular/state/government representatives professed a duty and a responsibility of Mexico to abide by the existing rules of the international economic game at all costs. Consul Rico Ferrat went so far as to claim Mexico's inability to manage the nation's economy in the face of a market governed by transnational corporations. For sure these are not Mexico-based corporations. Moreover, the examples proffered by Jesus Velasco to demonstrate the "transnational" market, the Border Industrial Program, GATT, and NAFTA were U.S. corporate-managed programs, all under the authority and the power of U.S. capital. Thus, more than a century of U.S. economic tutelage is camouflaged by asserting an irresistible and inevitable market that like an enchanter beckons the nation-state to shed its former self by abandoning traditional state functions and shuffle them to nongovernmental entities orchestrating the market. The odor of neoliberalism permeates the argument.

The loss of Mexico's sovereignty over the century seems not to impress the issue editor or the various authors seeking to establish new rules for historical explanation free from bondage to the nation-state tradition. In the case of the special issue, the venture led to a historical understanding that sustains, rather than undermines, the traditional relationship between powerful and weak states. To achieve that historical perspective certain alterations in the evidence become necessary. Jesús Velasco, for example, argues that Mexico (and therefore President Salinas de Gortari) led the struggle to implement NAFTA and that it was never a U.S.-inspired agreement but originated in Mexican governing circles. He then makes the novel assertion that Mexico's pro-NAFTA lobbying effort in Washington, D.C., exemplified the new "transnational history," the "intermestic" zone where "international politics" merge. On the other hand, Mexico's efforts to pass NAFTA serendipitously coincided with the foreign-policy objectives of the White House; as Velasco states, "the two governments were on the same side." This sleight of hand hides the centrality of the U.S. federal authorities in implementing GATT and its successor, NAFTA, and fails to convince. The latter emanated in its entirety from exclusive U.S. policy considerations, Mexico accepted the package, and as a junior partner launched lobbying efforts. Nonetheless, Velasco maintains that the lobbying efforts indicate the dwindling of the traditional notions and practices related to national sovereignty, yet the evidence supports the opposite conclusion—that the U.S. state is as central to constructing international and domestic politics as ever before. The overwhelming economic and military might of the hyperpower of the north has not weakened; on the other hand, the Mexican state is ceding national control of the economy to the United States. Even Mexican government representatives acknowledge Mexico's loss of economic independence.

The traditional understanding of sovereignty is allegedly outmoded and requires a new interpretation, according to Consul Rico Ferrat. Mexico, for example, has moved accordingly to adopt a "much more relaxed interpretation [of sovereignty] of what we have come to accept as valid."[42] The meaning of this "relaxed interpretation" devolves from the contention that the economic integration of the two countries is now so well advanced that it constrains Mexico from exercising traditional principles of national sovereignty. But the question is only halfway addressed: Who is integrating with whom?[43]

Is the Mexican economy moving northward or is the U.S. economy moving south (or shall we use the term "invading" preferred by writers of the early twentieth century)? Imagine for a moment the following:

- Mexican banks lending to U.S. state and nonstate agencies and setting terms for loans that include austerity measures that create unemployment, lowering welfare benefits, enforcing wage cuts, and deepening poverty.
- Mexican-owned maquilas setting up shop on U.S. territory, from Brownsville to San Diego and as far north as North Dakota.
- Mexican corporations crying for cheap U.S. migrant labor and lobbying their legislature for a new version of the previous temporary worker program.
- Mexican agribusiness interests dumping cheap corn on the U.S. market that ruins small farmers and sends them migrating en mass to Washington, D.C., to settle in shantytowns.
- Meanwhile, the Mexican legislature turns about and engages lengthy battles over "illegal" immigrants and implements "get tough" measures such as militarizing the border, exemplified in a Mexican version of "Operation Gatekeeper."

Were Mexico the actual rather than the imagined protagonist of these actions, it would be best to describe Mexico as the "dominant" agent in establishing transnational linkages. But in the real, objective world of nation-states, which nation-state, the United States or Mexico, is the dominant force? Which one scripts the transnational agenda?

There is another possible "imagined" scenario. Suppose for a moment that both countries mutually engaged maquilas, guest worker programs, foreign loan packages managed by international lending agencies, massive direct investments, and so on. Then perhaps we might have a "theoretical" space to argue, as do the Mexican government representatives, for a relationship based on economic integration. However, in light of the economic realities distinguishing the two nation-states, arguing for "integration" is neither a feasible nor an imaginable proposition, and is patently absurd. In fact, the new relaxed version of sovereignty, appropriated by the issue editor as a new way of understanding the nation-state, resonates with the late-nineteenth-century foreign-policy debates in Washington. The discourse revolved around a key question: Should the United States invade Mexico militarily and annex the territory, or should the United States, via corporate capital, conquer Mexico economically? Although the contentious discourse was quickly settled on the side of economic conquest, the two policy factions contended in Washington for more than fifty years. The Mexican foreign office, under Porfirio Díaz, acquiesced to economic conquest and welcomed the policy. Mexico stood squarely against military invasion, but opened the doors to the transnational economic linkages that have marked the relations between the two nation-states since the 1880s.

When Mexican government officials contend that "economic integration" and "relaxed sovereignty" are now keys to formulating Mexican foreign and domestic policy, they are in fact acquiescing to a century of economic dominance practiced by the northern power. The government has not the power to contend with economic forces, claims Consul Rico Ferrat, who argues, "It is not in the government's power to decide whether we want to become integrated into the international market economy" (i.e., integrated economically with the United States).[44] Mexico, then, is something like a leaf in the economic storm wrought by foreign capital. As that capital works its way through the sinews of the Mexican nation-state, the state loses degrees of power to determine national policy. Mexico has no choice and must abide by the new rules of the international game or lose out to those who join with it. To do so requires that Mexico relax its sovereignty and become an international player. In effect, the argument makes explicit that Mexico can no longer govern the national economy, the historical center of all nation-states. On this Consul Rico Ferrat defines the reasons for diminishing state sovereignty, and states: "Transnational corporations have ways of doing things that are beyond the central government. And you have to take that reality into account whenever you make your policy. . . . Very large private actors do things that are beyond the control of public actors." However, integration is a one-way street, or so he claims (and rightly in this case): that "without any specific policy of promoting integration with the north, the Mexican economy, and in fact Mexican society, became increasingly integrated with the United States economy." Not once do the three diplomatic representatives refer to the U.S. economy integrating with the Mexican economy. Why? That one is easy: the Mexican economy does not move north.[45]

On the other hand, never have any policymakers from Washington argued for relaxing U.S. national sovereign policies and practices or suggested that the United States is economically integrated with any nation, much less Mexico. Officials may speak of globalization and of its inevitability, but never of integration with another nation, nor of a loss of sovereignty. Has any national U.S. leader proposed a "relaxed sovereignty" or suggested that the federal government cannot govern transnational corporations? All evidence suggests that the United States, acting through national, regional, and international agencies such as AID, NAFTA, and WTO, within which it plays the dominant or leading role, opposes any alteration of its national institutional integrity, whether economic, political, or military.

Denying Empire

In sum, the special issue of the *JAH* appears as a classic top-down, ideological statement of defense of the status quo, or what is the same, the defense of U.S. imperial relations toward Mexico. There is really not much new here. Nationalist American intellectuals have avoided critiquing the U.S. empire for more than a hundred years, so in a sense the *JAH* is an inheritor of a well-grounded tradition. Despite the protestations about the relevance of the nation-state, the exercise as a whole is concerned with the building of an imperial nation. As was the case with the 1920s intellectuals discussed by Velasco, the *JAH* maintains the practice of discussing the two nations on the basis of equality and reciprocity, not of imperial domination of one by the other. The intellectuals not only had interests that "coincided" with those of Mexico, but also had a hand, as intellectual mouthpieces for the interests of the United States, in creating the agendas of Mexico.

Editor Thelen embraces the current political climate in Mexico. Much like Gruening, who praised Calles, the founder of PRI, for democratizing Mexico, Thelen also believes that the democratization of Mexico is in process. His supportive judgment, like that of Tannenbaum and of others before, upholds the interests of the United States, which stands solidly behind the current "democracy" movement in Mexico. Therefore, the economic substratum behind NAFTA, and the dismantling of the strong, populist state under the PRI, are not analyzed. Earlier unflagging support for the PRI by the United States, the subsequent withdrawal of support, and the orchestration of a mass media campaign against the presumed corruption of the PRI are not mentioned. The whole model of privatization that underlies the movement toward democracy is not interrogated, nor is the enormous state intervention that was required to put NAFTA into effect.[46]

A number of important questions related to the "democratic process" in Mexico are left unsaid. Why has the United States previously supported corruption, fraud, and even dictatorship around the world? Why does the

United States still support corruption, fraud, dictatorship, and even corrupt, dictatorial monarchies around the world? Might it be in the economic interests of the United States to act in such a fashion? These questions might well elicit answers that lead to greater understanding of the move toward democracy in Mexico and the significance of the nation-state.

As a whole, the special issue of the *JAH* appears more as a deliberate ideological project intending to obfuscate the new forms of imperialism, NAFTA and the like, while masking the old forms of imperialism that are at the root of the formation of the Chicano ethnic community and its history. There isn't a word about the historical subordination of Mexico, as if the history of U.S.–Mexico relations can be written off. In the face of the destruction of one nation, Mexico, by another, the United States, this concrete reality is ignored, in favor of abstract speculation about the irrelevance of all nations.

The elephant in the room, the weakening of a nation, Mexico, and its domination by another, the United States, is ignored. The *JAH*, like American writers of the early twentieth century, became a nationalist voice for U.S. imperialism.

Notes

1. David Thelen, "Rethinking History and the Nation-State: Mexico and the United States," *Journal of American History* 86, no. 2 (September 1999): 440.
2. We pay particular attention to articles by David Thelen, and David Gutiérrez, "Migration, Emergent Ethnicity, and the 'Third Space': The Shifting Politics of Nationalism in Greater Mexico," *Journal of American History* 86, no. 2 (September 1999): 481–517.
3. Rodolfo Figueroa Aramoni, "A Nation beyond Its Borders: The Program for Mexican Communities Abroad," *Journal of American History* 86, no. 2 (September 1999): 537.
4. Carlos González Gutiérrez, "Fostering Identities: Mexico's Relations with Its Diaspora," *Journal of American History* 86, no. 2 (September 1999): 547.
5. Ibid., 545.
6. Ibid., 551.
7. Gilbert G. Gonzalez, *Mexican Consuls and Labor Organizing: Imperial Politics in the American Southwest* (Austin: University of Texas Press, 1999). For a completely different and opposite take on the role of consuls, see Francisco Balderrama, *In Defense of La Raza: The Los Angeles Mexican Consulate and the Mexican Community* (Tucson: University of Arizona Press, 1982).
8. Gonzalez, *Mexican Consuls and Labor Organizing*, 56.
9. Ibid., 68–73.
10. Gilbert G. Gonzalez, *Mexican Citrus Worker Villages in a Southern California County, 1900–1950* (Urbana: University of Illinois Press, 1994), 130–31. From time to time, the Los Angeles Mexican consul visited segregated schools. According to late 1920s and early 1930s news reports, the special visitors soundly praised Americanization programs.
11. Camille Guerin-Gonzalez, *Mexican Workers and the American Dream: Immigration, Repatriation, and California Farm Labor, 1900–1939* (New Brunswick, N.J.: Rutgers University Press, 1994), 85; Gonzalez, *Mexican Consuls and Labor Organizing*, 31–36.
12. Lawrence Cardoso, *Mexican Emigration to the United States, 1897–1931: Socioeconomic Patterns* (Tucson: University of Arizona Press, 1980), 69.
13. See Devra Weber, *White Gold, Dark Sweat: California Farm Workers, Cotton, and the New Deal* (Berkeley: University of California Press, 1994); Clete Daniel, *Bitter Harvest: A History*

       of California Farm Workers, 1871–1994 (Ithaca, N.Y.: Cornell University Press, 1981); and Gonzalez, *Mexican Consuls and Labor Organizing*.

14.   Gilbert G. Gonzalez, *Labor and Community*, chap. 6; also *Mexican Consuls and Labor Organizing*, 115–21.

15.   Ernesto Galarza, "Big Farm Strike: A Report on the Labor Dispute at the DiGiorgio's," *Commonweal* (June 4, 1948): 178–82.

16.   Dennis Nodin Valdez, *Al Norte: Agricultural Workers in the Great Lakes Region, 1917–1970* (Austin: University of Texas Press, 1993), 103–4; Henry P. Anderson, *The Bracero Program in California* (New York: Arno Press, 1976), 89–90.

17.   Gonzalez, *Mexican Consuls and Labor Organizing*, 215.

18.   Ibid., 216.

19.   Arturo Santamaría Goméz, *La politica entre Mexico y Aztlan: Relaciones chicano mexicanas del 68 a Chiapas 94* (Culiacan: Universidad Autonoma de Sinaloa, 1994), 212; quoted in Gonzalez, *Mexican Consuls and Labor Organizing*, 218.

20.   Gonzalez, *Mexican Consuls and Labor Organizing*, 220.

21.   Helen Delpar, *The Enormous Vogue of Things Mexican: Cultural Relations between the United States and Mexico, 1920–1935* (Tuscaloosa: University of Alabama Press, 1992).

22.   Jesús Velasco, "Reading Mexico: Understanding the United States: American Transnational Intellectuals in the 1920s and 1990s," *Journal of American History* 86, no. 2 (September 1999).

23.   Robert Freeman Smith, *The United States and Revolutionary Nationalism in Mexico, 1916–1922* (Chicago: University of Chicago Press, 1972), 149, 201–2.

24.   Gregg Andrews, *Shoulder to Shoulder? The American Federation of Labor, the United States, and the Mexican Revolution, 1910–1924* (Berkeley: University of California Press, 1991), 28–29.

25.   Norman Caulfield, *Mexican Workers and the State: From the Porfiriato to NAFTA* (Fort Worth, Tex.: Texas Christian University Press, 1998), 73.

26.   See Andrews, *Shoulder to Shoulder?*, and Caulfield, *Mexican Workers and the State*.

27.   Andrews, *Shoulder to Shoulder?*, 153.

28.   Caulfield, *Mexican Workers and the State*, 89, 148.

29.   Andrews, *Shoulder to Shoulder?*, 153.

30.   Delpar, *The Enormous Vogue of Things Mexican*, 59.

31.   Andrews, *Shoulder to Shoulder?*, 149.

32.   Thelen, "Rethinking History and the Nation-State," 439–40.

33.   See, for example, Rodolfo Acuña, *Occupied America: The Chicano Struggle for Liberation* (San Francisco: Canfield Press, 1972); Mario Barrera, *Race and Class in the Southwest: A Theory of Racial Inequality* (Notre Dame, Ind.: University of Notre Dame Press, 1979); Gilberto Lopez y Rivas, *The Chicanos: Life and Struggles of the Mexican Minority in the United States* (New York: Monthly Review Press, 1973).

34.   David Gutiérrez, for example, praises the consulate for its service to the immigrant community in the early twentieth century and writes: "[T]he consulates continued to play an important role in both protecting the interests of Mexican nationals abroad and, in some cases, supporting civil rights activities of American citizens of Mexican descent . . . the consular corps actually sponsored the formation of labor unions on United States soil. In addition, the consular corps sometimes assisted in Mexican-American civil rights cases by providing technical legal advice and even financial support for litigation. . . . The consulates also exerted a strong and consistent symbolic presence in ethnic Mexican enclaves by helping to organize and support a vast network of *juntas patrioticas* . . . and *comisiones honorificas* . . . to celebrate Mexican national holidays." (David Gutiérrez, "Migration, Emergent Ethnicity, and the 'Third Space,'" 493). One could very well argue that Americans living in Mexico form a "third space" within Mexico. Recent reports place the numbers of Americans residing permanently in Mexico at six hundred thousand and increasing rapidly. This figure does not count the many Americans who come for annual stays, vacations, and weekend jaunts. Immigrating Americans have Americanized many a Mexican town. The example of Ajijic, near Guadalajara, which counts seventy-five hundred American residents out of the fifty thousand who live in the Guadalajara region, is a case in point. According to one journalist, "Ajijic is a rare blend of American and Mexican culture and language. Amused Mexican residents talk about how their American neighbors organize

themselves for every possible activity, from gardening classes to Saturday morning walking clubs." Mary Jordan, "American Retirees Flock to 'Paradise' in Mexico, *Washington Post*, February 5, 2001.

35. Juanita Darling, "Fearing a Bitter Harvest," *Los Angeles Times*, March 16, 1992; Juanita Darling, "NAFTA Buoyed Mexican Business and Consumers: But Now the Optimism Is Fading," *Los Angeles Times*, January 8, 1995; Chris Kraul, "Growing Troubles in Mexico," *Los Angeles Times*, January 17, 2000; Anthony de Palma, "Mexico's Rich Richer, Poor Angrier," *Orange County Register*, July 21, 1996; James F. Smith, "Sweeping Changes of Last Decade Translate into a Tale of 2 Economies," *Los Angeles Times*, January 10, 1999.

36. "La lucha por dirigir la economía de México," *La Opinión*, November 22, 2000; "Fox presenta su equipo económico," *La Opinión*, November 23, 2000; Mary Beth Sheridan, "Mexico's Cabinet New Cabinet Hailed as Business-Savvy," *Los Angeles Times*, November 11, 2000; "Fox: 'Let's Be Real Friends, Real Neighbors, and Real Partners'" (President-elect Fox interviewed by Nathan Gardels), *Los Angeles Times*, Novermber 28, 2000; Eduardo Garcia, "Investors Applaud Mexican Elections," *Orange County Register*, July 5, 2000.

37. If not corporate heads, political figures such as former New York mayor and staunch conservative Rudolf Giuliani have been called to duty. Giuliani, along with fifteen members "on the former mayor's team," were hired as "paid consultants" in October 2002 to design a project aimed at cracking down on crime and police corruption plaguing Mexico City. (*Orange County Register*, October 11, 2002).

38. Esther Schrader, "Mexican Opposition Candidate Hopes Trip North Plays Well Back Home," *Los Angeles Times*, March 21, 2000.

39. Esther Schrader, "Mexico's Diplomats Mull Future in Post-PRI Era," *Los Angeles Times*, November 11, 2000.

40. David Gutiérrez, "Migration, Emergent Ethnicity, and the 'Third Space,'" 497.

41. Pierrette Hondagneu-Sotelo, *Gendered Transitions: Mexican Experiences of Immigration* (Berkeley: University of California Press, 1994); also, Douglas S. Massey, "The Social Organization of Mexican Migration to the United States," in *The Immigration Reader: America in a Multidisciplinary Perspective*, edited by David Jacobsen (Malden, Mass.: Blackwell, 1998).

42. "Mexico, the Latin North American Nation: A Conversation with Carlos Rico Ferrat" (interview by David Thelen), *Journal of American History* 86, no. 2 (September 1999): 475.

43. Consul Rico Ferrat argues that the best demonstration of "intermestic" policy in action "is the example of migration." His argument runs like this: Since U.S. immigration policy reverberates across borders and affects Mexico's domestic policy, this presents compelling evidence for the existence of "intermestic" politics. However, he fails to provide a quid pro quo for Mexico. The latter's domestic policies seldom have such an effect on U.S. internal affairs, which makes the notion of "intermestic" extremely suspect, and speculative at best.

44. Thelen, "Mexico, the Latin American North American Nation," 476.

45. Mexican investment in the United States falls far short of equaling U.S. investment in Mexico. The example of California and Mexico is a case in point. In 1999, direct investment in Mexico originating in California amounted to $10 billion, as compared to only $504 million from Mexico invested in California. See James F. Smith, "Gov. Davis, Mexico's Fox Explore New Ways to Boost Cooperation," *Los Angeles Times*, November 11, 2000.

46. John R. MacArthur, *The Selling of "Free Trade": NAFTA, Washington, and the Subversion of American Democracy* (New York: Hill & Wang, 2000). See also the collection edited by Rodolfo de la Garza and Jesus Velasco, *Bridging the Border: Transforming Mexico–U.S. Relations* (featuring articles by *JAH* special issue contributors Carlos Gonzalez Gutiérrez and Jesus Velasco) (Lanham, Md.: Rowman & Littlefield, 1997). The authors in this volume contend that "intergovernmental conflict" rather than "integration" will increase in the decades to come. In a summary of the collection, Jorge I. Dominguez, Clarence Dillon professor of international relations at Harvard, writes that "state-based explanations go a long way to explain past and current patterns in U.S.–Mexico relations when the stakes are high, including the main changes in Mexico's foreign policy in the 1980s and 1990s," 185. These statements appear in a volume alongside articles from Jesus Velasco and Carlos Gonzalez Gutiérrez and are surprisingly at variance with the arguments that both avow in the *JAH* special issue.

Conclusion
Chicano History into the Twenty-first Century

Things are changing.
Jorge Castañeda, Mexico's foreign minister,
describing Mexico under the Fox administration

We want to deepen NAFTA. You could call it NAFTA-plus.
Vicente Fox, president of Mexico

It would be a cause for great joy and excitement if the processes of imperial domination we have described in the preceding chapters were coming to an end. Such a happy occurrence would allow the authors the pleasure of writing a traditional conclusion that mirrored the termination, in reality, of a historical epoch. Unfortunately, this is not the case. Thus this final chapter cannot be written entirely as a conventional conclusion. Instead we review the major arguments made in previous pages and point to a number of current policies and trends that demonstrate the persistent relevance of U.S. domination over Mexico for the Mexican-American community in the United States.

In the preceding explorations on the origins of Chicano history and its course over the twentieth century, the transnational economic relations between the nation-states of Mexico and the United States stand at the center of the analysis. The investigation underscored the late-nineteenth-century economic interventions carried out by the largest U.S. capitalist enterprises that began transforming Mexico from an economically sovereign nation into an economic colony of the United States. The evidence showed that this economic colonization uprooted the Mexican population on a massive scale, leading to migration within Mexico to the border and the United States, and the eventual formation of the Chicano community in the United States in the early twentieth century. The general outlines of this process continue to the present. The mass migration northward spurred by railroads, mining, and oil investments begun at the end of the nineteenth century continued with the Bracero Program, the Border Industrial Program, and, more recently, via NAFTA-inspired maquilas across the Mexican border states. In sum, the formation of the ethnic Mexican community in the United States, and its continued evolution and development, cannot be understood on the basis of U.S. territorial acquisitions following the Mexican-American War of 1846–48. Rather, its rise stems from the economic domination exercised by the United States over the Mexican nation beginning in the late nineteenth century. From this we conclude that U.S. imperial economic expansionism is at the root of Mexican migration to the United States and that Mexican migration is at the root of Chicano history.

In contrast to the traditional push-pull model, in which "pull" and "push" factors are viewed as separate and independent, and contrary to the variants of push-pull that emphasize the agency of migrants as the causal factor leading to pre- and post-1960 migrations, our analysis explains migration as, fundamentally, a by-product of U.S. imperial activities. In step with the initial economic domination exercised over Mexico, a culture of empire—based largely on travel writing—took shape in the United States and matured by the early 1900s, similar in many respects to the European Orientalism described by Edward Said. That body of travel literature, written by a broad collection of American writers, assigned cultural and genetic predispositions to Mexicans that explicitly defined them as a people incapable of modernization without foreign tutelage. That imperial vision impacted significantly on sociological theory and public policy directed at Mexican immigrants in the United States. The culture of empire flowed back into the United States to shape the experiences of Mexicans north of the border. The educational experience of Mexican immigrants was heavily influenced by this imperial mind-set, which was at the core of the "Americanization" programs of the 1920s (and which remains relevant today).

Rather than being powerless victims, migrants consciously exercise their agency—that is, their personal and shared power—but such actions are taken within the context of empire. Over the twentieth century, migration assumed a variety of forms; it has been cyclical and long-term; comprised of contract laborers, legal and illegal migrants, and border commuter labor. As part of the process, particular and unique forms of organizing the labor of women, men, and children evolved into patterns of common work experiences over generations. Specific systems of production utilized gender and legal status according to cost assessments made by management. Thus we see, for example, men exclusively in the Bracero Program and, more recently, women in particular rungs of the lettuce harvest, and undocumented men in others. Migrants and the power they wield function within the parameters of the imperial policies and the consequent social and economic conditions that lead to migration within Mexico and eventually to the United States. The formation of the Chicano ethnic community, its economic, social, and political integration into the United States, and thus Chicano history, follows from this imperial transnational process.

Contrary to the notion that the nation-state is losing historical significance, Chicano history can be neither understood nor explained apart from the interplay of the two respective nation-states. According to some interpretations, migrants transcend and defy borders and thereby redefine the traditional norms of the nation-state, even forming separate "third spaces." Such approaches appear to celebrate migration and the accomplishments that migrants are able to attain. However, what appear as "third spaces" are in fact immigrant communities integrated into the nation-state and, for the most part, internal sources of cheap labor.

At the dawn of the twenty-first century, Mexico's national economic policy continues to flow from the norms developed over the prior hundred years plus of U.S. economic colonization. The scenario points to the further breaking apart of the social fabric of the Mexican nation and guarantees the continuation of Mexican labor migration into the twenty-first century. Existing immigrant worker settlements will grow and new communities and enclaves will appear across the national landscape, extending a pattern of Chicano history into the new century. The elections of George W. Bush and Vicente Fox to their respective presidencies brought in their wake an effort designed to "regularize" the flow of Mexican labor as guest workers into U.S. agriculture and the service industry. Despite the severe consequences wrought by the tragedy of September 11, 2001, and the setback of deliberations for a guest worker program, negotiations have not been jettisoned, they have only been slowed. Reports indicate that both governments are reestablishing an agenda for an eventual guest worker program.[1] As one labor economist put it shortly after September 11, "we're just in a temporary pause."[2] A headline joined in: "U.S. and Mexico to Resume Talks on Immigration Policy." Mexican foreign minister Jorge Castañeda offered, "We would like to relaunch the agenda and recast it in the aftermath of September 11."[3] (Nonetheless, it appears at this writing that no significant obstacles stand in the way of an eventual guest worker program.) With or without September 11 and the ensuing threat by the Bush administration of a preemptive war against Iraq, that process exemplifies the continuity of, rather than any significant changes in, the basic pattern of economic relations between the two nations and portends continued immigration and the further development of a "Chicano nation" within the United States.

An overview of the deliberations occurring before September 11 between the leaders of Mexico and the United States over that guest worker program, and the ensuing high-level debate in Washington over the same program, reveal the predominance of the nation-state in matters related to migration. While the program underwent negotiation and intense debate, President Fox went on a campaign for two closely related programs. First, he asked emigrants to remain "loyal to Mexico," and, rather than send their remittances to their relatives, to send savings into a Mexican government-sponsored poverty program. Second, Fox proposed an expansion of the maquila industry from Mexico through Central America, named the Puebla-Panama Plan. Do these initiatives represent the rise of a new, more independent Mexico? Might these initiatives lead to a new pattern of relations that will impact the future development of the Chicano community in the United States? More than anything, the deliberations over a new guest worker agreement exemplify the imperial relations between the two governments. Lest there be any doubt that these policy initiatives arise from a political and economic template wrought by a century of U.S. domination, we take some time at the end of this book to analyze those policy proposals.

The United States, Mexico, and the Open Door

United States and Mexican media made much during the early months of the George W. Bush administration of the new "alliance" between the United States and Mexico. Cursory examination, however, reveals what defines the alliance for Mexico: concurrence on free trade; an open door to foreign investment; an eager reliance on foreign financing; the implementation of further privatization of the economy; the elimination of social safety nets as required by U.S.-dominated agencies such as the Inter-American Development Bank and the World Trade Organization; and the expansion of NAFTA. In other words, more of the same old Mexican national and foreign policies, which resonate with the basic features of U.S. foreign policy. Mexico's solid endorsement of a "free market" based on the maquila model, including the recently unveiled Puebla-Panama Plan, and the new cornerstone of U.S. economic policy toward Latin America, the Free Trade of the Americas Agreement, places Mexico securely within the ideological perimeter of the U.S. empire. And perhaps no other leader since the infamous dictator Porfirio Díaz at the end of the nineteenth century represents the interests of the United States in Mexico so well as the former president of Coca-Cola de Mexico, Mexico's president Vicente Fox.

Despite Fox's rhetorical statements rejecting the neoliberal economic model, proffered for public consumption, Mexico unabashedly implements the open door to foreign capital preferred by Washington and foisted on nations across the world under the mantle of "free trade."[4] No sooner had Fox been elected president than Mexico agreed to the terms of the World Bank's $1.12 billion loan to be used for road repair and construction and, among other things, for reforming the financing of health services. A deeply indebted Mexico added the $1.12 billion to the $165 billion already owed to a variety of international lenders.[5] Mexico's open door to foreign ownership is best exemplified in the recent takeover of Banamex, Mexico's largest independent bank, by Citigroup, the largest U.S. financial corporation. With the purchase of Banamex, Citigroup created the largest financial entity in Latin America. Former Clinton administration Secretary of the Treasury Robert Rubin serves as Citigroup's vice chairman and helped guide the takeover. News analysts noted that the Citigroup purchase means "foreigners will own Mexico's three largest banks," and as one headline read, "In Mexico, banking is mostly a foreign affair."[6] In contrast to the European Union, India, China, and other countries, Mexico explicitly engages a "good neighbor" policy supportive of U.S. foreign policy around the world. Whereas other world leaders are openly skeptical if not critical of U.S. objectives, such as regarding a missile defense shield and global warming, Fox stands "shoulder to shoulder" with U.S. foreign policy. Mexico talks the talk and walks the walk of the northern imperial power, calling for "human rights" and "elections," and even dropping references to "nonintervention," the ornamental nationalistic rhetoric that Mexican administrations have consistently proclaimed since the 1910 Revolution. Parrotlike, Fox reiterates daily the U.S. State Department neoliberal mantra that free trade and democracy are inseparable.

Fox, Bush, and U.S. Immigration Policy: Prepping for the New Bracero Program

Shortly after their election as presidents of their respective nations, Fox and Bush met twice. One of the gatherings turned into a celebratory "shirt-sleeve summit" (sometimes called the "cowboy summit") at the Fox family's expansive colonial hacienda in Guanajuato. The two made a point to dress in ranch style—boots and cowboy hats—and to embrace each other physically as well as politically.[7] High-level talks followed, engaging Secretary of State Colin Powell, National Security Adviser Condoleezza Rice, and Attorney General John Ashcroft with their Mexican counterparts. Under cover of a call for a general "open border" policy, Bush and Fox made clear that their goal was to secure an agreement for a new guest worker program, expanding the current H2 program and anticipating importing 250,000 Mexican workers annually into the United States. However, this figure is exactly the figure that American agriculture requires annually to care for fields and harvest crops.[8]

According to Jorge Castañeda, Mexico's foreign minister, Fox is well informed regarding migration and commands the expertise required to shape excellent policy. Castañeda explained the source of Fox's wisdom, stating, "This is not a guy who has to study about immigration . . . this is a guy who comes from a state that has been sending migrants to the United States for 100 years."[9] Castañeda could not have been more correct; Guanajuato is one of the leading "exporters" of migrants to the United States, and thus for Guanajuateños, "migration has become an accepted part of life."[10] Quite possibly Fox's hands-on education as Guanajuato governor formed his understanding of a century of migration framed by this short but illuminating statement: "Where before we saw migration as a problem, today we see it as an opportunity."[11] In step with a century of labor migration, that "opportunity" promises to provide Mexican labor to U.S.-owned maquilas around Mexico, with any excess labor going to the United States, an "opportunity" that will surely continue Guanajuato's and Mexico's tradition of worker migration to the United States, and further growth of the Mexican immigrant communities in the United States.

Planning for the New Bracero Program

In April 2001 a six-member Senate Foreign Relations Committee group led by the committee chairman, Senator Jesse Helms (Republican of North Carolina), and Senator Joseph Biden (Democrat of Delaware) journeyed to Mexico with the express purpose of hammering out some form of guest worker agreement. Three days of extensive policy discussions with Mexican counterparts and private meetings with Fox explored the important elements of such a program. According to onetime independent political critic Adolfo Zinser, now a national security adviser to Fox, Mexico "got the cooperative signals . . . wanted from U.S. officials."[12] Both sides congratulated each other for having deliberated in good faith, resulting in "unanimous support for a program to bring Mexican workers to the United States legally."[13] One commentator described the meetings as a "love fest between Helms and Mexican officials—especially [Foreign Minister] Castañeda."[14] Meanwhile, Senators Helms and Biden gushed that the United States and Mexico "are not just neighbors, we are democratic allies . . . we are potentially each other's solution."[15]

Not surprisingly, the visiting dignitaries poured lofty praise on Vicente Fox. Senator Pete V. Dominici (Republican of New Mexico), among others at the meetings with Fox, extolled the Mexican president in terms reminiscent of adulation for Díaz a century ago. "I've been senator twenty-eight years," remarked Dominici, "[and] I've never been privileged to sit with a chief executive of a foreign country that impressed me more."[16]A generally reserved Senator Helms chimed in, declaring, "I was mighty impressed with what President Fox is doing."[17] Enthusiastic congratulations from both sides of the border (and both sides of the aisle in the U.S. Congress) signified a seeming unanimity for resolving the thorny issue of immigration by importing thousands of cheap, unskilled Mexican laborers for temporary employment in the United States.

The Guest Worker Program

Under the plan worked out by the U.S. Foreign Relations Committee and largely shaped by Texas Republican Senator Phil Gramm in coordination with President Fox, workers would be hired under year-long contracts and returned to Mexico at the termination of the contract. In addition, the workers would have a portion of their wages placed into an IRA-like account for savings and health care costs. Unused health care accounts and the savings would be returned upon return to Mexico, a sort of incentive factor to return. Undocumented workers in the United States would be allowed to apply but would have to return to Mexico before applying. Senator Gramm succinctly defined the essence of the program: "A guest worker program means you come, you work, you accrue the benefits of working, and then you go home."[18] Under this revolving-door program, Mexican workers would be allowed into the United States on one-year contracts primarily for agricultural work and would be subject to "repatriation" at the end of the contract. In other words, Mexican labor would fall under legal restrictions that would effectively make guest workers a controlled labor force, here to meet the short-term requirements of corporate employers and to be legally expelled upon the termination of their utility.

Clearly, there is nothing new in this proposal for importing Mexican workers on temporary labor contracts. Mexican labor has been imported via state-sponsored programs at various times since 1908 and has been imported continuously since 1942, first through the Bracero Agreements and then through the H2 program initiated in 1952. The new version of a long-standing method for utilizing Mexican labor differs in few respects from the old Bracero Program. The new accord replicates the Bracero Program in that Mexico and the United States agree to systematically import cheap, unskilled labor into the United States to work in agriculture, the service industry, and similar lines of labor. Mexico actively cooperates with the United States, hoping to implement the latest version of an international labor contractor system by expanding the H2 program that at present allows for the importation of only about 42,000 workers from Mexico annually. Fox argues that by expanding the program to 250,000 workers annually the flow of illegal immigrants will be significantly curtailed.

Like the braceros before them, guest workers would have few if any opportunities to organize and form associations when they in fact would be subject to an annual termination notice. Without the benefit of time to organize, the guest workers would remain an unorganized mass of labor subject to the domination of the employer. Furthermore, there is no reason to believe that guest workers would stem the tide of "illegals." The Bracero Program had the effect of stimulating rather than ending the flow of the undocumented into the United States. Moreover, the Bracero Program did not contribute to the economic development of Mexico. Though some self-serving claims by Mexican and American authorities were made concerning a linkage between economic development and the Bracero Program, and purely anecdotal evidence at that, no reliable evidence was ever provided that the Bracero Program stimulated economic development in Mexico.

According to one report, the guest worker idea "has been supported by many farm-state politicians in the United States, and some labor unions."[19] However, what appeared as a "done deal" began to unravel as the final agreement, authored by Attorney General Ashcroft, Secretary of State Powell, and Mexico's Foreign Minister Castañeda and Interior Minister Santiago Creel neared completion. For sure the proposal elicited a controversy that flared over one issue: whether to grant "some form" of amnesty to the millions of undocumented Mexican immigrants.

Reformist critics of the initial agreement, in particular the AFL-CIO and the congressional Hispanic Caucus (which played a key role in approving NAFTA), both supporters of U.S. foreign policy and the Democratic Party (which played a key role in shaping the initial guest worker proposal), advocate a guest worker agreement with an amnesty provision.[20] Agribusiness understood amnesty as an opportunity to stabilize the labor force that they currently employ and explains their support. Despite the business-union-immigrant advocate coalition's support for the guest worker measure submitted to the House of Representatives in 2000 and authored by Representative Howard Berman (Democrat of North Hollywood, California), the legislation was narrowly defeated.[21] A period of negotiation among various interested parties then ensued.

Several months after negotiations between Mexico and the United States appeared to have been completed, Foreign Minister Castañeda declared that Mexico would agree to a guest worker program only if "some form" of amnesty or "some adjustment of legal status" for the undocumented were included. Before a July 2001 convention of the AFL-CIO–affiliated Hotel Employees and Restaurant Employees union in Los Angeles, Castañeda vowed to insist on amnesty in a package deal with the guest worker program. "It is," he said, "either the whole enchilada or nothing."[22]

Continued references to "some form" of amnesty left room for speculation as to the precise meaning of amnesty given by Castañeda. Nevertheless, "thrilled" union delegates, the majority Mexican immigrants, gave him four standing ovations. The appearance of demanding amnesty or regularization by Fox and Castañeda appeals to Mexican immigrants and the Chicano community. Since the guest worker agreement comes in a package deal, any support for amnesty automatically enlists support for a guest worker agreement and serves to neutralize any opposition to the latter.[23]

Notwithstanding Castañeda's colorful artifice, political "enchiladas" are more exacting, and amnesty would be defined by political winds in the United States. Consequently, Fox eventually stepped away from using a vaguely defined amnesty and emphasized an equally vaguely defined "regularization" of undocumented immigrants. The alterations made it appear that Mexico was accommodating to the objections to full amnesty from conservatives in the United States. Later, the Bush team also jettisoned amnesty and adopted "regularization" with good reason. By "regularization" Bush and Fox appear to define a new category for Mexican undocumented immigrants by granting work permits, Social Security cards, and driver's licenses, among other things. Such an amnesty would confer a right to continue living and working in the United States but is not equal to a residency card. In essence, those who qualify for the kind of "regularization" spoken of by Fox and Bush would form an internal commuter workforce—without having to return to Mexico daily.

Attachments to the guest worker proposal, regularization or "amnesty," and a legalization option for guest workers, nonetheless validate this latest international labor contracting system and present no obstacles to corporations long accustomed to exploiting Mexican workers. That corporate employers are willing to support "some form" of amnesty to secure a more permanent labor force and in the bargain lock in future guest workers speaks volumes.[24] One aide to a leading Democratic senator acknowledged, "Everybody has been clamoring for some kind of legalization program because they can't find sufficient low-skilled workers to fill jobs."[25]

For both nations, the guest worker agreement is the key issue around which they negotiate. Mexico is committed to continue exporting its most valuable commodity at bargain prices, and the United States is committed to continue exploiting that commodity. No amount of "packaging" will alter a transnational labor contracting system designed specifically to import unskilled labor into the United States. Nor will "regularization" and even full amnesty alter the course of a century of labor migration. Agribusiness, the service industry, and construction companies and others dependent on unskilled Mexican labor will secure their preferred workforce. All analyses indicate that a guest worker program will move forward with or without the vaguely worded amnesty provisions. While the outward contention seems to revolve around amnesty, or what is referred to as amnesty, the key issue has always been the guest worker agreement. There is no such thing as a reformed guest worker program, a "good" or a "bad" guest worker program, or anything in between. Legislators from both parties, interested corporations, the AFL-CIO leadership, and Latino rights groups, in alliance with Castañeda and Fox, support a transnational labor policy servicing the economic domination of Mexico. The transnational conditions that generate the varied forms of migration from Mexico to the United States, including guest workers, remain untouched.

U.S. "National Interests" and Guest Workers

The United States has several fundamental self-interests in promoting a guest worker program. For one, reports indicate that with the aging of the populations of the industrialized world, 99 percent of the world's labor supply in the twenty-first century will emanate from the underdeveloped world.[26] Consequently, the Carnegie Endowment for International Peace declared the planned guest worker agreement a "window of demographic opportunity" for meeting "U.S. industry's shortage of unskilled labor."[27] Within the meeting room where representatives of Mexico and the United States held discussions, Senator Helms represented a state whose demography and labor force have changed significantly through undocumented Mexican immigration and the importation of Mexican workers under the H2 program. North Carolina growers find themselves increasingly dependent on Mexican labor and, as one report put it, "are among the most vocal advocates for extending guest worker programs."[28]

Senator Gramm was heard to remark, "An effective guest worker program can help the American economy and dramatically decrease illegal immigration."[29] Note that Gramm, like his cohorts among the senators negotiating the agreement, referred primarily to the benefits accruing to the United States. For Mexico the only returns are the siphoning away of surplus labor and the possible increase of remittances.

The Office of Mexicans Living Abroad and Remittances

Under Fox, Mexico has continued the old policies of the PRI regarding the emigrant community, or *Mexico de afuera*, as it is sometimes called, with one exception. Fox has actively engaged a policy discourse relative to emigrants, and refers to them as heroes and hard workers, and pointedly rejects the old derogatory epithets heard for decades, such as *pochos* or "uppity Americanized Mexicans." While he refrains from critiquing the historical exploitation of Mexican labor, he lauds the potential of these "heroes" to assist the Mexican economy and seeks methods to "regularize" the export of this labor to the United States via a guest worker program. He has visited the border on several occasions to engage emigrants as they prepare to cross into the United States and has made a point of offering protections for the newfound "heroes."

Visiting various migrant enclaves in the United States, Fox carries the message that the Mexican government offers protection to its citizens abroad and plans to build strong ties with the expatriates.[30] The Fox administration maintains contacts with the emigrant community through outreach, originally via the Office of Mexicans Living Abroad, later superseded by the Council for Mexicans Abroad as the principal contact with the emigrant community. In the tradition of the PRI, the Fox administration sponsors such functions as delivering textbooks to school libraries and various cultural and sports programs in the emigrant communities. However, not much is new regarding the role of the consulates in relation to *Mexico de afuera*, and the old programs of the PRI survive. Not only have the old programs continued, but also many of the actors who worked for the PRI foreign offices are now enrolled in the Fox version of the Office of Mexicans Living Abroad. For example, Martha Irene Lara, the consul general recently selected to serve in Los Angeles, perhaps the most important of all Mexican consulate offices in the United States, served as a PRI senator from Chihuahua in the 1990s and was a career diplomat under the PRI before her selection to the "choice" office.[31]

Since the decade of the 1920s, when emigrants sent home $58 million in various forms, remittances intended to help support families and relatives have historically provided a major source of revenue for Mexico.[32] With the dramatic tenfold increase in emigration since the 1960s, the number of remittances has risen proportionally. In the 1990s alone, remittances increased from $4 billion to $6 billion, outdistanced the industrial output of Mexico, and stood behind only oil and tourism. However, while migrants use remittances as a form of family responsibility, the Fox administration seeks a political and business opportunity.

Given the historical utility of remittances, the Fox team has moved to "capitalize on the close links between Mexicans on both sides of the border" by expediting money transfers and thereby increasing the flow of dollars. Already Fox has successfully lobbied with money-order houses and banks to lower the cost of fees for sending funds to Mexico. Through formal meetings with transaction agencies Fox engineered agreements to lower the fees and other charges traditionally accompanying money transfers, thereby allowing for a greater amount of remittances to arrive without altering the amount of money placed by the sender.[33] Fox's appeal to the emigrant community has generated a positive response. Fox's overtures, titling emigrants "true heroes," have sent remittances soaring by 43 percent, reaching an annual estimated high of $8 billion and climbing. However, the business of remittances has more to do with the Fox administration securing any available source of revenue to incorporate into the deeply indebted national treasury. An important function, if not the most important, of the consulates and the Council for Mexicans Abroad (formerly the Office of Mexicans Living Abroad) will be coordinating remittances with small-scale economic assistance programs in the sending communities. Emigrants from a single community or city in Mexico often organize associations of various sorts in the United States, and by working actively with these associations the office hopes to channel the flow of remittances into projects dovetailed with a central economic plan, one obviously in tune with the neoliberal model.

The remittance scam ostensibly intends to counter the mean poverty that affects as many as 71 million, or 73 percent of the population, and potential political actions that poverty engenders.[34] Fox envisions remittances as an antipoverty program by channeling the funds in coordination with matching federal funds, and together engender small businesses and local infrastructure projects.[35] Juan Hernandez, former director of the now defunct Office of Mexicans Living Abroad, and at one time Fox's peripatetic ambassador for migrant affairs, contended that each remittance "goes directly to Mexico's poorest communities, where it has the potential to reduce immigration."[36]

Certainly it is not the wealthy who will be tapped to send their monies into the Mexican government's coffers. At least seven of every ten Mexican immigrants and their children live in poverty, clustering in largely segregated communities. Under the Fox formula, these very same emigrants, whether "regularized" or not (and those thousands of future guest workers), will finance a transnational economic program sponsored by the Mexican government in the name of the desperate migrant-sending villages and communities. In other words, the pockets of the Mexican poor in the United States are asked to support the poor in Mexico via a novel version of a privatized transnational poverty program. Or put another way, the imperial domination of Mexico will be cushioned by the poor themselves. Not only will migrants serve as cheap and disenfranchised labor while in the United States, they will also provide a "private" subsidy for resolving the social consequences of an empire built on "free trade."

Will remittances reverse the mass desertion causing widespread village extinction across central Mexico initiated by the dumping of American agricultural products? While remittances soften poverty, they do not eradicate it. Nothing argues this more persuasively than the millions of emigrants who today send an estimated $8 billion home, supporting 1.2 million homes in villages that are becoming ghost towns inhabited by the old and infirm, yet Mexico's enormous poverty rate remains without respite.[37] As in the case of the Bracero Agreements, guest worker remittances administered by the Fox government would be localized and short-term rather than national in scope. Remittances might serve to repair town streets, build family houses, paint village chapels, and send a child to school, but remittances can do little else than supply these and other limited forms of aid for economically depressed communities. Remittances have never provided the wherewithal to change the national economy. Rather than an economic development program sponsored and funded by the central government, emigrants will continue to foot the bill for ameliorating poverty in their increasingly abandoned home villages. Again, nothing is new here, such has been the role of emigrants throughout the twentieth century, and still the poverty rate increased and the economic distance between the United States and Mexico widened.

Furthermore, it is not clear that, as in the case of remittances sent home by workers of all legal statuses, the benefits will come in the form of direct support for those communities affected by acute conditions that spur migration. Fox's proposals aim at concentrating the flow of remittances into central banks, where they will then be utilized in coordination with administration economic programs. Fox's plan stands squarely within the pronouncements coming from the 2001 Summit of the Americas in Quebec. The summit's joint declaration "highlighted the significance of remittances as a source of developmental capital, and called on governments to . . . seek ways to channel some of this money into productive investments." Fox interprets "productive investments" to be "developmental zones" composed of extensive regional export platforms. The "job-generating projects" to stem the tide of migration envisioned by the Fox team fits within the export-oriented economy that spurs migration in the first place. Moreover, job-generating opportunities appear largely in the form of export platform employment, such as in the maquilas and agriculture for export. [38]

The Puebla-Panama Plan

Fox the "free trader" contends that job opportunities within Mexico will come in the form of expanding Mexico's role as an export platform (and thereby decrease "illegal" migration and the size of the informal economy). The Puebla-Panama Plan envisions a vast system of assembly plants employing indigenous peasants stretching from Puebla, near Mexico City, to Panama. Fox confidently declared, "We want to begin construction of great corridors of highways and railroads, of pipelines and electric lines, that quickly and efficiently connect the developmental zones of Panama to Mexico."[39]

Here Fox advances the favored "globalization" schemes of the past. Other than the huge scale of the proposed project, funded by foreign investors spearheaded by the Inter-American Development Bank, Mexico will remain, as one Mexican critic commented, "a nation of assembly plants and monoproducer for export."[40] A *New York Times* journalist observed that the plan "would have the peasants making consumer goods in assembly factories, as they do in Mexico's north, or harvesting food and wood in biotech plantations, for perhaps $10 a day."[41] Ten dollars a day is an exaggeration; peasants will be fortunate to earn $5 a day. The Puebla-Panama region contains, among other things, the largest coffee-producing area in Mexico and important oil and natural gas reserves. The planned infrastructure will assist in exploiting these natural resources and the production of agricultural commodities. Roads and airports will efficiently transport them as well as maquila products to foreign markets.

There is no reason to believe that a huge archipelago of maquilas will prevent migration. Migration soared while maquila production, fanned by NAFTA, rose significantly. It is a shot in the dark to propose that more migration in the form of guest workers, increased remittances, and more maquilas will resolve the conditions that spur migration. Despite President's Bush claim at the Summit of the Americas that "Free and open trade creates new jobs and income," the World Bank, a major sponsor of free trade, admits that Mexico's rate of poverty (by Mexican standards) rose significantly after the celebrated inauguration of NAFTA.[42] Other figures confirm the fallacy of Bush's "free trade" guarantees. From 1980 to 2000, the era of the opening of the Mexican market, the Mexican autoworkers' average wage dropped from one-third that of his or her counterparts in the United States to one-twelfth. Meanwhile, the informal sector, street vendors of all sorts, grew from 40 percent of the economically active population in 1990 to 50 percent in 2000.[43] Mass dislocations from farming villages propelled by NAFTA regulations, which allowed U.S. farmers to export 2.5 million tons annually of cheap duty-free corn into Mexico, have swelled the migratory flows. Undoubtedly, President Fox gained his "expertise" in migration theory by observing the fifty thousand Guanajuato families, one-fifth of the state's total, who abandoned (better, were forced out of) their village farms between 1990 and 2000 and who moved into cities, the northern border area, or the United States. In 2008 the ceiling on U.S. corn imports will be lifted and a saturated market will further erode village economies and increase the mass exodus from forsaken farming communities.[44]

The ominous situation is not lost on small landholders. After seven years of NAFTA, an Amatlán, Veracruz, farmer offered, "The entire Mexican countryside is a disaster." One commentator noted, "Farm failures are thought to be causing an exodus of peasants from the country to the cities—and the United States." At least one-third of all hog farmers have gone out of business due to unrestricted imports from the United States. A newspaper headline put it bluntly: "Free Trade Proves Devastating for Mexican Farmers."[45] Meanwhile, farmers throughout Mexico protest American shipments, protests that are becoming "increasingly common." At the Ciudad Juárez International Bridge, farmers have demonstrated on several occasions, and at one demonstration forced grain shipments back to the United States.[46] While Mexico's farmers are facing ruin, the guest worker program will conveniently absorb the uprooted mass by sending them to farms in North Carolina, Iowa, Arkansas, and Kansas, among other states. Rural discontent and its political ramifications will be conveniently exported as cheap labor, with the remainder to work in maquilas.

Mexico offers no plans other than "NAFTA-plus"—that is, the Puebla-Panama Plan (while the Bush administration offers the Free Trade of the Americas Agreement, which Fox also supports), tied to a guest worker program (with or without "regularization") and remittances for resolving a century of migration, of deepening poverty, and of emptying villages. For certain, "NAFTA-plus" and its hemispheric rendition, the Free Trade of the Americas Agreement, assure that the strangling economic domination by the northern superpower remains safely in place. The only plausible change that Mexico can envision, besides increased remittances to buoy the defunct treasury and fund a woefully short poverty program, is a gigantic transnational maquila-driven developmental zone, the Puebla-Panama Plan, which appears to be nothing more than a branch of the proposed Free Trade of the Americas Agreement.

In the above policy setting, with its attendant open door to imperial capital and a national economic strategy provoking the social and economic disarticulation of the Mexican nation, migration to the United States will escalate. To paraphrase Ernesto Galarza, "the slow but relentless pressure of United States' agricultural, financial, and oil corporate interests on the entire economic and social evolution of the Mexican nation" ensures that a century of Chicano history will continue to unfold along the same well-worn path. An intensification of an entrenched pattern in Chicano history stands on the threshold. The formative era of the Chicano ethnic community, an era of migration and settlement, constitutes a historical epoch that has yet to conclude.

Notes

1. According to Armand Pechard, Mexico Project chief for the Center for Strategic and International Studies (Washington, D.C.), the entire original agenda on immigration discussed by Presidents Bush and Fox before September 11 will come to fruition. In early May 2002

Pechard argued that an immigration pact will come "one ingredient at a time," signaling a "shift in the United States policy." A week or so after Pechard spoke those words, a party of U.S. lawmakers, including Senators Christopher Dodd and Jeff Bingaman and thirteen members of the House of Representatives, met with their Mexican counterparts for an airing out of perspectives on immigration. California representative David Drier commented that the meetings were "most successful." According to Representative Chris Cannon, Congress "is likely to approve" a bill in 2002 that legalizes some immigrants. Given the lobbying by agribusiness corporations and the rhetoric coming from U.S. lawmakers, a new guest worker program also will be pushed forward after national security issues stemming from September 11 and the imminent war against Iraq are satisfactorily resolved.

For articles that demonstrate the revival of immigration issues discussed previous to September 11 see the following: Alfredo Corchado and Ricardo Sandoval, "Fox Calls for Agreement on Rights of Immigrants," *Orange County Register*, May 10, 2002; Dena Bunis, "Bill Would Grant Migrant Stays," *Orange County Register*, May 10, 2002; Dena Bunis, "Mass Mailing Will Push Legalization of Immigrants," *Orange County Register*, May 15, 2002; Julie Watson, "Mexico Seeks Sign U.S. Is Serious on Immigration," *Orange County Register*, May 19, 2002; Fred Alvarez, "Picking a Fight over Guest Workers in California Fields," *Los Angeles Times*, May 19, 2002.

The continued postponement of deliberations has begun to rattle the Fox administration, given the huge economic depression affecting Mexico, particularly its small to medium farmers who are reeling from U.S. imports and driven into the migratory stream. The economic crisis in Mexico has no resolution in sight except to send the unemployed to the United States for temporary employment. See Richard Boudreaux, "Frustration Marks Fox, Bush Talks," *Los Angeles Times*, October 27, 2002; also, Chris Kraul, "Free Trade Proves Devastating for Mexican Farmers," *Los Angeles Times*, October 26, 2002.

2. Dena Bunis, "Immigrant Amnesty May Only Be Put Off," *Orange County Register*, November 30, 2001.

3. Mary Jordan and Kevin Sullivan, "U.S. and Mexico to Resume Talks on Immigration Policy," *Washington Post*, November 15, 2001.

4. "Fox Plans to Match Investments from Mexicans Abroad," *Orange County Register*, July 22, 2001.

5. Pilar Franco, "More Voices Join Call for Cancellation of Debt," Third World Network, *http://www.twnside.org.sg/title/voices-cn.htm;* Dr. Osvaldo Martinez, "Comments by Dr. Osvaldo Martinez," *http://www.cubaminrex.cu/versioningles/Comments%2oby%20dr. htm.* Martinez notes that Mexico's debt in 2000 was twice that of 1982, approximately the year when neoliberal policies began to be implemented.

6. John Moody, "In Mexico, Banking Is Mostly a Foreign Affair," *Orange County Register*, May 18, 2001.

7. While the meeting took place at the sprawling seventeenth-century hacienda, children labored for wages on the estate. According to UNICEF, the practice is widespread in Mexico, where 5 million children under fourteen are working in violation of the national constitution. Nevertheless, Fox distanced himself from the matter declaring, "This is not an issue for me. It is an issue for others whose names are Fox." Ginger Thompson, "At Home, Mexico Mistreats Its Migrant Farmhands," *New York Times*, May 6, 2001.

8. See Phillip Martin, "Guest Workers: New Solution, New Problem?" Pew Hispanic Center Study (March 21, 2002). Martin, an authority on agricultural labor, writes, "[I]t is likely that at least 250,000 new workers would be needed each year if farm labor conditions remain unchanged."

9. Minerva Canto and Elizabeth Aguilera, "Getting to Root of Immigration," *Orange County Register*, February 16, 2001; Ginger Thompson, "U.S. and Mexico to Open Talks on Freer Migration for Workers," *New York Times*, February 16, 2001.

10. Marion Lloyd, "Mexicans Hope for Prosperity from 'up North,'" *Orange County Register*, February 17, 2001.

11. Lee Romney, "Fox Focuses on Migrants' Role Sending Funds Home," *Los Angeles Times*, March 5, 2001.

12. Alfredo Corchado and Ricardo Sandoval, "U.S. Senate Panel's Visit to Mexico Marks a New Era for Neighbors," *Orange County Register*, April 16, 2001.

13. "Mexican Guest Worker Plan Backed," *Washington Post*, January 11, 2001.

14. Ricardo Sandoval, "Senators Impressed by Guest Worker Plan," *Orange County Register*, April 18, 2001.

15. Jesse Helms and Joseph Biden Jr., "Unique Visit to Mexico Builds Trust in Its Wake," *Los Angeles Times*, May 1, 2001.

16. "Mexican Guest Worker Plan Backed," *Washington Post*, January 11, 2001; similar expressions from American and British writers regarding Díaz were common. One author gave her all when she wrote: "That Porfirio was the greatest man of the nineteenth century may seem a strong assertion, but a glance, even one so cursory as this must be, will prove the fact. His life has been a long romance . . . in the career of this extraordinary individual." (Mrs. Alec Tweedie, *Mexico as I Saw It* [London: Hurst & Blackett, 1901], 116.) The list of admirers spans President McKinley; President Theodore Roosevelt; and, of course, many a writer like the famous Mrs. Tweedie.

17. William Safire, "Border Business," *Orange County Register*, April 3, 2001.

18. Dena Sunis, "Hispanics Draw Line on Work Plan," *Orange County Register*, March 9, 2001; Tara Copp, "Gramm Initiates Bill for Hispanic Workers," *Orange County Register*, January 23, 2001.

19. Tom Weiner, "In Mexico, Grim Resolve after Deaths," *New York Times*, May 26, 2001.

20. In anticipation of the Fox request for a guest worker agreement, a broad coalition, which included the AFL-CIO, agribusiness, and Latino civil rights groups, coalesced in support of a guest worker proposal. That plan allowed a limited form of amnesty for "at least some" undocumented immigrants and a provision for the eventual legalization of the guest workers based on the number of days employed in a set time frame. (Susan Ferris, "Unions Lobby for Immigration Change," *Orange County Register*, June 18, 2001.) See also Susan Ferris, "Unions Lobby for Immigration Change," *Orange County Register*, June 18, 2001, and Steven Greenhouse, "In U.S. Unions, Mexico Finds Unlikely Ally on Immigration," *New York Times*, July 19, 2001. Greenhouse writes, "The American labor movement and the Fox administration have worked intensely to improve ties, partly because they share an interest improving the lives of Mexican immigrants. In January, Mr. Fox met with John Sweeney, president of the AFL-CIO, and on Monday he met in Detroit with James P. Hoffa, the Teamsters president, and Stephan Yokich, president of the United Auto Workers.

    "Last month, Mr. Wilhem [president of the hotel employees union and chairman of the AFL-CIO's task force on immigration policy] and the presidents of the service employees, farm workers, and laborers unions went to Mexico to meet with Mr. Castañeda to discuss legalization of illegal immigrants and labor's concerns about the business community's push to expand the guest worker program."

    Arturo Rodriguez, president of the United Farm Workers of America, was widely quoted as saying, "We've made it clear that without legalization there will be no new guest worker program or revision of the current guest worker program." The leadership of the AFL-CIO, John Sweeney in particular, has been quiet and low-key in countering the guest worker agreement and thus has failed to dispel the widespread notion that organized labor stands solidly opposed to the guest worker agreement. See, e.g., John J. Sweeney, "No Joy This Labor Day," *San Francisco Chronicle*, September 3, 2001. In early September 2001, long after the guest worker agreement had been planned and discussed, Sweeney could only offer these few lines on the matter: "[T]he White House is currying favor with Latino immigrants by voicing support for immigration reform, but low-keying the fact that it would be linked to a guest worker program that would bind workers to employers, creating a new class of indentured servants. The AFL-CIO, in contrast, is working for policies to support all immigrant workers' rights." Sweeney appears a bit disingenuous in that a number of his unions and their leaders have given their approval to the Fox-Bush guest worker package. Futhermore, in the AFL-CIO's monthly magazine *America @work*, no mention of the guest worker agreement appears in the January through October 2001 issues, although some space is devoted to "immigration reform." In Sweeney's regular column he does not once mention the guest worker agreement.

21. A second guest worker proposal making its way through the Senate in 2001 would extend the length of time required for legalization of guest workers. That version garnered the backing of employers of undocumented labor and both political parties but is opposed by the AFL-CIO and Latino rights advocates objecting to the legalization provision. As the congressional tensions over the second proposal rose, Fox and Castañeda moved to enlist

broad support from both potential investors and the AFL-CIO. By then the U.S. labor federation had swung its weight in support of a guest worker measure.

22. James F. Smith and Ken Ellingwood, "Border Pact to Target Safety," *Los Angeles Times*, June 23, 2001; Eric Schmitt, "Bush Aides Weigh Legalizing Status of Mexicans in U.S.," *New York Times*, July 15, 2001.

23. While Fox claims to distance himself from the practices of the PRI, in the matter of guest workers he is digging deep into the PRI catalog of north-of-the-border strategies and opportunistically exploiting the Chicano ethnic community in classic PRI fashion to promote U.S. and Mexican national policies.

24. Schmitt, "Bush Aides Weigh Legalizing Status of Mexicans in U.S."

25. The aide added that the Bush-Fox proposal in final form would garner bipartisan support. Greg Miller and Patrick J. McDonnell, "New Amnesty for Migrants Possible," *Los Angeles Times*, July 16, 2001.

26. Gilbert G. Gonzalez, "El Fracaso de la Globalizacion Aumenta las Divisiones Mundiales," *Deslinde* (Bogota, Colombia) 26 (May–June 2000).

27. James F. Smith, "U.S.–Mexico Migration Plan Urged," *Los Angeles Times*, February 15, 2001.

28. Alfredo Corchado and Ricardo Sandoval, "U.S. Senate's Panel's Visit to Mexico Marks New Era for Neighbors," *Orange County Register*, April 16, 2001; Ginger Thompson, "Senators Led by Helms Meet with Mexican Leader," *New York Times*, April 17, 2001.

29. Minerva Canto, "Proposal to Import Workers Stirs Fears," *Orange County Register*, March 12, 2001.

30. James F. Smith and Dan Morain, "Fox's Visit to State Signals Improved Ties," *Los Angeles Times*, March 21, 2001.

31. Patrick J. McDonnell, "New Chief at Mexican Consulate," *Los Angeles Times*, February 2, 2001.

32. Gilbert G. Gonzalez, *Mexican Consuls and Labor Organizing: Imperial Politics in the American Southwest* (Austin: University of Texas Press, 1999), 29.

33. Lee Romney, "Fox Focuses on Migrants Role Sending Funds Home," *Los Angeles Times*, March 5, 2001.

34. The 73 percent figure is based on studies directed by El Colegio de Mexico economist Julio Bolvitnik and was presented at a symposium on poverty in Mexico City in 2000. The World Bank finds that 62 percent of the economically active population of Mexico live in poverty. In either instance the poverty rate in Mexico is enormous. See John W. Warnock, "Who Benefits from the Free Trade Agreements," *Regina [Canada] Leader Post*, April 18, 2001.

35. According to Mexican officials, the government expects to match each dollar of remittance with two to three dollars of federal funds. Either figure places a sizable responsibility on the shoulders of emigrants to fund a poverty program. However, the plans remain at the discussion stage. On this see Ester Hernandez, "Power in Remittances: Remaking Family and Nation among Salvadorans," Ph.D. diss., University of California, Irvine, 2001.

36. "Money sent home to Mexico up 43%," *Orange County Register*, June 5, 2001. More recently Juan Hernandez has been lobbying U.S. corporations to donate funds to an "adopt a community" campaign. The amount subscribed thus far has been infinitesimal. Interestingly, Tyson Foods, which has been charged by the federal government with smuggling Mexican workers into the United States, has "committed to helping farmers . . . by buying chickens from them." (NAFTA has opened the doors to the importation of poultry into Mexico; thus it appears that there is little of significance that can be expected from Tyson's offer.) United Parcel Service has promised "$1 million to 'adopt' communities." Along with several other "donations," the sum pales in comparison to the amount sent annually by migrants. (See Minervo Canto, "Sharing Prosperity," *Orange County Register* May 24, 2002.)

37. Jatziri Peréz Ojeda, "Sostienen migrantes hogares mexicanos," *Univision Online*, May 6, 2001; also Ginger Thompson, "Migrant Exodus Bleeds Mexico's Heartland," *New York Times*, June 17, 2001. Thompson writes of one typical village, Casa Blanca, in Mexico state: "Almost no one lives here anymore," and that migration is "leaving widening swaths of central Mexico abandoned."

38. See John Rice, "Mexico Looks for Business 'Godfathers,'" *Orange County Register*, July 7, 2001; The estimated $8 billion in remittances are among the opportunities that stand before Citigroup in its purchase of Banamex. With Fox pushing for lower fees on money transfers, California Commerce Bank, owned by Banamex, will actively engage the money transfer business. The expected increase in remittances will cause a spurt in the money transfer busi-

ness within the United States and a short-term cash flow in Mexico, assuring "Citigroup . . . a profit at both ends," according to one analyst. (Riva D. Atlas and Tim Weiner, "Citigroup to Buy Mexican Bank in a Deal Valued at $12.5 Billion," *New York Times*, May 18, 2001.)

39.   Morris Thompson, "Fox Hopes Development Plan Reduces Migration," *Orange County Register*, March 13, 2001.

40.   Carlos Fazio, *La Jornada*, May 28, 2001.

41.   Tim Weiner, "A Grand Plan Meets Skepticism in Mexico's South," *New York Times*, July 2, 2001.

42.   David E. Sanger, "Bush Links Trade with Democracy at Quebec Talks," *New York Times*, April 22, 2001.

43.   One program coordinated with remittances is the forcible elimination of the vast under-ground informal economy that Mexicans engage in when all other options disappear. Street vending has come under attack, and is one component of the general program to incorpo-rate remittances into a central economic plan. Thus we see the use of emigrant funding in coordination with a plan to eliminate street vending, a practice that, like remittances, has served as a major source of family income in Mexico. However, removing street vendors eliminates a large and popular tax-free market and forcibly channels consumer purchases into the formal (and higher-priced) government-controlled "free" market. (Traci Carl, "Fox Focuses on Sidewalk Vendors," *Orange County Register*, May 15, 2001.)

44.   Chris Kraul, "Growing Troubles in Mexico," *Los Angeles Times*, January 17, 2000; Victor M. Quintana, "La catastrófe maicera," *La Opinión* (Los Angeles), April 17, 1999; and Warnock, "Who Benefits from the Free Trade Agreements."

45.   Chris Kraul, "Free Trade Proves Devastating for Mexican Farmers," *Los Angeles Times*, Oc-tober 26, 2002.

46.   Ginger Thompson, "Farm Unrest Roils Mexico, Challenging New President," *New York Times*, July 22, 2001.

Subject Index

Author Index